# SOVIET
# COMBAT AIRCRAFT
## of the Second World War

## Volume Two:
## Twin-Engined Fighters, Attack Aircraft
## and Bombers

# SOVIET COMBAT AIRCRAFT
## of the Second World War

Volume Two:
Twin-Engined Fighters, Attack Aircraft and Bombers

# Yefim Gordon and Dmitri Khazanov
### with Alexander Medved'

## Midland Publishing
## Limited

*1999*

**Soviet Combat Aircraft
of the Second World War**
Volume Two – Twin-Engined Fighters,
Attack Aircraft and Bombers

ISBN 1 85780 084 2

Published by Midland Publishing Limited
24 The Hollow, Earl Shilton
Leicester, LE9 7NA, England
Tel: 01455 847815  Fax: 01455 841805

Midland Publishing Limited is a member of
the Ian Allan Group of companies.

Edited by Philip Jarrett and Ken Ellis

*Worldwide distribution (except Nth America):*
Midland Counties Publications (Aerophile) Ltd
Unit 3 Maizefield, Hinckley Fields
Hinckley, Leics., LE10 1YF, England
Tel: 01455 233747  Fax: 01455 233737
E-mail: midlandbooks@compuserve.com

*North America trade distribution by:*
Motorbooks International - Wholesalers &
Distributors, 729 Prospect Avenue,
PO Box 1, Osceola, WI 54020-0001, USA
Tel: 715 294 3345  Fax: 715 294 4448
US/Canada orders/service: 800 458 0454

Printed in Hong Kong via World Print Limited

*Photograph on half-title page:*
**A unit commander details the mission to a young
Il-2 attack pilot.**

*Title page:*
**Many DB-3 pilots were conferred with the highest
Soviet military decorations.**

# Contents

*Below:* **The Petlyakov Pe-2 proved itself to be a
fast and versatile bomber and attack aircraft;
over 11,000 were built.** *Philip Jarrett collection*

# Introduction

BILL GUNSTON
OBE FRAeS

I was pleased to be asked to write the Introduction to this book's companion volume, dealing with single-engined fighters. On that occasion I dwelt at some length on a lot of background topics: how aircraft design was organised in the USSR, the severe problems of territory and climate, structural materials, engines, armament and, not least, of the West's ignorance of almost everything east of Poland.

As I believe most people who read this volume will already have its companion, I will not cover all this ground again. Instead, I will concentrate on the aircraft, and how they were used in The Great Patriotic War of 1941-45 (as the Soviet Union termed its part in the Second World War). The authors have already produced a definitive work covering both subjects, so my job is to stand further back and take a broad view, and also relate developments in the Soviet Union to those taking place elsewhere at the same time.

## Twin-engined fighters

Between the world wars there were attempts in several countries to build fighters larger than the norm, with two engines. Most had a crew of two or three, the additional men manning pivoted guns. Two British types, the Bristol Bagshot and the Westbury, each had two gunners who strove to aim by hand the huge and awesome COW gun of 37mm calibre. Predictably, this idea got nowhere. In the USA, rather later, Larry Bell launched his new firm with the XFM-1 Airacuda, which likewise had two gunners who tried to aim pivoted

On 29th April 1942 the western Allies got to examine closely the awesome TB-7 heavy bomber when an example landed at Tealing in Scotland. The aircraft was bringing Vyacheslav Mikhailovich Molotov, Soviet Commissar for Foreign Affairs, to Britain to sign a treaty with his British counterpart, Anthony Eden. In late May, another TB-7 arrived at Tealing, this time transitting on to the USA on another diplomatic mission. Note the Hawker Hurricanes of 56 Operational Training Unit and a DH Hornet Moth in the background. *Philip Jarrett collection*

37mm cannon, but they were enclosed in the front of pusher engine nacelles.

There were several other attempts to produce twin-engined fighters with one or more gunners, perhaps the most misguided of all being the various Multiplaces de Combat of

France in which machine gunners aimed in all directions from aircraft slower and less manoeuvrable than those they were likely to encounter. Time was to show that the only sensible twin-engined fighter was one with fixed forward-firing armament similar to that of a single-engined machine (but possibly heavier). The Russians appreciated this from the start, and used two engines principally to obtain greater range.

Of the types featured here, Moskalev's SAM-13 stands out as being in a different class. Much smaller than the others, it resembled a scaled-down Fokker XXIII with push/pull engines of a mere 270hp (201kW) each, so it is astonishing that anyone took it seriously. It is even more remarkable that Mark Gallai (who not long ago retired after the world's longest and most interesting test-pilot career) thought it 'promising'. Similar engines were fitted to French Caudron light fighters, a few of which saw action in 1939-40 with Finnish and Polish pilots. In April 1953 I was complimented by W E W Petter for an article I had written about his beautiful little Folland Gnat. On reflection, I ought to have been less enthusiastic.

Tiny 'light fighters' do not appear to be likely to win in combat. On the other hand, 60 years ago twin-engined fighters were unable to dogfight with smaller machines. When it met the RAF the previously 'invincible' Messerschmitt Bf 110 fared badly.

Perhaps the most remarkable feature of the use of twin-engined fighters in the Great Patriotic War is that they played an insignificant role. Unlike the other warring nations at that time, the Soviet Union concentrated almost entirely on single-engined fighter and attack aircraft. This reflected the fact that they regarded the air war as an adjunct to the front-line in a land battle, where the required radius of action was seldom more than 60 miles (100 km). At the same time, their established single-engined fighters, despite being smaller than those of other nations, were readily modified to have remarkably long range (the brochure figure for the Yak-9DD was 1,420 miles (2,285km).

When this was coupled with the absence of airborne-interception radar in the Soviet Union it can be seen that there were few situations in which twin-engined fighters were needed. Incidentally, when in January 1942 German pictures of shot-down or captured Yak-4s became available, Western caption writers called this previously unknown type a 'twin-engined fighter'. As this book makes clear, none of the Yak-2 or Yak-4 aircraft were ever used as fighters.

This is surprising, because Yakovlev himself has recorded what a big impact the prototype Messerschmitt Bf 110 made when it appeared in May 1936. There is no doubt that this aircraft triggered responses in the Soviet Union, and the only astonishing thing is that nothing happened for nearly two further years, which was hardly Stalin's way. It was not until well into 1938 that the VVS issued a demand for a long-range fighter to escort the TB-7 bomber.

Designer V K Tairov (pronounced 'Taeerov') responded at once with the OKO-6, and in September Polikarpov was also charged with meeting this requirement. Petlyakov's '100' was similar in timing, but designed as a multi-role fighter and dive bomber, while Grushin and Mikoyan/Gurevich decided later to build aircraft in the same class. Perhaps surprisingly, none of these aircraft came to anything. Tairov's was very fast and heavily armed, and eventually flew well. Polikarpov's was almost as fast and had devastating armament. The MiG prototypes were the fastest of all, and also had heavy armament. The trouble was that they were too late, and the German invasion stopped Grushin's prototype (which looked just like a Bf110) from ever being completed.

Independently, Pe turned the '100' into the somewhat simpler Pe-2 bomber and then, from this, derived a fighter, the Pe-3. Though on paper it was markedly inferior to the purpose-designed heavy fighters mentioned previously, the Pe-3 was the only aircraft in this class to see active service. Though produced in several versions from 1940 through 1944 by Factories 22 and 39, total production was small (196 Pe-3 and 121 Pe-3bis). These were quite intensively used, some for day and night defence of Moscow and others (with the 95th IAP) mainly in the anti-ship role. Basically excellent aircraft (see Pe-2 later), they really needed more powerful engines. Initially lightly armed, some later carried BK and ShVAK guns in the nose, a ShKAS/BT/UBK/UBT in the rear cockpit, ShKAS in side windows, UBK/ShVAK in a ventral gondola, UBT/BT firing aft under the rear fuselage and ShKAS in the tailcone – though not all of these at the same time !

Thus, unlike the British Mosquito, the Pe-3 tended to have guns sticking out in all directions. Incidentally, DK296, an early de Havilland Mosquito FB.VI, was painted in Soviet markings and collected from RAF Errol, in Scotland, by a VVS ferry crew in 1942. So far as I know, no others followed it. In view of its high performance and wooden construction I would have thought the Mosquito would have been of intense interest to the USSR, but according to Leonid Selyakov, DK296 was not evaluated until spring 1944. It apparently prompted the development of the Pe-2I high altitude bomber.

I have read in several places that night-interception versions of the Mosquito would also have been welcome in the Soviet Union because of their ability to carry airborne radar, 'which', says one author, 'was something the Russians did not have'. For many years the history of Soviet airborne radar has been on public record. The Gneiss (Gneiss) interception radar began flight testing on a Pe-2 in June 1942, and pre-production radars were responsible for the destruction at night of many Luftwaffe aircraft trying to drop supplies to the 6th Army at Stalingrad in December of that year.

## Light bombers and attack aircraft

One of the seeming paradoxes of aircraft design is that there is often a fine line between success and failure. In 1939 Britain's RAF went to war with 18 squadrons equipped with the Fairey Battle, regarded as a modern fast light bomber. It proved to be a defenceless disaster, suffering catastrophic casualties. At the same time Sergei Ilyushin was perfecting what became the Il-2. This had roughly the same size, shape, engine power, gross weight and flight performance as the Battle, but was emphatically not a disaster. Josef Stalin said it was 'needed by the air force like it needs air and bread'. The number built, 36,163, exceeded that of any other single type of aircraft in history.

Going back in time, the VVS originally bought aircraft in this category in order to quell internal insurrections. Its first indigenous design produced in really large numbers was Polikarpov's U-2 (later redesignated Po-2) and one variant of this finds a place in this book. The U-2VS, or Po-2LNB, was so brutishly simple there was almost nothing to go wrong. Accordingly this machine, in the class of the British DH Tiger Moth (but with an engine of less power, a mere 115hp/85kW), was used in large numbers for almost every conceivable purpose. Often flown by female crews, they became adept at night attack with bombloads up to 441lb (200kg), not least of their achievements being to deprive the invaders of sleep. A decade later they did the same in Korea, the Po-2's 'Bedcheck Charlie' missions in that conflict being considered 'an annoyance out of all proportion to its apparent worth in combat'. The primitive nature of this fabric-covered biplane made it a difficult machine to shoot down, approaching quietly at night, offering a tiny target to radar, and with the ability to manoeuvre at speeds around 50 knots (93 km/h).

In the author's opinion, the RAF could have made good use of a few thousand aircraft in the same class for various front-line operations. The US Army had the Piper L-4, of only 65hp (87kW) – half the power of the Polikarpov – yet able to perform many tasks in addition to reconnaissance and liaison. A particular advantage of such aircraft is that they can be readily modified in the front-line, or fitted with locally devised armament or equipment. As late as 1945 the VVS (which was just one of the users) had over 9,200 Po-2s in the active inventory.

A little later Polikarpov designed the R-5. This was again a fabric-covered biplane, but with an engine of 680 to 730hp (507 to 544 kW). Designed to replace the R-1 (R-2), which was based on a British aircraft of 1917, the R-5 was the Soviet counterpart to the prolific British Hawker family of two-seat biplanes. Like the Audax, Hardy, Hind and Hector, it continued to serve into the Second World War. It remained in production to 1937, output being 6,726, and though completely replaced by later types in its original bomber/reconnaissance role, gave good service with various later add-ons such as passenger/cargo cassettes, loudspeakers, searchlights, glider tow hooks, a wide range of guns, up to eight rails for RS-82 rockets, and containers for no fewer than 18 types of bomb.

Unlike the Po-2 versions, these add-ons were usually factory designed and made, some dating from the mid-1930s. After 1941 the R-5's numbers dwindled sharply, but much more slowly than (for example) the RAF's Hawker biplanes. The VVS and other Soviet air arms had absolutely no hang-ups about keeping in service seemingly obsolete equipment that still served a useful purpose. They have also done better than Britain in preserving aircraft for posterity.

After the R-5 came the R-6, one of the early monoplanes based on Junkers light alloy technology by Tupolev. Though the last was made in 1936 almost all had been withdrawn by 1941, or consigned to non-combatant roles. The next of the R (tactical reconnaissance) category to be produced in numbers was the KhAI-5, designed at the Kharkov Aviation Institute by J G Neman. First flown in 1934, this was almost in the class of the Battle, but rather lighter and less powerful. Though the series version, designated R-10, was a competent and quite good-looking machine, the original force of 528 had dwindled to 399 by the end of The Winter War with Finland, and so far as I am aware by June 1941 none remained in front line service except as transports and hacks.

Sukhoi's Su-2 was identical in concept but a later design with a more powerful engine. On paper this was an excellent aircraft, similar in concept to the Battle yet smaller, faster, more agile and better protected. Sadly, the '109s hacked down Su-2s in droves. Even the Su-4, with a much more powerful engine and better protection, suffered severe combat casualties from both fighters and ground fire. Quite apart from the fighters of the Luftwaffe, which until 1943 virtually controlled the sky over the battlefront, the murderous flak from German ground forces made it almost suicidal for any normal aircraft to press home bomb or rocket attacks at low level.

Thus, even Yakovlev's speedy twin-engined Yak-2 and Yak-4 experienced heavy attrition, compounded by the fact that these apparently beautiful aircraft suffered from endemic problems of their own. On paper they ought to have been war-winners, despite having airframes made variously of wood, steel tube, aluminium alloy and fabric. Whereas Britain's Mosquito really was a war-winner, the superficially similar Yaks were made only in modest numbers, were quickly shot down or rendered unserviceable, and altogether did little in 1941 to interfere with the progress of the invaders. By 1942 hardly any were left. By then Yakovlev was so busy with single-engined fighters that he had no time or manpower to think about twins.

With their fixation on invasion by a hostile army, such as actually happened, the Soviet leaders were naturally intensely interested in tactical aircraft designed to operate against such an army. From 1930 various designers had produced some 20 different solutions to the problem, not one of which appeared really effective. It was left to Sergei Ilyushin to produce a really effective aircraft, and to say the course of its development did not run smoothly is an understatement. The authors have outlined how, burdened by the onerous appointment of Director of GUAP, Ilyushin had hardly got started on the design of his BSh-2 armoured attacker when he was hospitalised by the crash of his AIR-11.

Gradually, and overcoming many technical problems, the BSh-2 was placed in production as the Il-2. Though suffering barely adequate engine power, keys to this classic design were not only adequate wing area and the availability of a succession of devastating armaments, but above all the first really useful armour protection for a mass produced aircraft. The obvious problem of doing this was weight. It was logical for Ilyushin to try to save weight by making the armour an integral part of the structure, but this was very difficult to do.

Eventually he had to retain normal fuselage structure, and in turn this posed the desperate problem of creating sufficiently accurate jigging for the large (5 or 6 mm) rivet holes to line up precisely with the light-alloy airframe. Case-hardening the massive pieces of armour caused slight but variable distortion, and it took a long time for production to build up. There is no doubt that, because the problems were so difficult, the number delivered on 22 June 1941 was just 249, instead of the 2,000 plus that would have been the case had ordinary armour been fitted. Nobody equalled the armour protection of this aircraft until Republic (later Fairchild, now Northrop Grumman) created the USAF's A-10 Thunderbolt II, in which the protection takes the form of a giant 'bath' of titanium.

Ceaselessly goaded by Stalin, it is perhaps remarkable that Soviet aircraft designers were just like those of other countries in not 'getting it right' until thousands of brave men had died in second-rate aircraft. There was little about the Avro Lancaster that could not have been put into production in 1937 instead of the Battle and Bristol Blenheim. In the same way, the Il-2 could have been put into production at the outset, in 1940, with a more powerful engine, guns of 23 or 37mm calibre, rockets of 82 or 132mm calibre and a rear gunner. The problem was that such developments came only after bitter experience.

In the critical summer of 1940 Britain schemed such emergency measures as the Miles M.20 fighter (which, with the same engine and armament as a Hurricane, flew faster despite having more ammunition and fixed landing gear), also bomb racks on Tiger Moths and Percival Proctors. In the same way, in late 1941 D L Tomashevich proposed a simple 'emergency' wooden aircraft powered by two Po-2 engines, carrying heavy guns (or other weapons), with armour round the pilot. The result, called Pegas, resembled a 'poor man's Henschel 129'. Despite the armour its poor turn of speed would have made it exceedingly vulnerable, so it was sensible to proceed no further than four dissimilar prototypes.

## Bombers

In June 1941 almost all Soviet bombers were of two totally different designs by A N Tupolev. One was the monster TB-3, which in 1930 was by far the greatest and most formidable bomber in the world. The last of the 819 built came off the line in 1938. The TB-3 was a major type in the Winter War, and nearly all survivors were still in service when Hitler invaded, but by 1941 these noble aircraft – despite repeated updates and numerous interesting armament fits – were no longer modern enough for combat duty. Instead they performed prodigious feats as transports.

The other Tupolev was the SB. Though unashamedly inspired by the American Martin Bomber of 1932, this classic design was actually a natural successor to the ANT-21, ANT-29 and ANT-37. Created as the ANT-40, its service designation of SB meant 'fast bomber' in Russian. It was common practice at the time to link the aircraft designation with

Ilyushin's family of attack aircraft centred around the Il-2 became the most produced aircraft of all time. *Top:* Fine air-to-air study of the two-seat Il-2M3. *Bottom:* Mass production of the Il-2 was aided by its relatively simple airframe. *Philip Jarrett collection*

the number of engines; thus documents of the day record the 'TB3-4M34' and 'SB-2M100'. This confused Western magazines and books, which reported that this bomber was called the 'SB-2'. This belief has taken as long to die as 'Me109'.

Even today the SB looks modern. Its sleek stressed-skin airframe was the smallest that could be wrapped round the engines, fuel, bombs and crew of three. Predictably, when the first production version got into action over Spain in October 1936 it did extremely well. It could fly high, aim bombs accurately, manoeuvre impressively and, not least, outrun any fighter sent against it. Tupolev kept introducing improvements, but gradually the fighters got faster, and it was then discovered that lack of armour and self-sealing fuel tanks was combined with a serious propensity for catching fire.

Total production amounted to 6,831, plus a further 111 made in Czechoslovakia. On 22nd June 1941 the SB accounted for 94% of VVS bomber strength. By 25th June about 1,000 had been destroyed on the ground, and survivors were suffering severe attrition in the sky. Despite this, the later SB versions remained important aircraft until 1945, many serving with bomber regiments until late 1943, but most being used as trainers, transports, trials testbeds and for other purposes.

While the SB was always a tactical aircraft, Sukhoi's brigade within the Tupolev bureau had in parallel created the ANT-37 long range bomber, intended to go into production as the DB-2. Factory 39 had already tooled up to put this excellent aircraft into production when Stalin was impressed by seeing a bomber prototype perform three successive loops over Red Square. He summoned the designer and pilot to the Kremlin, and after that there was no future for the DB-2. Against all professional advice he said 'Our long-range bomber is Comrade Ilyushin's DB-3'! Thus, no matter how good or bad it was, the DB-3 and its successors were to become the most important Soviet bombers of the war. A year after Operation *Barbarossa*, after Luftwaffe intelligence officers had clambered all over hundreds of modern Soviet aircraft, virtually nothing about these aircraft was known to the Soviet Union's allies in the West. Before the war British magazines had heard about a bomber prototype called the TsKB-26, because it had set so many world records. They described it as 'derived from the Boeing Y1B-

9A', which was a prototype of 1931. One might as well have said of the Gloster Gladiator 'derived from the Sopwith Camel'.

Returning to sanity, while Stalin sometimes put all his political weight (which was total) behind badly chosen weapons, the DB-3 was not one of his mistakes. The whole family had a remarkably good performance, especially in the matter of range with bomb load. They were generally in the class of the British Handley Page Hampden and American Douglas B-18, but unlike these types served in front line units until 1945. Total production of all versions nudged 7,000, and among other things they carried a remarkable variety of bombs, torpedoes, mines and other stores. Of course, over hostile territory they were vulnerable, though later Il-4 versions often had a 20mm ShVAK in the dorsal turret. Like most Soviet aircraft the Ilyushin bombers were not easy to fly. They required a lot of muscle power, even at light weights an overshoot with full flap was a touch-and-go procedure (and absolutely a non-starter on one engine) and it was only as a result of endless modifications that such seemingly essential add-ons as leading-edge de-icing and cockpit heating were added. But they were tough and survived being maintained by semi-skilled people in extremely harsh conditions, with runways made of straight tree trunks.

I cannot think of the TB-7, later called the Pe-8, without thinking of Stalin's brutality and repression. Tupolev was in prison, and the commanding general of the air force was tortured and shot (along with his wife, who, it was said 'must have known about his treasonable activities'). His crime was merely that he told Stalin the existing heavy bombers were 'old crates'. He ought to have followed the dictum 'Find out what the boss wants and give him lots of it'. However, had General Rychagov done this, they might have had to stay with the 'old crate' TB-3.

What has never been explained is why Stalin, who called all the shots, loved bigness and was happy to see getting on for 1,000 of the 'old crates' delivered, should apparently have lost interest in strategic aircraft. The development task expended on the Pe-8 was enormous by any standard. Compared with the Lancaster or Boeing B-17 it was larger and considerably more complicated. It was built with three totally different families of engines, and carried a vast range of stores including the awesome FAB-5000 which weighed over 11,900lb (5,216kg) and over which the bomb doors could not close fully. With all this effort one might have expected the Pe-8 to play a major role in the war, yet the number which went could usually be counted on the fingers. The greatest number produced in any year (1942) was 20! The greatest number operationally available in one year (1944) was 30,

and serviceability in that year averaged 65.6%, compared with 93.9% for the NA B-25 Mitchells operated by the same regiments.

Petlyakov's other bomber, the Pe-2, could hardly have been a greater contrast. Small, graceful, agile and very like an all-metal Mosquito, it maintained a serviceability rate nudging 90%, and deliveries totalled 11,427. Derived from the '100' prototype of December 1939, this aircraft was not necessarily better than others in the same class, but its development was quicker and so it received production orders first. After that, no rival could find a factory with spare capacity.

By 22nd June 1941 the VVS had received 459, a number which rose to 1,626 by the end of that year. Nothing was known of it in Britain, but in September the pilots of RAF 151 Wing, based in the Petsamo region of arctic Russia, had a shock when they found that their Hurricanes had to fly at full throttle to escort Pe-2s on a bombing mission. Despite this, photographs did not appear in the West until 1942, along with garbled information. Unfortunately, Petlyakov himself was killed on 12th January of that year, and this combined with a shortage of light alloys to make production and further development difficult.

Over the years, snippets of information have emerged about the work of the Pe-2 in its many variations. Whereas in 1941 this aircraft was difficult to intercept, by 1943 it was experiencing quite heavy attrition from the Bf109G and Fw190, and not even the FT ('frontal demand') BS gun was much of a deterrent. From the 275th production series the Pe-2 was equipped to eject ten AG-2 grenades, which immediately streamed a small parachute and exploded in 3 to 5 seconds to deter fighters coming up astern. These retarded grenades were also useful against ground targets. A wealth of evidence exists regarding the use by Pe-2s of these and other unconventional weapons.

I cannot help commenting on the fact that, if one can read documents written in a design bureau, or official papers from military or government offices, it is usually safe to treat them as gospel. In contrast, anything that might have been written for public consumption is inevitably suspect, and sometimes arrant nonsense.

For example, come aboard the Pe-8 of the famed Colonel E K Puusepp, as they head for the electricity generating station (a target maybe 50 yards [45m] across) in the city of Riga. I quote: 'The bomber has now climbed to 8,000 metres [26,250ft] ... Shtepenk shouts 'Combat course 185 degrees!' ... five to the left ... three wider ... keep it there' ... the aircraft slides noticeably upwards, 3.5 tonnes of bombs have left ... all the lights in the town below and partly in the surrounding area are suddenly extinguished. The gunners shout

*Opposite page, top:* **Tupolev's SB initially saw operational service during the Spanish Civil War.** *Philip Jarrett collection*

*Bottom:* **A Naval Aviation SB being loaded with mines. The SB remained an important type in the Soviet inventory until 1945.** *Philip Jarrett collection*

'Direct hit!' With free-fall bombs from that altitude nobody could do this even today, except by sheer chance.

Alternatively, we are told the dive attacks by the Pe-2 were very accurate. 'On 16th July 1943 airmen of 3-BAK destroyed 55 tanks, 229 vehicles, 11 AA guns, three field guns, 12 machine gun and mortar nests and seven stores of fuel or ammunition'. British writers of Air Ministry press releases put out the same kind of precisely quantified nonsense in the first year of the war. By 1943 they usually just wrote the names of cities. This is in no sense intended to cast doubt on the colossal effort made by over 11,000 of these superb attack bombers, whose work may one day be collected into a definitive treatise.

Another aircraft, whose combat record is still far from completely known in the West, is the Yer-2. Originally flown as the DB-240 prototype, this was an outstanding bomber with capability far surpassing its modest dimensions and power. I am delighted to see it feature in enhanced detail in this book. Myasishchev's succession of rather more powerful twin-engined bombers is even less familiar to Western audiences, and again we can read about these aircraft – which never managed to progress beyond the prototype stage – in more depth. As for Polikarpov's 'T' or NB, despite its complicated and rather dated structure, this also showed every sign of being a most useful machine, thwarted only by the lack of factory space and, especially, by internal politics.

This leaves just the Tu-2. Not many really successful aircraft have been designed in prison. The remarkable history of this aircraft which, one supposes, pleased Stalin and so won Tupolev his freedom, is well known. Tupolev himself did not like to discuss his incarceration, though when I asked him to his face, he just said 'I was required to breathe purified air for a time'.

For various reasons, it took longer than expected to get the Tu-2 into full production. Though deliveries began in about September 1942, and in December one photographed the Demyansk bridgehead, very few were available until mid-1944. Thus, the Tu-2 made little contribution to the war until the final stages, when other aircraft had done all the most difficult work. Twin ASh-82 engines had been used on various other aircraft, even including the smaller and lighter Pe-2, but the Tu-2 was an ideal match with this excellent engine. I find it difficult to comprehend why such German aircraft as the Dornier 217 and Junkers 188, identical in concept, should have been in most respects outperformed by the Tu-2. The Soviet aircraft gave rise to numerous later variants which served well into the jet age. Indeed, one version was a jet!

## New technology

Like the single-engined fighters, the aircraft in this book exhibited an astonishing diversity of airframes. In the West, once (in the case of the UK, belatedly) manufacturers had learned how to make cantilever stressed-skin monoplanes, airframes tended to become 100% aluminium alloy, the Mosquito being the only notable exception. In the Soviet Union a severe shortage of light alloys resulted in a profusion of methods for using wood, in most cases based on birch veneer. Welded steel tubing naturally persisted where possible, and in any case the designer always had to recognise that his creation would have to survive in the harshest and most extreme environments on Earth, on primitive airfields and maintained by servicing crews with no technical background whatsoever and who had received only the briefest course of instruction.

By December 1941 the shortage of light alloys was so crippling that production of several aircraft, in particular the all-metal Pe-2, was slowed considerably. Fortunately, by this time shiploads of aluminium ingots were arriving from the Western Allies, notably Canada, and this enabled production to pick up again. By 1944 there was no longer a problem, and (as particularly explained in the companion volume on single-engined fighters) several mass-production aircraft were redesigned with wood and other materials replaced by light alloys.

One major new development in which they did lag was in turbojet engines, but even here the position in 1945 was not what we then imagined. It was taken for granted that nobody in the USSR had even heard of such engines until the joint UK/US announcement of 6th January 1944, and that Russians had never seen one until in spring 1945 they captured German engines. Even today not many Western aviation buffs know that Arkhip Lyul'ka completed calculations for an axial turbojet in 1936 and, having been sent to Chelyabinsk to work on other projects until 1942, began testing his first turbojet in spring 1943.

In such fields as the installation of air-cooled radial piston engines and cooling radiators for liquid-cooled engines the Soviet engineers were at least on a level with Western teams. In the matter of fitting combat aircraft with comprehensive equipment, especially for the comfort of the flight crew, they were on a par with the Americans and significantly ahead of the British. Not least, they were far ahead of everyone else in the great diversity of proven mass-produced weapons available.

Though Soviet designers did not develop bombs larger than the FAB-5000 (11,900lb), nor (until after 1945) nuclear weapons, they provided their various air arms with an unrivalled variety of free-fall stores, dispensers, sprayers, projectors and rocket weapons. Not least, no other Allied country came anywhere near the diversity and excellence of Soviet aircraft guns, in calibres up to 57mm. In amazing contrast, the RAF relied on two families of guns, one American and the other French, designed in the First World War!

During the Great Patriotic War, we in the West found it hard to slough off the strange belief that Soviet engineers could never think of anything for themselves, and had therefore to copy others, and especially the British and Americans. In almost every aeronautical field the Soviet Union was well up with the latest technology, and in several important areas was ahead.

*Left:* **Rare view of a Neman R-10 in operational use. The type had its origins in the KhAI-5 of 1934.** *Philip Jarrett collection*

*Photographs on the opposite page:*

*Top:* **Tupolev's Tu-2 was introduced to service late in the war, but went on to a long service life afterwards. Post war variants included the Tu-12 (or Tu-77) twin-jet bomber.** *Philip Jarrett collection*

*Bottom:* **An unusual adaption, the Tu-2 special transport and parachute supply aircraft, carrying a GAZ-67 scout car in its modified bomb bay.** *Philip Jarrett collection*

# Glossary

**ADD** Aviatsiya Dal'nevo Deistviya – Long Range Air Arm.

**ATsN** Agregat Tsentralnovo Nadduva – on-board independently-powered turbo-supercharger.

**A-VMF** Aviatsiya Voenno-Morskovo Flota – Naval Air Force.

**B** Bombardirovschik – as a prefix, bomber.

**BAP** Bombardirovochny Aviatsionny Polk – Bomber Air Regiment.

**BB** Blizhnii Bombardirovshchik – as a prefix, short range bomber.

**BBAP** Blizhne-bombardirovochny Aviatsionny Polk – Short Range Bomber Air Regiment.

**BBS** Blizhny bombardirovschik, skorostnoy – short range bomber, high speed.

**bis** as a suffix, literally from the French or Latin 'again' or encore, more practically, a rethought or developed version, or even Mk.2. Designation used by only a few OKBs; e.g. MiG with their MiG-21 jet.

**BSh** Bronirovanny Shturmovik – armoured attack aircraft.

**cg** Centre of Gravity.

**D** Dalny – as a suffix, long range.

**DB** Dalny Bombardirovshcik – long range bomber.

**DDBSh** Dvukhmotornyi Dalny Bronirovannyi Shturmovik – twin engined, long range armoured attacker.

**DIS** Dvukhmotorny Istrebitel Soprovozhdeniya – twin-engined escort fighter.

**DVB** Dalny Vysotny Bombardirovshick – long range, high altitude bomber.

**GKAT** Gosudarstvenny Komitet Aviatsionnoi Teknniki – State Committee for Aviation Equipment.

**GKO** Gosudarstvenny Komitet Oborony – State Committee for Defence.

**GN** Golos Neba – as a suffix, literally voice from the sky, psychological warfare.

**GUAP** Glavnoye Upravleniye Aviatsionnoi Promyshlennosti – Chief Directorate of Aircraft Industry.

**HSU** Hero of the Soviet Union.

**I** Istrebitel – as a prefix, fighter, or literally 'destroyer' – see also I - Izdelie.

**I** Izdelie – as a prefix, product, or item, used by an OKB to denominate an airframe prior to acceptance, see also I - Istrebitel.

**IAP** Istrebitelny Aviatsionny Polk – Fighter Air Regiment.

**IAS** Inzhenernaya Aviatcionaya Sluzhba – Engineering/Maintenance Service.

**KBF** Krasnoznamenny Baltiisky Flot – Red Banner Baltic Fleet.

**KhAI** Kharkovskii Aviatsionny Institut – Kharkov Aviation Institute.

**KOSOS** Konstruktorskii Otdel Opytnovo Samolyotostroeniya – Experimental Aircraft Design Section.

**LB-S** Legky bombarovschik-sparka – light bomber, two-seater.

**LII** Letno-Issledovatel'skii Institut – Ministry of Aviation Industry Flight Research Institute.

**NAK** Nochnoi Artilleriiskii Korrectovovshchik – as a suffix, night artillery observation.

**NB** Nochnoi Bombardirovshchik – night bomber.

**NII** Nauchno Issledovatelyskii Institut – scientific and research institute (of VVS).

**NKAP** Narodny Komissariat Aviatsionnoi Promyshlennosti – State Commissariat for the Aviation Industry – People's Commissariat for Heavy Industry.

**NKVD** Narodny Komissariat Vnutrennikh Del – People's Commissariat of Internal Affairs, forerunner of the KGB.

**OKB** Opytnoye Konstruktorskoye Byuro – experimental construction bureau.

**ON** Osobogo Naznachueniya – as a suffix, personal assignment or special use.

**ORAP** Otdel'ny Razvedyvatelny Aviatsionny Polk – Independent Air Reconnaissance Regiment.

**PB** Pikiruyushchii Bombardirovshcik – as a suffix, dive bomber.

**S** Skorostnoy – as a prefix or suffix, high speed.

**SB** Skorostnoy Bombardirovschik – high speed bomber.

**SBB** Skorostnoy Blizhniy Bombardirovshchik – high speed, short range bomber.

**SBP** Skorostnoy Bombardirovochny Polk – High Speed Bomber Regiment.

**SDB** Skorostnoi Dnyevnoi Bombardirovshchik – fast day bomber.

**SFR** Skorostnoy photorazvedchik – high speed photographic reconnaissance aircraft.

**ShAP** Shturmovoy Aviatsionny Polk – Attack Air Regiment.

**ShKAS** Shpitalny-Komaritski Aviatsionny Skorostrelny – rapid-firing aircraft machine gun (designed by Shpitalny and Komaritski).

**ShVAK** Shpitalny-Vladimirov Aviatsionnaya Krupnokalibernaya – large calibre aircraft cannon (design by Shpitalny and Vladimirov).

**SPB** Skorostnoy Pikiruyuschy Bombardirovshchik – high speed dive bomber, also denominate the TB-3/Polikarpov Zveno composite.

**T** Torpedonosyets, as a suffix, torpedo.

**T** Tyazhelowooruzhenny – suffix, heavily armed

**TB** Tyazhyoly Bombardirovshchik – heavy bomber.

**TIS** Tyazhelyi Istrebitel Soprovzhdeniya – heavy escort fighter.

**TsAGI** Tsentral'nyi Aerogidrodynamichesky Institut – Central Aerodynamic and Hydrodynamic Institute.

**TsIAM** Tsentral'noye Institut Aviatsionnogo Motor-ostoeniya – Central Institute of Aviation Motors.

**TsKB** Tsentral'noye Konstruktorskoye Byuro – central, ie state, design bureau.

**VAP** Vylivnoy Aviatsionny Pribor – literally pour out airborne unit, precursor of napalm tanks.

**VI** Vysotny Istrebitel – suffix, high altitude fighter.

**VIAM** Vsesoyuzny Institut Aviatsionnykh Materialov All-Union Institute for Aviation Materials.

**VIT** Vozdushny Istrebitel Tankov – anti-tank fighter.

**VR** Vysotny razvedchik – as a suffix, high altitude reconnaissance fighter.

**VS** Voiskovaya Seriya – as a suffix, military series, re U-2/Po-2.

**VVS** Voenno-vozdushniye Sily – air forces of USSR

## Airframe and Engine Design Bureaux

Accepted abbreviations to denote airframe (surname only used for the abbreviation) or engine design (first name and surname) origin within this volume are as follows:

**AM** Alexander Mikulin

**Ar** Arkhangelsky, Aleksandr

**ACh** Aleksei Charomskii

**ASh** Arkadi Shvetsov

**Gr** Grushin, Pyotr

**Gu** Gudkov, Mikhail (see also LaGG)

**Il** Ilyushin, Sergei

**La** Lavochkin, Semyo.

**LaG** Lavochkin and Gorbunov

**LaGG** Lavochkin, Gorbunov and Gudkov (see also Gu)

**MiG** Mikoyan, Artyom and Gurevich, Mikhail

**Pe** Petlyakov, Vladimir

**Po** Polikarpov, Nikolay – but only applied to the U-2, which became the Po-2.

**ASh** Arkadi Shvetsov

**Su** Sukhoi, Pavel

**Ta** Tairov, Vsevolod

**Tu** Tupolev, Andrei

**VD** Viktor Dobrynin

**VK** Vladimir Klimov

**Yak** Yakovlev, Alexander

**Yer** Yermolayev, Vladimir

# Notes

## Measurements

In the narrative, all measurements are given in Imperial figures (of British FPSR – foot, pound, second, Rankine) and then decimal units (or SI – Système International d'Unités, established in 1960) second in brackets. The states that comprised the Soviet Union embraced the decimal system from the earliest days, although it should be noted that power was measured up to the Great Patriotic War, and beyond, using the established Western horsepower measurement. The following explanations may help:

**aspect ratio**  wingspan and chord expressed as a ratio. Low aspect ratio, short, stubby wing; high aspect ratio, long, narrow wing.

**ft**  feet – length, multiply by 0.305 to get metres (m). For height measurements involving service ceilings and cruise heights, the figure has been 'rounded'.

**ft²**  square feet – area, multiply by 0.093 to get square metres (m²).

**fuel**  measured in both gallons/litres and pounds/kilograms.
The specific gravity (sg) of Soviet fuel varied considerably during the war and conversions from volume to weight and vice versa are impossible without knowing the sg of the fuel at the time.

**gallon**  Imperial (or UK) gallon, multiply by 4.546 to get litres. (500 Imperial gallons equal 600 US gallons.)

**hp**  horsepower – power, measurement of power for piston engines. Multiply by 0.746 to get kilowatts (kW).

**kg**  kilogram – weight, multiply by 2.205 to get pounds (lb).

**km**  kilometre – length, multiply by 0.621 to get miles.

**km/h**  kilometres per hour – velocity, multiply by 0.621 to get miles per hour (mph).

**kW**  kilowatt – power, measurement of power for piston engines. Multiply by 1.341 to get horse power.

**lb**  pound – weight, multiply by 0.454 to get kilograms (kg). Also used for the force measurement of turbojet engines, with the same conversion factor, as pounds of static thrust.

**litre**  volume, multiply by 0.219 to get Imperial (or UK) gallons.

**m**  metre – length, multiply by 3.28 to get feet (ft).

**mile**  Imperial length, multiply by 1.609 to get kilometres (km).

**m²**  square metre – area, multiply by 10.764 to get square feet (ft²)

**mm**  millimetre – length, the bore of guns is traditionally a decimal measure (eg 30mm) and no Imperial conversion is given.

**mph**  miles per hour – velocity, multiply by 1.609 to get kilometres per hour (km/h).

## Russian Language and Transliteration

Russian is a version of the Slavonic family of languages, more exactly part of the so-called 'Eastern' Slavonic grouping, including Russian, White Russian and Ukrainian. As such it uses the Cyrillic alphabet, which is in turn largely based upon that of the Greeks.

The language is phonetic – pronounced as written, or 'as seen'. Translating into or from English gives rise to many problems and the vast majority of these arise because English is not a straightforward language, offering many pitfalls of pronunciation!

Accordingly, Russian words must be translated through into a *phonetic* form of English and this can lead to different ways of helping the reader pronounce what he or she sees.

Every effort has been made to standardise this, but inevitably variations will creep in. While reading from source to source this might seem confusing and/or inaccurate but it is the name as *pronounced* that is the constancy, not the *spelling* of that pronunciation!

The 20th letter of the Russian (Cyrillic) alphabet looks very much like a 'Y' but is pronounced as a 'U' as in the word 'rule'.

Another example, though not taken up in this work, is the train of thought that Russian words ending in 'y' are perhaps better spelt out as 'yi' to underline the pronunciation, but it is felt that most Western speakers would have problems getting their tongues around this!

This is a good example of the sort of problem that some Western sources have suffered from in the past (and occasionally some get regurgitated even today) when they make the mental leap about what they see approximating to an English letter.

## Designations of German aircraft

Is it 'Bf' or 'Me' for the Messerschmitt designs? This work has used official documentation and Reichsluftfahrtministerium (RLM – Reich Air Ministry) nomenclature has been adhered to. The RLM transition from 'Bf' to 'Me' occurs between the unsuccessful Bf 162 Jaguar (whose number was subsequently allocated to the He 162 Volksjäger) and the Me 163 Komet; all Messerschmitt types below the RLM number 162 being prefixed 'Bf' and all those from 163 and upwards being prefixed 'Me'.

## Design and Illustration considerations

In this work we have utilised our well-proven format, aiming as always to provide a high level of readability and design.

A conscious decision was made to include peripheral details where they appear on the original illustrations; photographs have not been printed across the fold and cropping has been kept to an absolute minimum.

Unfortunately, in this two-volume work, many of the photographs received were copies of those from official sources and proved to be lacking in definition and tonal range. Although no effort has been spared to achieve the highest standard of reproduction, priority for inclusion has, of necessity, been given to historical significance over technical perfection.

*Overleaf:*
**Of the millions of posters displayed widely as a constant reminder of the importance of Soviet air power, this particular design, featuring stylized DB-3 bombers, appeared in mid-1943, after the Battle of Kursk, when the Soviet Air Force gained a decisive edge against the Germans. The legend translates as 'Glory to the Soviet Air Force'.**

Part One

# Twin-Engined Fighters

# Grushin

### Gr-1

In 1940 Russian aircraft designer Pyotr Grushin initiated development of the Gr-1 long-range single-seat escort fighter, powered by two water-cooled AM-37 engines each giving 1,400hp (1,044kW) at 23,600ft (7,200m).

The aircraft was all metal and of twin-fin configuration, and the cockpit was protected by armour plate. Armament comprised four ShKAS 7.62mm machine guns, two ShVAK 20mm cannon and eight RS-82 or RS-132 rocket projectiles. Bombs of up to 1,100lb (500kg) could be carried in a fuselage weapon bay.

The fighter was developed and built in nine months, and in the spring of 1941 static structural testing was completed. Due to the outbreak of war it was arranged to move the aircraft to inner Russia, but the train on which it was being transported was bombed by the Luftwaffe and the Gr-1 was destroyed.

# Mikoyan-Gurevich

### DIS-200 (MiG-5)

In the second half of 1940 the design bureau of Artyom Mikoyan and Mikhail Gurevich set to work on a single-seat, long range twin-engined escort fighter. Their experience with MiG-1 and MiG-3 development proved beneficial in shortening the time spent designing the new aircraft and, owing to the good production capabilities of the Stalin Aircraft Plant No.1, production of the first prototype was significantly speeded up. As a result the DIS-200, (Dvukhmotorny Istrebitel Soprovozhdeniya - twin-engined escort fighter) redesignated MiG-5 in January 1941, made its maiden flight on 11th June 1941. By then the bureau had redefined the roles of the MiG-5, the tasks of reconnaissance, strafing and torpedo attack being added to those of escort and bomber interception. Thus the MiG-5 became a multimission aircraft rather than a pure fighter.

Powered by a pair of 1,400hp (1,044kW) AM-37 water-cooled engines, the MiG-5 had to attain a maximum speed of 412mph (664km/h) at 24,000ft (7,300m), and its estimated range at cruising speed was 1,460 miles (2,350km). Although the MiG-5 was larger than the Tairov Ta-3 (or OKO-6) fighter, the specific loads of the two aircraft were almost the same because of the former's significantly greater weight.

The MiG-5's airframe was designed with full scale flow-line production in mind. For this purpose its structure was divided into several major components to allow field as-

sembly. The fuselage had a composite structure and consisted of three main parts. The forebody was made from Duralumin, the structure being based on three solid heavy section beams to carry the bomb/torpedo load, as well as the gun pod. These beams, together with their cross-members, formed the solid cockpit floor. Two large calibre Berezin machine guns were installed in the forepart between the beams. A streamlined nose cone was fitted in front of the cockpit compartment, and could be easily removed to allow maintenance of the equipment. To improve the downwards field of view, the lower segment of the cone was made of glass. The MiG-5's canopy structure was the same as that of MiG-3, but the view forward and especially rearward was much better. Unfortunately the lateral fields of view were worse because of the engine nacelles. The canopy could be jettisoned in emergency.

The forebody was bolted to the front spar as well as to the first frame of the centre section. The central part of the fuselage was a wooden monocoque with longerons of phenol-impregnated modified wood, pine wood frames and stringers, and a veneer skin. A 168 gallon (765 litre) fuel tank was installed in this section through a hatch edged with steel tubes in the bottom covering. The tail section was a steel tube girder which carried the tailwheel mounting and the variable incidence tailplane, and was faired with Duralumin. It had two side access hatches.

The wing was a twin-spar composite struc-

ture with a Clark YH aerofoil section. The centre section longerons were made of metal, the front ones having steel T-shape flanges connected with screwed tubes, and the aft ones having steel angular flanges and a Duralumin wall. The ribs were of Duralumin, and the structure was skinned with veneer. Four ShKAS machine guns were installed in front of the central fuselage section, the lower panels of which were covered by three rigid hatches, as in MiG-3 construction. The outer wing panels were entirely of wood, with box spars of phenol-impregnated modified wood and pine ribs. Automatic leading edge slats occupied two-thirds of their span, and Shrenk-type flaps made of Duralumin and covered with a veneer skin were mounted beneath the centre section and the outer panels. The ailerons were also made of Duralumin, but had fabric covering. The wing panels were connected to the central fuselage section along the longerons.

The tailplane was similar in construction to the wing panels, being based on two wooden spars, and had a special electrically operated mechanism to change its incidence. The elevators were made of Duralumin and fabric covered. An electrically controlled trim tab was installed on the port elevator. The twin fins were also wooden and covered with veneer. The rudders were similar in construction to the elevators, each rudder having its own trim tab. The main undercarriage units had single struts and retracted rearwards into the nacelles using an hydraulic system. There were several different undercarriage position indicators, including warning lights and audible and mechanical signalling.

The Mikulin AM-37s were suspended on special frames in front of the wing centre section. The oil radiators were installed in the inboard ends of the outer wing panels, and the water radiators in the aft part of each nacelle, as in the Yakovlev BB-22 bomber. An additional ethylene-glycol loop was used for aftercooling. There were six fuel tanks, four in the wing centre section and two in the fuselage.

Avionics included an RSI-4 receiver/transmitter and an RPK-2 hand-operated direction-finding loop. Retractable landing lamps, KPA-3bis oxygen equipment and an AFA-I camera were also provided.

The flight test programme for the first prototype was carried out at the Letno-Issledovatel'skii Institut (LII - Ministry of Aviation Industry Flight Research Institute) from July to October 1941. At the time the armament was not ready and was therefore not subject to test, and the aircraft was flown without the pod for the two 23mm MP-6 guns. Four versions of torpedo-bomber armament were considered; three FAB-250 bombs, two FAB-500s, one FAB-1000, or a parachute equipped torpedo. During the tests the MiG-5's high speed manoeuvring characteristics were evaluated. When maximum speed at high altitude was investigated, it became clear that there was a deficiency on the estimated figure of more than 62mph (100km/h) at 24,600ft (7,500m). The 348mph (560km/h) attained was totally inadequate. At first it was suggested that poor performance of the engine and propeller combination was the main reason, but this was disproved by ground-rig tests in which the high speed power conditions were simulated. The performance of the engines was sufficient, though they overheated during the maximum rate-of-climb tests. The aerodynamic configuration was then carefully evaluated in a special programme of wind tunnel tests at the Tsentral'nyi Aerogidrodynamichesky Institut (Ts AGI - Central Aerodynamic and Hydrodynamic Institute), using a MiG-5 model.

After this, technical shortcomings became evident and design errors in the structure of the engine exhaust gas manifold, the oil radiator pipes and the inlet branch pipe were un-

The configuration of the DIS was very much like other aircraft in its class.

Frontal aspect of the AM-37-engined DIS

The exhaust pipes of the AM-37 vented over the trailing upper surface of the DIS's wing.

When fitted with the radial M-82, the DIS took on a different appearance.

covered. When the necessary modifications and improvements were made, and AV-9BL-149 four-bladed propellers were installed, the MiG-5's maximum speed immediately increased to 379mph (610km/h) at 22,300ft (6,800m) on the second test flight. Moreover, specialists at the LII claimed that the maximum speed could have been increased fo 391 to 397mph (630 to 640km/h) if some further technical improvements had been carried out. These improvements concerned the quality of the camouflage finish and of the covering itself; the leading edge slats, which did not fit snugly into the wing when retracted; and the ShKAS machine gun installation in the front of the central fuselage unit, which caused localised stalling.

At a normal take-off weight of 17,636lb (8,000kg) the MiG-5 could reach 16,400ft (5,000m) in 5.5 minutes, but manoeuvrability and stability were not so good. While the aircraft was excessively stable in the rolling plane, it had insufficient longitudinal and lateral stability. It proved hard to resolve these problems because there was considerable friction in the control wiring, especially in the aileron channelling, which imposed unacceptable loads on the control column during manoeuvres.

In addition, the armour was deemed insufficient (an armoured backrest was all that protected the pilot from bullets of up to 7.92mm calibre), and the long pipelines between the engines and the water radiators made maintenance very difficult, especially in winter. There were problems with the engines as well. For instance, all efforts to eliminate vibration were in vain.

The main problem was lack of perspective regarding the AM-37 engine, which was not yet ready for full-scale production. Moreover, building AM-35s for the production MiG-3 had been cut back to increase output of AM-38s for the Ilyushin Il-2 attack aircraft. When the MiG-5 test programme had been completed it was concluded that: 'The aircraft cannot be recommended for full-scale production. Continuation of the flight test programme might be useful only for data acquisition in order to improve future aircraft of this type'. But the

MiG Optnoye Konstruktorskoye Byuro (OKB - experimental construction bureau) thought this conclusion ill-founded, and decided to install two Shvetsov M-82s.

According to estimates, the new version would attain a maximum speed of 376mph (605km/h) at 16,400ft (5,000m), and it would reach that height in 6.3 minutes. The service ceiling was estimated at 31,500ft (9,600m), 3,300ft (1,000m) lower than the MiG-5 with AM-37s.

The second prototype MiG-5 was completed in the spring of 1942, but it had not even begun flight testing. It then became clear that such an aircraft was not of sufficient importance to justify reorganisation of an entire factory for its production, even if it was successful. The needs of the Soviet Army Air Force and Naval aviation for such an aircraft were met by large scale production of the Pe-3*bis*. Although it had slightly inferior performance, production had already been established.

*For technical data, see Table A, page 163.*

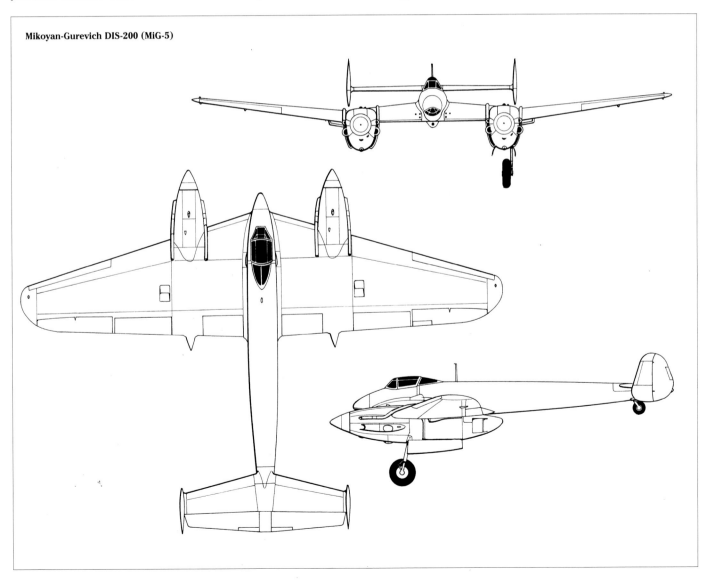

**Mikoyan-Gurevich DIS-200 (MiG-5)**

# Moskalev

## SAM-13

Most of the aircraft designed by Alexander Moskalev, of which there were about 20 in all, were for peaceful purposes. His prototype/experimental design bureau was established in 1936, and most of its products were cargo/transport, passenger or ambulance aeroplanes designed according to the limited capabilities of the Soviet aircraft industry of the 1930s. For this reason the SAM-13 fighter project, powered by two Renault-Bengazi MV-6 engines rated at 220hp (164kW) each, was unusual. During 1936-1938 Moskalev worked as a part-time director of the aviation technical secondary school in Voronezh, and his aeroplanes were designed and built in the school's workshops. Later, the experimental workshop of an aircraft factory in Voronezh became the production centre.

The new fighter had a twin-boom configuration with two engines in tandem, with the pilot's cockpit in between. It was similar to Andrei Tupolev's ANT-23 prototype fighter of the 1920s, but had much greater aerodynamic efficiency and was very small, with a wingspan of only 23ft 11½in (7.3m) and an overall length of 25ft 2⅛in (7.68m). Construction was entirely of wood. The wing, of 96.8ft² (9m²) area, was two spar one-piece structure with a plywood skin. The two-row air-cooled engines were mounted on frames of Chromansil steel tube which were attached to oval frames protecting the cockpit, and drove two-blade variable pitch Ratier-type propellers of 7ft 2⅜in (2.2m) diameter. The rear propeller had a locking device to allow safe escape from the aircraft in an emergency.

The wooden tailplane was attached to the ends of the two tubular tailbooms, and the fin and rudder were mounted at its centre. The control surfaces had Duralumin frames and were fabric covered. All surfaces were carefully filled and smoothly finished.

The SAM-13 was one of the first aircraft in the USSR to have a retractable nosewheel undercarriage. The main legs retracted into the wing each side of the fuselage centreline, and the front leg, which had a nosewheel shimmy damper, retracted rearward beneath the engine and front part of the cockpit. The cockpit had a Plexiglas canopy.

At a flying weight of 2,608lb (1,183kg) the fighter had a low wing loading of 26.7lb/ft² (131kg/m²) and a power loading of 5.9lb/hp (2.7kg/hp), corresponding to the best single-engine fighters of the time. Its armament comprised four ShKAS machine guns, two in the wings and two over the front engine.

The SAM-13's rated sea level speed was 292mph (470km/h), and its speed at critical altitude (19,000ft - 5,800m) was 422mph (680 km/h). It made only two test flights, which were conducted at the factory by Nikolay Fikson late in 1940. It was planned to record speeds at different altitudes during the second flight, but unfortunately the nosewheel leg failed to retract. Nevertheless, the maximum speed at 18,700ft (5,700m) with the leg down was 348mph (560km/h). Although the small flaps were deflected 90° during the subsequent landing, they proved ineffective, and consequently the take-off and landing runs were too long. Redesign of the undercarriage and flutter tests in the Tsentral'nyi Aerogidro-dynamichesky Institut (TsAGI - Central Aero-

dynamic and Hydrodynamic Institute) full scale wind tunnel took a long time, and the new fighter was not transferred to the Letno-Issledovatel'skii Institut (LII - Ministry of Aviation Industry Flight Research Institute) until the summer of 1941.

During its tests at the LII it displayed several outstanding qualities:
- a good field of view forward and downward owing to the pilot's cockpit being located above the wing leading edge;
- better manoeuvrability in the horizontal plane compared with conventionally configured twin-engined fighters, owing to the longitudinal concentration of mass (or centre-line thrust);
- the propeller arrangement cancelled out torque reaction.

However, there were some shortcomings:
- unfavourable conditions for the pusher propeller owing to slipstream disturbances caused by the wing;
- the rear propeller had a disturbing effect on the tail surfaces, which were close to it;
- there were deficiencies in the cooling of the rear engine;
- during taxying, take-off and landing the nosewheel threw small stones into the rear engine's cooling system and propeller;
- the airframe structure did not protect the pilot from the rear engine in the event of a head-on collision and nose-over.

The advent of the Second World War forced the development of this unconventional fighter to be abandoned.

Although the SAM-13 was similar in configuration to the twin-finned Dutch Fokker D.XXIII, which had appeared a year and a half earlier, the resemblance was purely superficial. The D.XXIII was twice as heavy, one and a half times larger and had an all-metal airframe. Each of its engines was more powerful than the two MV-6 engines combined, but its maximum speed at 13,500ft (4,100m) was only 326mph (525km/h). It can therefore be confidently asserted that Moskalev had designed an original and promising fighter for the Soviet Army Air Force, but its destiny was decided when the Nazis attacked the USSR.

*For technical data, see Table A, page 163.*

**The SAM-13 during wind tunnel testing.**

*Opposite page:*
**While the Moskalev SAM-13 resembled the Dutch Fokker D.XXIII, it was a much more lightweight fighter and had only a single fin.**

**Moskalev SAM-13**

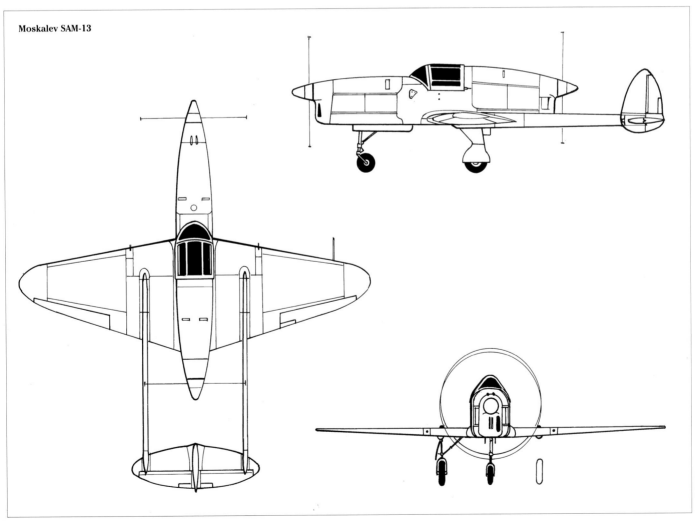

# Petlyakov

Up to November 1937 Vladimir Petlyakov, the senior deputy director of the ZOK prototype development plant and head of its design department, could not bemoan his lot. He was one of Andrei Tupolev's nearest associates, and enjoyed the confidence of the Tsentral'nyi Aerogidrodynamichesky Institut (Ts AGI – Central Aerodynamic and Hydrodynamic Institute) administration and high-ranking authorities.

Petlyakov had designed the wing for the ANT-6 (TB-3) heavy bomber, which was considered an advanced aircraft for its time, and he also headed the development of the still more advanced ANT-42 (or TB-7) high altitude multi-engined bomber. Petlyakov was a member of a Soviet technical delegation which visited the USA and France in the summer and autumn of 1937, respectively. The visit resulted in the purchase of licences for a number of foreign aircraft, including the famous Douglas DC-3, designated Lisunov Li-2 in the Soviet Union.

However, on the eve of the 20th anniversary of the October Revolution Petlyakov was suddenly arrested on a charge of intentionally prolonging the development of the ANT-42. The accusation was ridiculous, but, according to the practice and 'traditions' of Stalin's security forces, undeniable.

Only in the summer of 1938 was he permitted to resume his professional work in a special department formed at the Narodny Komissariat Vnutrennikh Del (NKVD – People's Commissariat of Internal Affairs, forerunner of the famed KGB), named the Special Engineering Department. Leading a group of 50 designers, Petlyakov had to design a new long range high altitude fighter with powerful offensive armament. The new aircraft clearly inherited a great deal from the ANT-42, with which it had much in common, and it is worth describing the earlier aircraft briefly.

One of the key aims in the development of the ANT-42 was the attainment of high speeds at high altitudes. It was required that the bomber should be able to outpace enemy fighters, thus giving it high survivability in combat.

The ANT-42's development was considerably delayed, and the work which began in July 1934 was seriously affected by powerplant problems. The attempt to solve the survivability problem of the heavy bomber by endowing it with high speed at high altitudes failed because the new fighters that appeared in the second half of the 1930s were much faster than those of the previous generation. It seemed that it was impossible to keep pace with the development of the likely Luftwaffe fighter opposition

## Type '100'

A concept was formed for a high altitude escort fighter to provide cover the ANT-42 during its long range flights. In addition, the '100' fighter had to intercept high altitude bombers and reconnaissance aircraft. Its designation was apparently derived from the abbreviation of the name of the office where the fighter was developed, STO, which is spelt identically to the Russian language numeral 'one hundred'. An aeroplane designed by another detainee, Vladimir Myasishchev, was named STO-2 or '102', and Andrei Tupolev's design was designated STO-3 or '103'.

The designation '100' outlived the Special Engineering Department itself, which was soon renamed the Special Engineering Bureau (OTB) and headed by state security officer Major V Kravchenko of the NKVD. It is interesting to note that all papers, including those of a purely technical nature, were signed by Kravchenko before they left the bureau. The names of the chief designers were not mentioned anywhere. However, there was another class of documents for which their authors, the detainees, were responsible. The NKVD was determined not to multiply the signatures of 'people's traitors'. Each of the specialists who had the right to approve the documents was given a seal with figures stamped on it. It is known that at first three and then four design teams worked at the bureau. To avoid confusion of the stamped documents, it was decided that the sum of the figures on the author's seals should be equal to the number on the seal of 'their' chief designer. Quite a model of resourcefulness!

The detainees worked very hard, up to twelve hours a day without any days off or rest periods. The time scheduled for the development of the aircraft was very limited, and it was required to fly in 1939. However, the 'people's traitors' at the OTB coped with their important task and the '100', built at Plant No.156, took off for the first time on 22nd December 1939.

The fuselage, designed by Alexander Putilov, was of almost monocoque structure. It consisted of three production units of circular section, with a lightweight dorsal fairing located between the cockpit and the navigator's and gunner's cockpit. The fuselage skin was relatively thick, averaging $\frac{1}{16}$ to $\frac{1}{12}$in (1.5 to 2mm), and the frames were closely spaced, at 11½in to 1ft 7½in (0.3 to 0.5m). There were no skin stiffening stringers. The wing was a tapered two-spar structure with a virtually straight leading edge, and consisted of a centre section and two outer panels with stringers and ribs closely spaced and covered

with a skin $\frac{1}{42}$ to $\frac{1}{32}$in (0.6 to 0.8mm) thick. The wing was fitted with split ailerons and Schrenk-type trailing edge flaps. The tailwheel landing gear was designed by Timofey Saprykin. The twin-strut main undercarriage units rotated backwards into wheel wells in the engine nacelles. The tailwheel retracted into the fuselage.

The aircraft's exterior was covered with varnish but left unpainted to maintain its natural silver colour. The ailerons, rudder and elevators were painted red, and there were black-edged stars on the fuselage sides and on the lower wing surfaces.

In general, the '100' fighter, with its two Klimov M-105 engines equipped with TK-2 turbochargers, and two pressurised cockpits, was really a pioneering design. Its most significant features were as follows:

- Its two advanced M-105 engines with TK-2 turbochargers, structurally integrated with the engine nacelles and driving VISh-42 variable pitch propellers, were estimated to ensure a speed of 385mph (620km/h) at 32,800ft (10,000m). The turbochargers were positioned on the nacelle sides under the wing leading edges. There were no exhaust pipes or manifolds on the nacelles, as found on other M-105 powered aircraft;

- the two pressurised cockpits designed by M Petrov provided comfortable conditions for the three-man crew. Compressed air for the system was bled from the turbochargers, and cockpit pressure was kept constant from 12,000ft (3,700m) up to the 32,800ft (10,000m) operating ceiling;

- a safety factor of ten allowed all aerobatic manoeuvres and high speed dives to be performed;

- the wide use of electrically-signalled control devices developed by A Yengibaryan and I Sklyansky included electro-hydraulic undercarriage retraction and electrically-operated trailing edge flaps, radiator louvres, trim tabs, and governors for the P-3 constant speed propellers;

- powerful offensive armament included two ShVAK guns with 300 rounds per gun and two ShKAS machine guns with 900 rounds each. To protect the fighter from stern attacks, provision was made for the installation of a fixed ShKAS machine gun with 700 rounds in the tailcone. This last

Side elevation of the Petlyakov Type '100' high altitude fighter.

Testing of the Type '100' was carried out during the winter months.

The Type '100' rigged for gun and sight calibration.

weapon, however, was not installed on the aircraft used in the '100' flight tests;

- provision for two 551lb (250kg) and 1,102lb (500kg) free-fall bombs on external stores carriers located outside the propeller arcs to permit safe bomb release in an almost vertical dive. In addition to the above, provision was made for a new form of armament consisting of a cluster of 40 x 200mm projectiles to be dropped on enemy bomber formations. The projectiles were detonated by means of time fuses.

There is a saying that disadvantages are the outcome of advantages, and this can apply to aircraft. Its numerous innovations proved a handicap to the '100', and its flight tests revealed many deficiencies.

The starboard engine failed on the maiden flight. Pilot Peotr Stefanovsky, who was flying the prototype, described the situation: 'I was flying with only one engine running. The landing gear was down, as always on the first flight, and the aeroplane was losing height, making flying still more difficult. God, low, too low. Dead ahead was a hangar roof and beyond it, on a servicing apron, were all kinds of ground equipment, including a large wooden rig used to lift aircraft off the ground for inspection. I flew the yawing aircraft over the roof at full power, then it suddenly lost altitude as if it had hit a bump and rushed towards the rig. Collision was imminent and unavoidable. Flaring slightly, the aeroplane touched the ground with its wheels and immediately made a gigantic leap, then a second and a third, finally coming to a halt. The 2m wooden rig was behind us; we had jumped over it!'

The bouncing of the '100' was caused by an error in the design of the main undercarriage shock absorbers, which affected their damping properties. Petlyakov, who was a very gentle person and usually did his best to avoid blaming people, reproved Saprykin: 'Well Timosha [Saprykin's nickname], how did you manage to fail, eh?' The landing gear was redesigned in the shortest possible time.

More serious problems were associated with the engines. The oil cooling system was found to have insufficient capacity at altitudes above 1,600ft (500m), and water temperature exceeded its maximum permissible value at 21,600ft (6,600m) and above. Although the engines, oil pumps and other equipment were replaced twice during the flight tests, the predicted altitude/speed performance envelope was not achieved. The rate of climb tests remained uncompleted, too.

Surprisingly, the TK-2 turbocharger, which was potentially the most troublesome unit and was expected to be a great cause of concern, was practically faultless. Consequently the directors of the aircraft's test programme

drew the optimistic conclusion that the design speed of 372 to 385mph (600 to 620km/h) at 32,800ft (10,000m) was really attainable. In general, the design speeds and actual speeds obtained during flight tests at low and medium altitudes agreed well. The maximum speed achieved on a flight leg flown at 21,600ft (6,600m) was 334mph (538km/h). At a typical flying weight of 16,016lb (7,265kg) the fighter climbed 13,000ft (4,000m) in 6.8 minutes.

During the period of manufacturer's flight tests, from 20th December 1939 to 10th April 1940, the prototype underwent repair following a belly-landing due to ski landing gear retraction failure, and it flew on 11 days only. During this time the fighter made 23 flights, amassing 6 hours 55 minutes total flying time.

From 11th April 1940 the '100' underwent official State tests at the Nauchno Issledovatelyskii Institut (NII – scientific and research institute) of the Voenno-vozdushniye Sily (VVS – air forces of the USSR). The first prototype was flown by Major Peotr Stefanovsky and his navigator, Major Nikitin, while NII test pilot Khrypkov and navigator Perevalov flew the second, 'back-up', prototype. The latter aircraft turned out to be an unlucky machine. During the second flight its cockpit caught fire due to a fuel system leakage. The pilot had to make an immediate force-landing. Because of its high sink rate the fighter nosed over and was damaged beyond repair. The crew members escaped with injuries, but several onlookers were killed. The NKVD interfered in the matter again, and only Petlyakov's resolute stand in the ensuing conflict enabled the flight crew and equipment designer K Rogov to escape violent repercussions.

The first '100' prototype, now the only remaining example, continued the flight tests. To improve directional stability the fin area was increased by approximately a third, but the longitudinal stability was still insufficient and it was suggested that the outer wing panels should be swept back to improve these characteristics. A three-point landing with the trailing edge flaps fully down was impossible, as the effectiveness of the control surfaces was inadequate. It was therefore recommended that the trailing edge flaps should not be extended fully, and that the stabiliser's angle of incidence should be changed on series production aircraft.

But the most unpleasant characteristics resulted from the aerodynamic behaviour of the aerofoil sections at speeds corresponding to those for an approach to a landing. In endeavouring to achieve high speeds the designers had selected two sharp-nosed sections developed by TsAGI; 'B' at the wing root and 'BS' at the tips. At low angles of attack they had lower drag while providing a lift coefficient equal to that of ordinary aerofoils, but at the high angles of attack typical of a

landing approach they suffered an asymmetric stall. This disadvantage had to be accepted, though later more than one rookie pilot paid for it with his life.

During the official state tests 34 flights were made, the total time flown being 13 hours 25 minutes. On 1st May 1940 Stefanovsky displayed the new fighter in the aerial parade over Moscow. In his excitement he forgot to retract the undercarriage, and performed a zoom over Red Square with the gear extended. Petlyakov and his associates watched the flight from the roof of the prison building, the former TsAGI Konstruktorski Otdel Opytnovo Samoloyostoyeniya (KOSOS – Experimental Aircraft Design Section).

Despite the deficiencies, the results of the '100's evaluation were mainly favourable. A summary of the Flight Evaluation Report stated:

- The '100' aircraft offers the best solution to the problem of creating a pressurised-cockpit armed machine. It is necessary to build a development batch of the '100';
- to make use of the '100's high aerodynamic properties it is advisable that an unpressurised cockpit dive bomber should be designed using this aircraft as a basis. A development batch is required to be built;
- submit a mock-up of the bomber for approval by 1st June 1940.

Bearing in mind that the '100' had completed the official tests on 10th May, the schedule was very tight. The fate of the aircraft was greatly changed by the report's request for a dive bomber and an official resolution accompanying the document, which stated: 'The statement is approved with the Flight Evaluation Report amended as follows: series production of the dive bomber version of the '100' aircraft is considered advisable'.

On 10th May 1940 German dive bombers attacked French territory for the first time. At that time the Soviet Air Force did not have a mass-produced dive bomber, and the series-built SPB medium dive bomber designed by Nikolay Polikarpov was considered a failure. The priority of the need for a dive bomber was quite justified. In the second half of 1940 and early in 1941 the question concerning the necessity to proceed with a fighter version of the aircraft was raised several times, along with the equally urgent need to begin series production of the PB-100 dive bomber, the future Pe-2. Three hundred designers were sent from the Yakovlev, Sukhoi and Alexander Arkhangelsky design bureaux to the Special Engineering Bureau to develop production drawings for the PB-100. People's Commissar of the Aviation Industry Alexey Shakhurin demanded that the first flight of the PB-100 be made on 7th November 1940. Full scale development and production of the dive bomber at Moscow Plants No.39 and No.22

suffered so much from multiple delays and slippage that the design team was unable to work on the high altitude fighter version. Lavrenty Beriya, the feared head of the NKVD, intervened, ordering a search for those who caused delays at the production plants; the design had been conceived under his authority, and he could not allow it to fail. The first pre-production PB-100 dive bomber eventually made its maiden flight on 15th December 1940, and this was just the first step in the difficult life of this aeroplane, later to become famous. All trace of the '100' high altitude fighter was lost somewhere in the fuss of getting the Pe-2 bomber into series production.

## Pe-3

A month after the opening of the German assault on the Soviet Union, the Luftwaffe executed its first mass night bomber raid on Moscow. In a fitting manner, the pilots of the 6th Fighter Air Corps met the enemy and repulsed the raid, and only 11 or 12% of the bombers managed to reach Moscow. However, owing to the lack of a guidance system for the fighters and their insufficient endurance, it was very difficult to achieve a successful interception. Pilots spent the greater part of their time searching for enemy aeroplanes that were invisible in the night beyond a range of 1,000 to 1,300ft (300 to 400m). Anti-aircraft searchlights were also useless.

Well-known Soviet test pilot Mark Gallay described his first combat action like this: 'The enemy bomber, which I could scarcely find in the intersection of searchlights, had disappeared before I could approach it. That was simple to explain – it had fulfilled night bombing and was flying to the west at full speed. The searchlights were still following it, but with every second the distance became greater, the illuminating sharply decreased and soon the bomber disappeared.'

The night environment was not only useful to an enemy. German bombers approached Moscow without a fighter escort, and in such conditions the interceptor needed good endurance, powerful armament and a wide field of view from the cockpit. Such properties were inherent to the twin-engine, two-seat aeroplane, and the Soviet Air Force Command had a wide selection of such fighters: the Tairov Ta-3, Mikoyan-Gurevich MiG-5, Polikarpov TIS and Grushin GR. The Ta-3 was even recommended for full scale production in accordance with a joint decision reached by the Narodny Komissariat Aviatsionnoi Promyshlennosti (NKAP – State Commissariat for the Aviation Industry Promyshlennosti – People's Commissariat for Heavy Industry) and VVS Administration on 4th June 1940.

This was the same day that a decision on series production of the Pe-2 bomber and Il-2 Shturmovik attack aeroplane was accepted.

Meanwhile, the need to produce an interceptor to counter enemy bomber and reconnaissance aircraft became evident. Such an aircraft could only be produced quickly by using a production aeroplane as its basis. Then the recent 'fighting past' of the Pe-2 tactical bomber was recalled.

In accordance with the decision made by the National Defence Committee on 2nd August 1941, Moscow Aircraft Plant No.39 and its chief designer, Vladimir Petlyakov, were ordered to develop a fighter version of the Pe-2 by 6th August. Only four days were allowed for modification of the fuel system, armament and radio-electronic equipment. Nonetheless, the first prototype of the Pe-3 twin-engine fighter made its maiden flight on 7th August, piloted by test pilot Major Fedorov. The next day NII VVS test pilot Colonel V Stepanchyonok completed the production acceptance flight tests, and the Pe-3 then went for its state flight tests. There can be no better example of expeditiousness in the history of aviation; only seven days had elapsed from the issuing of the request for a proposal to the passing of the State tests.

To suit the aeroplane to its intended purpose considerable attention was paid to increasing its endurance and range. The standard Pe-2 wing contained a total of eight fuel tanks, and it was impossible to increase their capacity without making considerable changes to the wing structure. There was simply no time for that, so additional tanks were placed inside the fuselage, increasing the range to 1,242 miles (2,000km). It was necessary to squeeze fuel tanks with a total capacity of 153.9 gallons (700 litres) into the centre and aft fuselage sections, and they could not be too far from the wing's centre of pressure if the aircraft's centre of gravity was to be kept within the limits. One of the additional tanks was therefore located inside the fuselage bomb bay, and two more replaced the gunner's cockpit. As this left no room for the gunner/radio operator, the aeroplane became a two-seater. However, the hatch in the aft section of the fuselage was retained to enable the aircraft to carry its ground crew technicians during redeployment.

The attack armament was reinforced with an additional UBK 12.7mm machine gun with 150 rounds in the forward fuselage. Thus, on the Pe-3 prototype the nose ammunition comprised two large calibre UBK machine guns and one ShKAS with 750 rounds. In production Pe-3s the ShKAS machine gun was omitted but ammunition for the UBKs was increased to 250 rounds per gun.

The upper turret ShKAS machine gun was taken from the Pe-2. Because there was no

tail gunner in this version of the aircraft, the fixed ShKAS machine gun tail mounting from the '100' high altitude fighter, with 250 rounds, was fitted in the fuselage tailcone. The bomb load was considerably reduced. Only four of the bomb racks of the conventional Pe-2 were retained; two in the bomb hatches in the engine nacelles, and two mounted externally on the fuselage underside. The total normal bomb load was 400kg, and the maximum or overload was 700kg (two 250kg bombs and two 100kg bombs). The electrical bomb release control system was removed, leaving only the mechanical emergency system. Also removed were the dive-brake grids under the wings, together with their mechanism, but this was a mistake, because the Pe-3 was used more often as a bomber than as a fighter, and in that role the airbrakes would have been very useful.

The RSBbis bomber radio was replaced by the RSI-4 radio conventionally fitted in Soviet fighters, installed in the navigator's cockpit. This substitution was not very successful, as the fighter's communication range with a ground command station was 110km (between fighters it was only 50-60km), and its combat range was 700-800km. As a result, the aircraft had no communication with ground control during combat operations. To save weight the radio compass was also removed, which made the situation even worse.

The Pe-3 prototype's normal loaded take-off weight was 7,800kg, and its empty weight was 5,890kg. During its flight tests at the NII VVS this aircraft produced the following performance figures: maximum speed at 5,000m, 530km/h; service ceiling, 9,000m; maximum range, 2,150km. The flight test data were considered satisfactory, and on 14th August Aircraft Plant No.39 received a government order to begin full-scale production of the fighter, being given only until 25th August to assemble five pre-production aircraft. A pilot production Pe-3 was under flight test at the NII VVS from 29th August 29 to 7th September 1941, the tests being conducted at the central airfield in Moscow. The aircraft's performance was the same as that of the prototype, and it is interesting to compare it with the performance of the German Messerschmitt Bf110C fighter of very similar design. The range, sea-level speed (445km/h) and time to climb to 5,000m (8.5 to 9min) were practically the same, but the Messerschmitt was lighter by 1,350kg, had better manoeuvrability in the horizontal plane and its nose battery of four MG 17 machine guns and two MG FF cannon had a heavier salvo per second compared with the Pe-3's armament. However, the Soviet fighter was 10km/hr faster than the Bf110C at the engines' critical altitude.

The initiation of Pe-3 series production was beset with great difficulties. Sets of drawings

*Top:* Pe-3 fighter built at Plant No.22, 1944.

*Above left:* **Pe-3 armament was installed on a single-gun mount in the lower fuselage section.**

*Above:* **Fixed hatch-mounted machine gun, used to protect the Pe-3 from attack from below and behind.**

*Centre left:* **Fairings removed from the Pe-3's tail cone-mounted rear defence machine gun.**

*Bottom left:* **Long before napalm appeared, the Vylivnoy Aviatsionny Pribor (VAP) was tested on a Pe-3. VAPs were used for pouring out combustible fluids over troop concentrations.**

for some components were not ready, and the first batch was assembled using sketches, detail parts being adjusted to fit *in situ*. The new large-scale assembly units – the fuel tanks, the nose mounting for the additional UBK machine gun and the tail-mounting for the ShKAS machine gun – were not accurately machined, and this reduced the production rate.

During firing tests of the lower UBK machine gun the Plexiglas nosecone could not withstand the pressures of the gases emitted from the gun barrel, and was shattered. It was first replaced by a nosecone of Duralumin, and then by one of steel. In general, the absence of part of the nose glazing was the main external feature distinguishing the Pe-3 from the Pe-2 dive-bomber. The shellcases and links ejected by the large-calibre guns damaged the wing leading edges and the fuselage underside, causing scratches, dents and even jagged holes in the skin, and cartridge cases sometimes entered the radiator intakes. Altering the shape of the ejection chute openings proved unsuccessful, so it was finally decided to collect the spent cases and links in the ammunition boxes.

According to engineer Makarov and pilot Stepanchyonok, the production Pe-3 had to undergo the following modifications:

- enhancement of the offensive armament by the installation of an additional ShVAK cannon;
- enhancement of the defensive armament by replacing the ShKAS machine gun in the navigator's turret with a UBT machine gun of larger calibre;
- provision of front armour for the crew, and extension of navigator's aft armour plate;
- replacement of the RSI-4 radio with another having greater radius of action;
- installation of a photographic camera on the Pe-3 reconnaissance aeroplane.

It was impossible to introduce all of these modifications quickly into series production, and aeroplanes were delivered to combat units without frontal armour and cannon.

The 95th High Speed Bomber Air Regiment was the first Soviet Air Force combat unit to introduce the Pe-3 into service and the first in the Moscow military district to receive the Pe-2 in 1941, demonstrating it to the general public during the aerial flypast on 1st May.

Having already mastered the Pe-2, the pilots and navigators quickly grew accustomed to the fighter version, but the shortcomings mentioned earlier caused bewilderment and even protest from some pilots. The absence of frontal armour made the crew very vulnerable to the defensive fire from enemy aircraft. Colonel S Pestov, commander of the 95th Regiment, noted in a report that if the armour was not installed, 'the regiment will disappear after two combat actions'. A squadron commander of the regiment, Captain A Zhatkov, was of the same opinion, and even sent a personal letter to Secretary Malenkov which began: 'I, being the Air Squadron Commander, wish to inform you regarding the inferiority of aeroplanes entering service with the VVS'. Zhatkov enumerated practically all of the aeroplane's weak points as already noted in the NII VVS report. In Zhatkov's opinion it was an urgent necessity to install ShVAK cannon and replace the ShKAS machine gun with a large calibre UBT machine gun on the Pe-3.

A study of the aircraft's night combat capability had been made at the NII VVS aircraft weapon testing range at the beginning of September 1941. Test pilot Stepanchyonok and his navigator Nos, a first rank technician, conducted firing trials against a ground target and found that the flames from the gun muzzles dazzled the crew and rendered the K-8T aiming reticule invisible. For that reason visual sighting during the trials was conducted down range. The armament specialists quickly installed flame dampers on the gun barrels, and these eliminated the dazzle. It was also necessary to fit night curtains to the lower cockpit glazing to eliminate the glare when the aircraft was caught in a searchlight beam, and these were quickly designed and installed. Later, for the first time in the USSR, ultra-violet cockpit lighting and electric luminescent lighting for instruments was tested during night flights. All such modifications were recommended for inclusion in production aircraft.

## Pe-3*bis*

Captain Zhatkov's letter to Malenkov served as a powerful incentive for the rapid modification of the Pe-3. Its weaknesses and defects had to be eliminated quickly, and this task was accomplished by the Petlyakov Design Bureau in September 1941. The updated Pe-3*bis* aeroplane that appeared as a result of this work was tested at the NII VVS by pilot A Khripkov in September and October 1941, a total of 40 flights being made during the test programme.

The main differences between the Pe-3*bis* and the production Pe-3 tested earlier were:

- two UBK updated large calibre machine guns with 250 rounds per gun were installed in the nose in place of the UBK machine guns; the lower machine gun was attached to mounting used for the ShKAS machine gun in the Pe-2;
- a 20mm ShKAS cannon with 250 rounds replaced the lower UBK machine gun;
- a 12.7mm UBT machine gun with 180 rounds replaced the TSS-1 in the navigator's turret;
- automatic slats were installed to improve low speed stability;
- the cockpit canopy was shortened and the anti-nose-over frame was moved forwards 1ft 6in (0.48m);
- frontal pilot's armour was installed and the navigator's seat armour was reinforced, bringing the total weight of armour to 299.8lb (136kg);
- the nitrogen fuel tank filling system was replaced by a neutral gas system using engine exhaust gases;
- a hood was installed in the cockpit to prevent the pilot being blinded.

The aircraft's flying weight increased to 17,724lb (8,040kg) – 396lb/180kg greater than that of the Pe-3. The speed at service ceiling was reduced to 329mph (530km/h), but sea level speed increased to 278mph (448km/h). The automatic slats simplified handling, especially during approach and landing.

The ShVAK cannon doubled the striking power of the Pe-3*bis*. At a range of 1,968 to 3,280ft (600 to 1,000m) at a diving angle of 25 to 30° up to 50% of the shells hit a 129ft² (12m²) target. However, the port UBK seriously affected gun firing due to its blinding the pilot, especially at night. Moreover, the nose gun mounting proved to be very difficult to manage, up to 45 minutes being required for the armament specialists to rearm the fighter. Again, as on the first Pe-3 fighters, the ejected shellcases and links from the ShVAK gun damaged the skin of the fuselage underside and wing centre section. Because it was very difficult to devise a means of collecting them in the ammunition boxes, the damaged areas were patched with steel sheets. The UBT machine gun mounting in the rear of the canopy was designed by specialists at Plant No.39. To simplify handling of the heavy machine gun, they decided to remove the belt feed sleeve and replace it with a purpose-designed cartridge box containing a 30 round belt. The box was fastened to the machine gun, ensuring a wide firing angle, with an azimuth deviation of 90° and a vertical angle of up to 70°.

It subsequently transpired that the greatly extended barrel of the gun imposed an unacceptable load on the navigator's arms at angles of deflection greater than 40 to 50° and speeds above 248mph (400km/h). Even the strongest gunners found it impossible to deflect the machine gun to 90° under such conditions. The NII VVS specialists demanded that an aerodynamic or mechanical balance be designed for the UBT turret mounting. Another shortcoming of this unit was the low capacity of the cartridge box and the long time required to change it - more than a minute. In the midst of a dogfight such delay was unacceptable. Moreover, vibrations due to insufficient stiffness of the turret made long bursts of fire impossible, and the mounting in the navigator's turret needed to be completely re-designed.

The armament designers never thought much of the effectiveness of the fixed ShKAS machine gun in the tail, and after the Pe-3*bis* tests it was recommended that a remote-controlled movable mount be designed to protect of the aircraft's lower hemisphere. The task was given to Aircraft Plant No.32.

In spite of the repeated demands of its military customers, Plant No.39 was unable to install RPK-10 radio compasses in the initial series Pe-3*bis* owing to irregular deliveries. When the ShVAK gun was mounted in the fuselage nose, the residual deviation of the A-4 magnetic compass exceeded 20˚. This, combined with the reduced cockpit glazing and the inevitable aggravation of conditions during visual reference navigation, caused acute problems during long range flights, especially over unfamiliar territory.

In addition to the shortcomings of the Pe-3*bis* described above, there were yet more inherent to the Pe-2 bomber, mainly regarding the powerplant.

After completion of the Pe-3*bis* flight tests the modifications were gradually introduced into production aircraft. The updating of some aircraft (but not all) was undertaken in the field by specialist engineering servicing teams. In combat units the ShVAK guns were installed, the navigator's turret machine gun was replaced by the large calibre UBT without a shield over the standard 'tortoise shell', and a carrier for DAG-10 aerial grenades was mounted in the tail as a defensive measure. In some memoirs it is stated that a gun was installed under the Pe-3's wing centre section or even in the wing. The first seems improbable, but the second is simply out of the question, because the wing structure did not permit such a modification, especially under combat unit conditions.

The desire for improved performance resulted in the design of the second and final version of the Pe-3*bis*. Soviet Air Force test pilot M Nyukhtikov flight-tested this aeroplane in May and June 1942.

The new version differed from earlier ones in several respects. The UBK machine guns were moved from the forward fuselage to the wing centre section, where the Pe-2's bomb bay had been located. Both guns were mounted on the same frame, shielded by a light side hatch. This frame was similar to the structure designed for the two ShVAK guns of the Pe-2I at Plant No.22, but its axis of rotation was in the front section. When the rear attachment point was released, the machine guns together with their ammunition boxes were lowered, considerably improving their accessibility. The starboard UBK was provided with 230 rounds, and the port with 265.

A production unit designed by I Toropov of specialised Plant No.32 was installed in place of the turret in the initial Pe-3*bis* batch built at aircraft Plant No.39. The ammunition belt of the UBK wing-mounted machine gun designed by M Berezin held 200 rounds. To improve the reliability of the mounting, the gun was equipped with an electric belt drive. During flight tests it proved impossible to deflect the machine gun to angles greater than 40 to 50˚ with the navigator's help, owing to the excessive aerodynamic load. To overcome this, a twin-petal compensator was mounted on the shield, but it was not sufficiently effective.

The anti-nose-over frame in the crew cockpit was dismantled to improve the navigator's working conditions, and the crew armour was reinforced, the total weight of armour increasing to 362lb (148kg). The pilot's frontal armour plate was 2½in (6.5mm) thick, which would have been impossible in the first version of the Pe-3*bis* owing to the armament in the fuselage nose. The pilot's rear armour was made of 5in (13mm) steel plate, and the lower hatch of the cockpit was also armoured to protect the crew against accidental firing of the UBK during ingress.

The nose glazing was removed. Only a small access hatch in front of navigator was left for aiming (visual sighting) during level flight.

Repositioning of the armament in the wing centre section reduced the capacity of fuel tank No.7 by 21.9 gallons (100 litres). To insulate the tank from heat, an asbestos bulkhead was fastened to the structure. At the same time, the bulkhead served to shield the machine guns from gasoline leakage.

The fin area was increased by 15% to improve directional stability. According to pilots, however, this modification did not prove effective, and it was not incorporated in series production aircraft.

An anti-icing system was provided for the propellers and the canopy windscreen, and R-7 engine speed governors operated by a wheel control in the cockpit replaced the automatic R-3s with electrical remote control, which had an inherent fault that allowed the possibility of propeller overspeeding during recovery from a dive.

The aeroplane's centre of gravity, especially when landing with empty fuel tanks, moved forward owing to the cannon and armour in the forward fuselage. This reduced the anti-nose-over angle and made effective braking impossible, and the aeroplane always tried to go on to its nose. To eliminate this tendency the braces of the main undercarriage legs were lengthened, moving the wheels forward 2⅓in (60mm), enough to improve the Pe-3*bis*'s landing characteristics.

The normal flying weight of the Pe-3*bis* was 17,641lb (8,002kg). Compared with the first

version of the aeroplane its maximum speed was slightly reduced to 272mph (438km/h) at sea level and 327mph (527km/h) at altitude – owing to the turret compensator and increased fin area. In a combat turn the aircraft gained some 1,770ft (540m) of height, the time to complete a turn at 330ft (100m) was 30 seconds, and the time taken to reach 16,400ft (5,000m) was 9.65 minutes. This performance was typical for a Pe-3*bis* production fighter of 1942.

As described above, full-scale production of the Pe-3 fighter began at Plant No.39 in August 1941. During that month only 16 were manufactured, and all of them were apparently delivered to the 95th Istrebitelny Aviasionny Polk (IAP – Fighter Air Regiment). In September the delivery rate increased significantly, 98 aircraft being produced at the plant. These were delivered to the 95th Fighter Air Regiment and the 9th, 40th, 54th, 208th and 511th Bombardirovochny Aviatsionny Polks (BAP – Bomber Air Regiment). In addition, 82 aircraft produced in October were delivered to the 3rd and 13th Reconnaissance Air Regiments. It is well known that Pe-3s were later delivered to the 121st and 603rd Bomber Air Regiments and to the 65th Air Regiment of the Soviet Army Navy (VMF). All of the aircraft produced in 1941 were of the Pe-3 type, armed only with machine guns. Some already in combat units were fitted with the ShVAK gun and large calibre machine guns installed in the navigator's cockpit in addition to a pair of UBK machine guns. During three months of combat actions, Pe-3 losses totalled 50 aircraft, about a quarter of number delivered.

Because of its evacuation to Irkutsk, Plant No.39 ran down Pe-3 production and initially built only Pe-2 bombers at the new location. Production of twin-engined fighters was not resumed until April, but the monthly output never reached the level of September 1941. In April 1942 the last eleven Pe-3s and one Pe-3*bis* pilot pre-production aircraft with a ShVAK gun in the forward fuselage and UBK machine guns beneath the wing centre section were built. Thus the total number of Pe-3s built was 207.

From May the plant began producing the Pe-3*bis* at a rate of 20 aircraft per month. Forty were manufactured in July, and then production began to decrease. By the fourth quarter of the year Plant No.39 had been tasked with starting production of the Il-4 long range bomber. To complete work already started, some Pe-3*bis* were also produced during this period. Altogether, 132 aeroplanes were produced in 1942, including eleven Pe-3s. Another 13 were built and delivered in early 1943. The majority of the 134 produced at the plant were turned over to the 2nd, 4th and 40th Long Range Reconnaissance Air Regiments and Navy aviation units.

*Top:* **First prototype of the modified Pe-3bis fighter, as tested as the NII VVS in October 1941.**

*Above:* **The Pe-3bis did not have the under fuselage and tailcone machine guns of the Pe-3.**

In May 1943 the State Committee of Defence decreed that production of heavy twin-engined fighters would be established at Aircraft Plant No.22. It was implied that they would not be modelled on the Pe-3 or Pe-3bis of Plant No.39, but on their forerunner, the Pe-2I with a pair of ShVAK guns under the wing centre section, designed at Plant No.22 in 1941. The design was slightly changed; the front armour, the tailcone ShKAS gun and the UBK navigator's turret machine gun were added. It was estimated that this version would have a speed of 335mph (540km/h) at 11,500ft (3,500m) and would climb to 16,400ft (5,000m) in 9.6 minutes. After building two pre-series aircraft, the plant would deliver 25 new fighters (based, it was now implied, on the Pe-3) in July, and would deliver two aircraft daily from August. But the decision to put the Pe-3 in production for a second time was cancelled in July, when Plant No.22 was given the new task of manufacturing the Pe-2 bomber powered by Shvetsov M-82s.

A final bout of interest in the Pe-3 arose in the summer of 1944, when another 19 aircraft were produced at Plant No.22. They differed from the previous version in having only one ShVAK gun with increased ammunition in the wing centre section, and only one UBK machine gun in the fuselage nose. A standard VUB-3 turret with a UBT machine gun was installed in the navigator's cockpit, and the tail-mounted ShKAS gun was removed. The engine nacelle bomb carriers were also eliminated. As a result, on this last version of the Pe-3 only two external beams with MZD-40 locks under the wing centre section were retained, to which bombs of up to 551lb (250kg) could be attached. Two DAG-10 carriers for 20 AG-2 aerial grenades were mounted in the rear fuselage.

Thus a total of 360 Pe-3s of all variants was built during the war, and they were used in combat actions right up to the last days of the conflict.

## Pe-3s in combat

The 95th, 208th and 40th Air Regiments were the first Soviet Army aviation units to introduce the Pe-3 long range fighter into their in-

ventories, in August and September 1941. The aircraft of the initial batch were delivered to the 95th Skorostnoy Bombardirovochny Polk (SBP – High Speed Bomber Regiment), commanded by Colonel S Pestov. By that time the regiment had a short but commendable history. Formed in April 1940, it received the SB-2 bomber but was quickly converted to the new version, the Arkhangelsky Ar-2 dive bomber. The regiment's pilots flew over Moscow in five perfect nine-aircraft formations during the parade marking the 23rd anniversary of the Great October Socialist Revolution.

During February and March 1941 the regiment converted to the newest Pe-2 dive bomber, becoming the first aviation unit in the Moscow Military District to fly the type. Aircraft Plants Nos.22 and 39 delivered 40 aeroplanes of the initial batch to complete the regiment's inventory. During the flying parade on 1st May 1941 the 95th again demonstrated its modern bombers, and later it began operational testing of the Pe-2. The final two pre-war months were spent in combat training. On 15th June the first night flights using the Pe-2 took place. It was planned to stage a regimental competition for firing accuracy using ShKAS machine guns on 22nd June, but on that day the regiment was called to the alert.

At the outbreak of war the 95th SBP was based at Kalinin airfield in the interior of the USSR, and for that reason its losses were significantly less than those of many other bomber regiments located near the frontier in the early days. Moreover, its personnel were generally better prepared for action than other units, having begun to master the new aircraft in May and June.

Having completed a series of reconnaissance flights, the 95th was turned over to the VVS of the Western Front on 6th July. The situation was very difficult. Most of the combat missions undertaken by the regiment's bombers were flown without fighter escort. On 11th July five crews failed to return from missions, and by 23rd July only three combat capable aircraft remained in the squadron commanded by Captain A Zhatkov. On that day the squadron's aircraft, led by the commander, performed their last bombing raid, to the region of Yartsevo. While heading home the three Pe-2s were attacked by 15 Messerschmitt Bf 109E and 'G fighters, which were mistaken for Heinkel He 113s by Zhatkov's pilots, and in an intense dogfight four of the enemy fighters were brought down. One was accounted for by the canopy of Zhatkov's Pe-2, which was thrown from the bomber and struck a Bf 109G's propeller. However, the Luftwaffe pilots shot down all of the squadron's aircraft, their crews taking to their parachutes and returning to their regiment on foot.

In August the 95th Regiment was withdrawn to the reserve of the VVS of the Western Front to be reformed. In late August and practically throughout September the regiment converted to the new Pe-3 long range fighter, its gunner/radio operators being detached to other units. Navigators had to undertake a deep study of radio engineering, because they became responsible for radio communications, and the pilots were studying fighting tactics. Having gained combat experience in dogfights with German fighters, the latter already knew that the Pe-3 could achieve success in combat only by attacking the enemy's low speed bombers and reconnaissance aircraft. Different methods of attack were proposed, ranging from loitering in pairs as an airborne surveillance post and destroying lone enemy aircraft before calling for reinforcement if there was a massing of enemy machines, to the direction and guidance by radio of single-engined fighters during air combats. The latter case resembled the naval ship-leader concept; heading an attack by lighter forces. Nautical terminology was widely used in the Luftwaffe, where such aircraft were called destroyers, and in the Netherlands, where the concept of an 'airborne light cruiser' was born.

It was quickly realised that, with its long range, the Pe-3 could be used as high speed reconnaissance aircraft. Its lack of defensive armament was compensated for by the cloud cover provided by the Russian autumn, which pilots used to their advantage when attacked by the enemy.

On 25th September 1941, by order of the Soviet Air Force Commander-in-Chief, the 95th Regiment, which had 40 Pe-3s, was converted into the Air Fighter Regiment and incorporated in the 6th Fighter Air Defence Corps. A few days later six Pe-3s under the command of Captain Zhatkov performed the regiment's first escort mission, protecting Douglas C-47s carrying a British military delegation from Vologda to Moscow. The long range fighters fended off three German attacks and returned to base without loss.

On 3rd October 1941 First Lieutenant Fortovov of the 95th Regiment shot down a Junkers Ju 88 bomber, thereby opening the Pe-3's combat account, and another Ju 88 was attacked and set on fire the same day by Lieutenant Kulikov. But a day later the regiment suffered its first combat loss when Fortovov and his crew failed to return to base. According to the evidence of his wingman, Fortovov noticed a lone German aeroplane and, having ordered his wingman to continue loitering over the target, sped off to intercept the adversary. The exact circumstances of his death remained unknown.

Early in October the aircraft of the 95th Regiment took part in strike missions against ground targets. On 4th October the squadron led by Major A Satchkov bombed and strafed a large column of German armoured vehicles, dropping 40 bombs of 110lb (50kg) and 220lb (100kg) and machine gunning selected targets. The pilots observed direct hits on tanks and automobiles, and many vehicles were set alight. On their return flight the squadron was attacked by German Bf 109s, and in the ensuing dogfight each side lost one aircraft. Another Pe-3 was damaged while landing because its pilot was injured.

On 28th November the crews of First Lieutenants L Puzanov and V Streltsov flew a mission to provide air cover over Alexandrov railway junction. Three Ju 88 bombers were intercepted by the Pe-3s as they attempted to reach the railway station using cloud cover, and were dispersed. Puzanov quickly shot down one of them and Streltsov attacked another, but he was not so skilful. During his second attack he set fire to a Ju 88's engine, and the third pass finished off the German machine, but Streltsov had been wounded by a shell burst. His eye was injured and blood was pouring over his face. Nevertheless, guided by his navigator he managed to land his aeroplane at his base airfield, losing consciousness on the landing run.

Late in November 1941 Major A Zhatkov,

who had shot down several German aircraft, was appointed Commander of the 95th Fighter Air Regiment. The Pe-3s were operational in Moscow's air defence system until March 1942. To maintain a high level of combat readiness, the water radiators were not drained, even on frosty nights.

In the autumn of 1941 the regiment's aircraft underwent modification. The navigator's ShKAS guns were replaced by large calibre UBT machine guns, and ShVAK guns were installed in the forward fuselage. Some Pe-3s were equipped with RO-82 rocket projectiles in sets of eight, and some with eight RO-82s and a pair of RO-132s. A salvo could comprise two or four rockets fired simultaneously. Some of the regiment's aircraft were fitted with AFA-B cameras. Nevertheless, the main task of the 95th Regiment was the bombing of troops, and in only two months the regiment dropped more then 1,500 bombs on Hitler's forces.

On 1st March 1941, in accordance with an order issued by Stalin and the National Defence Committee, the 95th Fighter Air Regiment was turned over to the VVS of the Northern Fleet of the Soviet Navy. On 5th March many of the regiment's pilots and navigators were honoured with State military awards, and its commander, Major A Zhatkov, and his navigator, Captain N Morozov, received Orders of Lenin. On 7th March the regiment's aircraft took off and, forming up in two columns, headed north.

The 9th and 511th Blizhne-bombardirovochnyye Polki (BBAPs – Short Range Bomber Air Regiment), flying Pe-3 fighters, entered into combat on 10th October 1941 as a part of the VVS of the Western Front. Compared with the 95th Fighter Air Regiment, these regiments had only 20 aircraft apiece, formed into two squadrons.

This was the 9th Regiment's 'second attempt'. On 22nd June 1941 the regiment, flying SB-2s, had established its base on airfield in Panevezhis, Lithuania. After only four days under attack by German aircraft, both in air combats and in ground attack operations, the regiment lost almost all of its aircraft and was put in reserve. In July and August the regiment was re-staffed and divided into the 9th and 723rd BBAPs, and in September 1941 it received Pe-3 long range fighters in place of its Pe-2 dive bombers, though its title was not changed. From October 1941 to February 1942 the regiment was based at Frunze Central Airfield in Moscow, where the city's air terminal is now located, and was commanded by V Lukin. Most of the 9th BBAP's missions during October and November 1941 comprised bombing strikes against German troops. Another important task was the aerial protection of parts of the Moscow-Zagorsk and Moscow-Dmitrov railways.

**Oversized mainwheels gave the Pe-3*bis* the ability to operated from unpaved airfields.**

**Plant No.39 at Irkutsk started building the Pe-3*bis* in April 1942.**

In air combats from October 1941 to February 1942 the regiment's pilots shot down eleven enemy aircraft, including six Bf109s, and more than 130 reconnaissance flights were performed in the same period. In November 1941 the regiment was subordinated directly to the Main Headquarters of Soviet Air Force for special missions. One task was to lead regiments of fighter and strafe aircraft to the front, and the Pe-3s of the 9th Regiment led more than 2,000 combat aeroplanes to their new bases. The most skilled pilots performed another important task, escorting government aircraft, and carried out 95 escort flights during three months in 1941. Winter came early in 1941, and the flights were often made in difficult weather conditions. On 21st November Major Lukin, leading six Pe-3s, was escorting a C-47 carrying Marshal Semyon Timoshenko and Nikita Khruschev (Soviet premier 1958-1964), who was then a member of the Political Bureau of the VKP Central Committee. Owing to the thick cloud cover

the aeroplanes were flying in a tight formation. At one point, as they emerged from cloud, Lukin saw the tail of the Douglas looming in front of him and banked left to avoid it. As a result his aircraft collided with the wingman and crashed, killing both Lukin and his navigator. The crew of the other aircraft managed to bale out.

While leading a squadron of Lavochkin LaGG-3 fighters to its airfield at the front, Captain K Danilkin's Pe-3 was set upon by German fighters near Voronezh. The attack took place when the LaGG-3s had insufficient fuel reserves for a dogfight, and in addition the pilots' skills were not of the highest level. The Luftwaffe pilots concentrated their attention on the leader. Danilkin's navigator, K Manturov, shot down two Bf109s with his turret machine gun, and another was shot down by salvo from the UBK nose guns. A fourth Bf109 was shot down by Danilkin when his own aeroplane was enveloped in flames, and the navigator's machine gun was silent when German fighters made a final pass at their target. A moment later Danilkin's aeroplane exploded. This was the only Pe-3 lost in a dogfight by the 9th BBAP during eight months of combat operations. However, another two were shot down by German anti-aircraft

guns, one failed to return from a combat mission, and a fifth was destroyed on the ground when German attack aircraft strafed the airfield in Grabtsevo. Another four Pe-3s were lost in emergencies or accidents.

Late in December 1941 the rest of the Pe-3s in the 9th Regiment were upgraded by the installation of a ShVAK gun in the forward fuselage and a large calibre UBT machine gun in the navigator's turret. Almost all of this work was done by the regiment's Inzhenernaya Aviatcionaya Sluzhba (IAS – Engineering/ Maintenance Service. By the evening of 31st December the work was complete, and the regiment entered the new year possessing significantly greater capabilities.

The 511th BBAP was formed in the middle of September 1941 from the 40th BBAP, which was divided in two. Captain A Babanov was appointed commander of the 511th Regiment, and in September it was completely equipped with two dozen new Pe-3s. On 10th October it was engaged in action with the Soviet Air Force of the Western Front, being used for bombing and strafing attacks against German ground troops during the offensive against Moscow. Based at an airfield in Noginsk, the regiment flew more than 320 combat missions and destroyed over 30 tanks, eight aircraft on the ground, four railway trains and about 30 artillery pieces. The German troops lost some 200 vehicles along with equipment, ammunition and staff. But the regiment's losses were also considerable. By May 1942 it had only seven fighters, and only four of those were operational. On 16th and 18th March the Pe-3s of Lieutenants G Potapochkin and L Drevyatnikov, returning from a combat mission, were shot down near their own airfield by a German 'intruder' flying a Bf 110C fighter. Later, the 511th Regiment converted on to the Pe-2 reconnaissance aeroplane and became an Otdel'ny Razvedyvatelny Aviatsionny Polk, (ORAP – Independent Air Reconnaissance Regiment).

Late in October 1941 one more regiment flying Pe-2s was in action in the Western Front. This was the 54th Red Banner High Speed Bomber Air Regiment and as in the case of the 9th Regiment, this was the 54th's second appearance at the front during the Second World War. On 22nd June 1941 the regiment was based at an airfield near Vilnius when a surprise attack by German aircraft destroyed more than a half of its aeroplanes on the ground. By 14th July almost all of its remaining SB bombers had been lost in the relentless dogfights, and it was taken out of combat, re-equipped with new Pe-3 fighters and retrained.

During Moscow defensive and counterattack operations the regiment, under the command of Major Skibo, performed about 400 combat missions, wiping out enemy troops near Klin, Solnechnogorsk, Istra and Volokolamsk. According to its combat reports the regiment destroyed 33 tanks, up to 780 automobiles, 35 freighters and two ammunition depots, and its aircraft shot down six German aircraft during air combats. Its own losses totalled eleven aircraft. In January 1942 four Pe-3s of the 54th Regiment attacked the airfield in Belskaya, dropping 16 x 220lb (100kg) bombs on Luftwaffe aircraft lined up on the ground. While leaving the target four Pe-3s were reportedly attacked by He 113s (most probably they were the Bf 109Gs). One of the enemy aircraft was shot down by a navigator, and a second, miscalculating a manoeuvre, ran into the tail of the leading Pe-3, flown by Captain Karabutov, and lost its wing. Although his aeroplane was severely damaged, Karabutov managed to fly back to the airfield in Tula. The crew were uninjured.

Judging by the type of ammunition used, the aircraft of the 511th and 54th regiments, unlike those of the 9th and 95th regiments, were apparently not upgraded and rearmed.

Late in January 1942 the 54th Regiment's base in Zhashkovo was discovered by German reconnaissance aircraft, and during the night of 1st/2nd February about two dozen Bf 110Cs flattened the airfield. A second attack

followed in the morning, and that evening several Ju 88s bombed the location. As a result the regiment lost seven aircraft, three of which were set alight. After this onslaught the regiment was suspended, basically because it had no combat capable aircraft. The last of its aircraft were turned over to the 511th Regiment, and its personnel were placed in reserve. In May 1942 its remaining crews were sent to the 9th Reserve Air Regiment, where they underwent special training and later flew Pe-2 bombers.

Having joined the Northern Fleet, the 95th Fighter Air Regiment underwent training to navigate without reference points, and, beginning from the middle of April 1942, engaged in combat actions. The Soviet Navy had only a few bombers, and the heavy fighters were used first and foremost for bombing attacks on enemy ships and airfields.

On 15th April 1942 four Pe-3s led by Captain V Kulikov attacked the naval base at Linahamari, sinking a transport vessel of 4,000 tons displacement and damaging some others ships, the moorage and naval port installations. No aircraft were lost.

On 22nd April in the region of the port of Kirkenes the crew of Lieutenant V Streltsov opened his combat score in the north. During a 'lone ranger' patrol the Pe-3 successfully attacked a tanker of 5,000 tons displacement, stealing up on it from the offshore side. After the attack, Streltsov's machine became a target of the anti-aircraft artillery of all the ships in the port. The pilot made an Immelmann turn to evade the hostile fire, then dived on the burning tanker and destroyed it with rocket projectiles. Soviet navy reconnaissance confirmed the sinking of the tanker.

Less then a month later the regiment's aircraft again reminded the Kriegsmarine of their existence. On 16th May four Pe-3s led by Captain Kirikov were scrambled to Varde Island, where reconnaissance forces had discovered a German combat ship. As they approached the island they came upon a German T-type destroyer, which opened fire on the aircraft and began to perform evasive manoeuvres, changing its course and speed. But a salvo of 16 FAB-100 bombs released in level flight determined the destroyer's fate. During the second attack a pair of Pe-3s fired their rockets, and the destroyer disappeared beneath the waves.

Lieutenant V Streltsov was a participant in this combat. During three years of war this outstanding pilot flew 146 combat missions, sank three ships and damaged two, and destroyed 12 enemy aircraft, nine tanks, two trains and 45 automobiles. He became the only wartime Hero of the Soviet Union among the pilots of the 95th Regiment.

In the spring and summer of 1942 Luftwaffe strikes against Allied 'PQ' convoys making

their way from England to Murmansk and Arkhangelsk grew in intensity. In March German torpedo-boats and bombers sank four ships of PQ-13. The arrival of the regiment of Pe-3s in the north made it possible to launch strikes against the enemy's airfields even in daylight. On 23rd April the regiment's 1st squadron attacked the airfield at Luostari, destroying 16 aircraft on the ground and shooting down one more Bf 109 in the air. The squadron returned to base without loss.

However, the bombing of the airfield at Hebugten was less successful. This large airfield could accommodate up to 100 German bombers and fighters at any one time, and was therefore both a very tempting and dangerous target. The seven Pe-3s sent there were met by more than two dozen German fighters, but this did not prevent them from bombing their target. To gain time, Captain B Shishkin, the group's leader, manoeuvred and met the enemy fighters with a salvo of rockets. This unexpected use of the RS-132s and RS-82s served to delay the German interception and allowed the group to bomb the airfield, but on their return the bombers were torn to pieces by German fighters, only one Pe-3 returning to its base. One other landed at a neighbouring airfield. The pilot of a third, who baled out, was the last to return alive. Twenty-six German aeroplanes were destroyed or damaged.

Late in April 1942 the crews of the 95th Regiment again took on the fighter role. Three Pe-3s led by the regiment's commander, Major Zhatkov, met convoy PQ-15 a great distance from the USSR's northern airfields, and gave the German torpedo-carriers and bombers, who were unaccustomed to aerial opposition, an unpleasant surprise. The German aircraft did not dare to attack the convoy while it was under fighter escort.

Early in June 1942 the convoy PQ-17 approached the operational zone of the Soviet Northern Navy. Because of a mistake by the British Admiralty the ships were unescorted, and they were still far from Soviet protection when German submarines and aircraft began to strike repeatedly. In the short period from 4th to 10th July the convoy was attacked by 130 Ju 88 bombers, and 43 He 111 and 26 He 115 torpedo-carriers.

The aircraft of the 95th Fighter Air Regiment then began to cover the remaining ships of PQ-17, operating at the limit of their range. At the extreme end of the Kolsky Peninsula an airfield was organised, permitting a zone of air protection to be established in the north west. Groups of four Pe-3s performed two or three escort flights per day, each lasting four to five hours. On 13th July the leaders of one such group, Captain K Volodin and Lieutenant A Suchkov, attacked the German bombers and brought down seven Ju 88s with rockets and machine gun fire. Suchkov, the leader of the second pair, was badly wounded by return fire, and his navigator took control and, after an 1½ hour flight over the sea, landed the damaged aeroplane back at its airfield.

On 19th September 1942 four Pe-3s led by Lt Colonel Zhatkov intercepted 24 Ju 88s that were trying to attack PQ-18 in the proximity of Molotovsk Harbour. Two German aircraft were shot down and several damaged.

The Pe-3s' next important duty was to provide cover for Soviet torpedo-carriers and bombers attacking enemy convoys. Thus, on 25th April 1943, five Il-4 torpedo-carriers protected by three pairs of Pe-3s attacked a convoy in Kongs Fjord. Four Bf 110 heavy fighters and one He 115 floatplane were loitering over the ships, and the Pe-3s had an opportunity to engage with German aeroplanes of a similar type which had been confused with their Soviet counterparts owing to their similar configurations. However, nothing came of it, as the 'air umbrella' scattered after the Pe-3s' first attack. While the Messerschmitts hid in the clouds, the less manoeuvrable He 115 crashed into the fjord, engulfed in flames. A moment later the torpedo-carriers launched their attack, sending two enemy transports and a patrol ship to the bottom.

Finally, the majority of the reconnaissance tasks in the north were performed by camera-equipped Pe-3s of the 118th Reconnaissance Air Regiment of the VVS of the Northern Fleet. One crew, led by Captain Rodion Suvorov, who was honoured in May 1944 with the Golden Star of the Hero of the Soviet Union, performed more than 300 reconnaissance flights during the Second World War and located more than 800 German vessels. Suvorov also destroyed three railway trains, 13 tanks and 75 automobiles, and shot down four German aircraft.

In April 1942 aircraft Plant No.39, relocated in Irkutsk, resumed production of the Pe-3 and Pe-3*bis*. The last unarmed Pe-3s were turned over to the 9th Short-range Bomber Air Regiment, while the Pe-3*bis* were sent primarily to long range reconnaissance air regiments such as the 40th Regiment.

This regiment had received its first Pe-3s as early as September 1941, using them against attacking German troops. From 22nd to 24th September its aircraft struck the Stara Russa railway station, rendering it inoperative for a whole week.

During the Battle of Moscow the regiment flew 365 combat missions and dropped 218 tons of bombs on the Nazi forces. As the result of one of such bombing attack, a bridge over the Ugra river in the Yukhnov region was destroyed. A second attack destroyed a bridge in Kalinin, making it difficult for German troops to cross the river.

From December 1941 the regiment was given a new task, being transformed into a reconnaissance air regiment of the High Command of the Soviet Army. Pilots underwent retraining in reconnaissance while still flying combat missions. The Pe-3s of the 40th Long Range Reconnaissance Air Regiment performed reconnaissance on the Western, Bryansk, South-Western, Stalingrad, Don and Voronezh fronts. They made regular observation flights over the main railway stations and German air bases near Sesha, Orel, Bryansk, Roslavl and Vyazma. In 1942 alone, the cameras of the 40th Regiment's Pe-3s pinpointed the locations of 9,050 tanks, 229,000 automobiles, 1,500 guns, 11,000 trains and 19,680 aircraft. In 1943 'for great merit in the struggle against the German fascist invaders' the regiment was awarded a Guard title and reformed as the 48th Guards Regiment.

# Pe-2I

In late August 1941 yet another fighter version of the Pe-2 tactical bomber was in existence. This development was the work of the design staff of aircraft Plant No.22. It was called the Pe-2I (I – Istrebitel, fighter), and had more powerful armament. A ShVAK twin-cannon mounting with of 160 rounds per gun was installed in place of the Pe-2 bomb bay. The nose armament was not changed, and consisted of ShKAS and UBK machine guns.

Like the Pe-3, the Pe-2I was two-seater. A fuel tank of 52.7 gallons (240 litres) capacity was installed in the radio operator/gunner's cockpit, and the capacity of the centre-section fuel tanks was increased by 15.3 gallons (70 litres). Even so, the total internal tankage was insufficient for the specified range of 1,242 miles (2,000km), and, for the first time on a Petlyakov designed aeroplane, two external 39.5 gallon (180 litre) drop tanks were fitted to the shackles of the under fuselage bomb racks.

Another upgrading was similar to that made in the Pe-3 fighter, but instead of a ShKAS machine gun in the tailcone, the Pe-2I had a large calibre UBT machine gun installed in the fairing, in the position occupied by the radio operator/gunner. As a result of flight tests it was recommended that a remote-control system be designed for the UBT.

The greatest weakness in the Pe-2I's design was the absence of frontal armour for the crew, but it was thought that its installation would not be difficult. The Pe-2I was more updated than its direct competitor from Plant No.39, especially regarding armament, it was faster by 6.2mph (10km/h) at all altitudes, and it took 30 seconds less to climb to 16,400ft (5,000m).

To study aerial combat tactics using twin-engined fighters, simulated combats were flown by a Pe-2I with an SB bomber and a MiG-3 fighter. The Pe-2I's greater speed allowed it to overtake and attack the SB from any direction, but owing to its inferior manoeuvrability in the horizontal plane dogfighting during turns was not recommended. In its clash with a MiG-3 the Pe-2I found itself in trouble. Two aerial combat tactics were recommended for Pe-2I crews in such a situation: either attack head-on or escape in a steep descent at full throttle.

The Pe-2I did not go into production. The twin-engine fighter version was reconsidered some time later, after Vladimir Petlyakov's tragic death.

*For technical data, see Table A, page 163.*

**Based upon Petlyakov's Pe-2 bomber, the Pe-2I fighter was designed by Vladimir Myasishchev.**

# Polikarpov

## TIS

The request for proposals for a Tyazhelyi Istrebitel Soprovzhdeniya (TIS – heavy escort fighter) was received by the Nikolay Polikarpov Design Bureau in November 1938, during the planning of the annual programme of prototype designs. However, owing to the bureau's difficulties with the development and introduction into series production of the I-180 and SPB aeroplanes, full scale development of the TIS fighter did not begin until the third quarter of 1940. Mikhail Yangel, destined to become a well-known designer of Soviet space launch vehicles, including the famous Proton, was appointed chief designer of the new fighter. During the design stage the role of the aeroplane was repeatedly changed and confirmed owing to the multiplying of its intended functions, including interceptor, dive bomber and reconnaissance aeroplane.

The first TIS prototype aeroplane was produced at Plant No.51 during the first half of 1941. An all-metal, two-seat, low wing monoplane, it was powered by two AM-37 water-cooled engines designed by Alexander Mikulin. It had a cigar-shaped monocoque fuselage of oval cross-section assembled from four main units: F1, F2, F3 and F4. Four ShKAS machine guns were installed in the front part of F1, with 1,000 rounds per gun (as on the Messerschmitt Bf110). The machine guns were covered by a light cover allowing easy access. There was a hatch on the port side for inserting ammunition boxes, and there was a landing light in the nose.

The F2, or middle section, of the fuselage contained the crew cockpit with an access hatch underneath. The canopy consisted of four parts; a panelled windscreen, a front rearward-sliding unit to protect the pilot, a middle fixed part covering the gunner/radio-operator, and a rear forward-sliding unit which, in the open position, allowed fire upwards and astern by a ShKAS machine gun on a TSS-1 mounting, with 750 rounds. In addition to armour plate behind the pilot, armour plate was installed behind the gunner, with a hatch to a lower gun mounting in the forward part of F3. The TIS was the only Soviet twin-engined fighter of the Second World War to have a rear under fuselage gun position. To reach the lower ShKAS machine gun the gunner had to raise the armoured hatch and, kneeling down, squeeze his way through beneath the armoured bulkhead. The lower machine gun was provided with 500 rounds. The tail section of the fuselage, F4, contained the tailplane and tailwheel attachment points.

The two-spar wing, of NACA-230 aerofoil section, comprised five parts: the wing centre section, two engine sections and two cantilever outer panels. The centre section spars were made from T-section steel spar booms and solid Duralumin walls reinforced by struts. On each side between No.1 and No.2 ribs the Duralumin walls were replaced by drag struts for the attachment of a ShVAK gun with 350 rounds and a large calibre UBK machine gun with 400 rounds. Ribs, stringers and the smooth wing covering were also of Duralumin, the engine nacelles had a Duralumin framework and skin, and the engine mounts were made of steel tube. Each nacelle was covered by eight removable panels ensuring easy accessibility to the powerplant. Split flaps for landing were located in the aft of the wing centre section and engine sections. The two-spar outer panels were fitted with leading edge slats and a small flap between the ailerons and the engine nacelle section. The ailerons were unslotted, and there was a trim tab on the starboard side and a tab adjustable on the ground on the port side. To ensure simultaneous opening, the slats were interconnected by a tubular pushrod.

The aeroplane had a twin-fin tail. The tailplane was assembled as two halves and attached to the F4 fuselage tail unit. Each half of the tailplane had two spars, 20 ribs and Duralumin skinning. Each elevator was hinged at three points, and had a tubular spar and a framework of formed ribs. Apart from the nose section, which had a Duralumin skin, it was fabric covered. The structure of the fins and rudders was the same as that of the horizontal surfaces. All control surfaces had electrically controlled trimmers.

The tailwheel undercarriage had twin-leg retractable main landing gear units which retracted rearwards into the engine nacelles. The tailwheel retracted into the rear fuselage. The legs had oleo-pneumatic shock-absorbers, and the undercarriage dual control system was pneumatic.

The TIS(A) was powered by two AM-37 engines each providing 1,044kW) 1,400hp at 20,700ft (6,300m) and driving VISh-61FS variable-pitch propellers. The powerplant differed from previous ones in having an additional oil cooling loop in the water/oil cooler for after-cooling of the water. All radiators were housed in the nacelles. It was estimated that the aircraft would attain a maximum speed at a sea level of 301mph (485km/h), and 394mph (635km/h) at the service ceiling of 24,250ft (7,400m). The climbing time to 16,400ft (5,000m) was set at 7.3 minutes, and the range with total fuel of 492 gallons (2,240 litres) was expected to exceed 1,242 miles (2,000km).

The aeroplane had no bomb bay, but it could carry 1,102lb (500kg) bombs, bomb clusters or spray tanks on two external carriers. Because the second member of the TIS's crew was a gunner/radio-operator, not a navigator, bomb dropping was always performed by the pilot. In a dive the pilot used a PBP-1A sight, and during level flight bombing was accomplished with the help of leader aeroplane or without aiming at specific targets. In addition to the standard equipment for fighters, the aeroplane had the GMK-2 gyro-magnetic compass, an air-driven gyro horizon, an RSR-1 radio and an RPK-10 Chayenok directional radio-compass.

The TIS(A) prototype first flew in September 1941, pilot N Gavrilov making the test flights from Moscow's Schyolkovo Airfield. During these flights speeds of 279mph (450 km/h) at sea level and 344mph (555 km/h) at 19,000ft (5,800m) were achieved. The main shortcomings were unsatisfactory directional stability and faulty operation of the AM-37 engines. Late in September at Plant No.51 the size of the fin was increased, albeit insufficiently as it transpired. Engine vibration at altitudes above 16,400ft (5,000m) was not eliminated.

In October 1941 the flight tests were continued at Novosibirsk, to where the Letno-Issledovatel'skii Institut (LII – Ministry of Aviation Industry Flight Research Institute) facilities had been evacuated. Enlargement of the tail and upgrading of the powerplant had been completed by early March 1942. Then, after several flights, the problem of directional stability was solved, but engine reliability was not improved.

The first stage of the TIS fighter's tests at the LII was finished with a flight on 8th May 1942. By the summer of 1942 it was clear that the AM-37 could not be put into production (as was the case with the MiG-5), because the engine needed to be updated. Moreover, it should be noted that the Polikarpov Design Bureau of 1942 was not the same as it had been in 1938. Nikolay Polikarpov's first deputy, Vsevolod Tairov, had gone to the factory in Kiev to work on his own designs, and some of the bureau's other designers, including Dmitri Tomashevitch, were arrested following the failure of the VIT and I-180 aeroplanes.

Lastly, Artyom Mikoyan and Mikhail Gurevich, the designers of the MiG-1, also left the Polikarpov Bureau, along with the greater number of its engineers. As a result of these events, and also the evacuation, only 100 designers remained at the bureau in the spring of 1942, and their main efforts were focused on updating the I-185 and ITP fighters.

Only in the second half of 1943, after the

*Above and right:* **TIS(A) heavy escort fighter.**

*Below:* **The modified TIS, designated TIS(MA).**

cessation of work on the I-185, was it decided to power the TIS with AM-39s. The new version, the TIS(MA), differed not only in having the more powerful engines, but also in armament. In the F1 forward fuselage section two 20mm ShVAK guns with 120 rounds each replaced the four ShKAS machine guns. The wing centre section mounting included yet another two guns of 45mm 111P-type with 45 rounds per gun (the prototype had two 37mm guns). The lower mounting for a ShKAS machine gun was removed, and in the aft part of the canopy the standard upper gun mounting of a VUB-1 bomber was installed, carrying a UBT machine gun with 200 rounds.

The powerplant installation was designed for AM-39s but, owing to the non-availability of these engines, AM-38Fs from the Il-2 attack aeroplane were installed, supposedly as a temporary measure.

Compared with the first version of the fighter, the radiators were moved from the engine nacelles into the wings, where they were housed in special tunnels with leading edge air intakes and outlets in the undersurface of the wing. The altitude tolerance of AM-38F was only 5,400ft (1,650m), which made it impossible to achieve high speeds at altitude. The TIS(MA)'s speed at ground level 319mph (514km/h), and at its critical altitude the speed was 332mph (535km/h). The service ceiling was only 21,600ft (6,600m), but its rate of climb at sea level at a flying weight of 18,235lb (8,280kg) was 13.5m/sec, which was not bad for a twin-engine fighter. The performance differed from the estimated figures by no more than 1.5%, and on the basis of the flight test data it was concluded that the TIS with AM-39s could reach a maximum speed at 23,500ft (7,150m) of 403mph (650km/h)

and climb to 16,400ft (5,000m) in 6.4 minutes.

During the flight tests undertaken by Gavrilov from June to September 1944, 15 flights were made with a total flying time of about nine hours. Damage caused to the fighter by a brake failure on 29th June was repaired in a month, but the TIS was ill-fated. On 16th September 1944 it was damaged again during a belly-landing caused by non-lowering of the undercarriage. It was not restored. Its chief designer, Nikolay Polikarpov, had died earlier, on 30th July 1944.

*For technical data, see Table A, page 163.*

**Externally, the TIS(MA) differed from the TIS(A) by its protruding gun barrels.**

**Polikarpov TIS(A)**

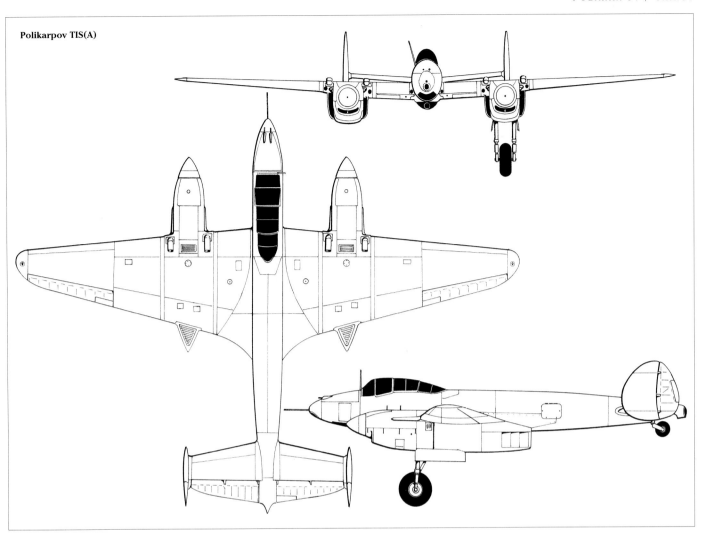

# Tairov

## OKO-6 (Ta-3)

The OKO-6 experimental twin-engined fighter was built at the end of 1939 at Plant No.43, under the guidance of Vsevolod Tairov. Everything in its design was directed at two main goals; high speed and heavy offensive fire. The OKO defined the role of the aircraft as escort fighter and attack aircraft for the destruction of armoured forces. Its high speed was achieved by the use of two Tumanskii M-88s, rated 1,000hp (746kW) at 24,700ft (7,550m) – the second limit of the engine's altitude capability – and by keeping the aircraft as small as possible, with the minimum cross section and a streamlined configuration. For example, the OKO-6's length, wingspan and wing area were almost the same as those of the single-engine Hawker Hurricane, though its power and wing loading were almost twice as great.

The fuselage consisted of three parts. The front section was mounted on the back-ar-

mour plate, which was of ⅜in (8mm) gauge, and ½in (13mm) in the upper part. The sidewalls of the cockpit were made of sheet Duralumin. The cockpit was shielded from the front with ⅜in (8mm) armour plate and from below with steel sheet, which protected the construction from the muzzle blasts of the guns. The fuselage nose fairing, which housed a light, could be opened to the right to allow maintenance of the ShKAS machine guns installed in forward fuselage. This provided access to the weapons and equipment. The cockpit was covered by a rearwards-sliding canopy.

The rear fuselage was built as a wooden monocoque with hatches for inspection of the control runs. The centre fuselage was made as a single unit with the wing centre section, and the forward and rear fuselage units were bolted to it. The wing's centre section outer panels had two spars with steel spar caps and Duralumin spar webs. The wing frame and covering were also of Duralu-

min, and the engine nacelles were of Elektron alloy. The aircraft had Frise-type ailerons and pneumatically-operated Shrenk-type flaps on the centre section and on the outer panels. Its tail unit was of metal construction, with a tailplane of Duralumin and elevators and a single fin and rudder of Elektron. The same material was used for the aileron frames, and to cover the wing leading edges and tips. The control surfaces were fabric covered.

Armament comprised two ShKAS machine guns with a total of 800 rounds in the forward fuselage, and four ShVAK guns with 200 rounds per gun under the wing centre section and cockpit. The guns had a system for automatic reloading after each burst.

The powerplant consisted of two air-cooled M-88s driving counter-rotating propellers (left clockwise, right anti-clockwise). Unusual features of the engine nacelles were the inlet and outlet cowl flaps. Owing to the inlet cowl flaps the propeller spinners seemed disproportionately large.

The pneumatically operated undercarriage was of the conventional tailwheel type. The two-strut main legs retracted into the engine nacelles, leaving part of the tyres protruding. The tailwheel retracted into the fuselage.

Flight tests of the OKO-6 began on 31st December 1939. At a flying weight of 11,574lb (5,250kg) it had a speed of 303mph (488km/h) at sea level and 352mph (567km/h) at 24,700ft (7,550m), and the ascent to 16,400ft (5,000m) took 5.5 minutes. However, the longitudinal and directional stability of the single-finned, short-fuselaged aircraft was inadequate, and radical changes to the empennage were required. Moreover, during one flight an engine connecting rod broke and the flight tests had to be postponed. Although the estimated maximum speeds had not been attained, the aeroplane was promising, and at a joint session of aviation industry ministry leaders and air force representatives, the following decisions were taken:

- to use Plant No.43 to organise the series production of the OKO-6 2xM-88 armoured fighter;
- to finish all the necessary preparations for production by the end of the year;
- to build before the end of the year ten aeroplanes with the revised, twin-fin tail unit and M-88 direct-drive engines with opposite rotation;
- to order Vsevolod Tairov to prepare the modernised OKO-6, with M-88P geared left-hand-rotation engines, for factory tests by 1st August 1940.

With the M-88 direct-drive engines the propeller revolutions were too high, especially at maximum speed, and propeller efficiency was increased by using M-88s with 0.666 reduction gearing. The tail of the modified aircraft was lengthened and the tail unit area considerably increased. To increase directional stability additional endplate fins were installed on the tailplane, and later the central fin was removed. Aileron control was made easier by changing the control rod arms and the balance. To restore the correct centre of gravity position with the heavier engines, the sweepback of the outer wing leading edges was reduced. Other minor improvements were also made.

This work took longer than expected, mainly owing to the limited production and test facilities. The OKO-6bis second prototype was completed before September, but its Tsentral'nyi Aerogidrodynamichesky Institut (TsAGI – Central Aerodynamic and Hydrodynamic Institute) tests did not begin until January 1941. These tests were performed by factory pilot A Yemelyanov, and on the whole the results were satisfactory. The maximum speed at ground level was 296mph (477 km/h), and at 23,100ft (7,050m) it was 366mph (590km/h); time to climb 16,400ft

(5,000m) was only 6.33 minutes. The aircraft could perform all aerobatic manoeuvres and maintain altitude on one engine. It was given the new designation Ta-1, in accordance with the name of its chief designer, and everything indicated that series production would soon begin, but on 14th January 1941 an engine failed during a test flight and the aircraft crashed.

Nonetheless, this accident did not change aircraft industry ministry leaders' generally favourable interest in the aeroplane. Late in January Tairov received government instructions to develop two Ta-3s, improved developments of the OKO-6bis. In February aircraft Plant No.43 was reorganised as ordered by Alexey Shakhurin, the Minister of the Aircraft Industry, and the Tairov OKO prototype production plant became the new Plant No.483. Almost simultaneously it was decided to cease development of the OKO-8 twin-engine fighter powered by AM-37 engines and concentrate the bureau's efforts on the Ta-3. Unfortunately it proved impossible to repair the badly damaged OKO-6bis and tests were halted until May 1941.

In the meantime the first OKO-6 was rebuilt to the standard of the OKO-6bis, with a twin-finned, lengthened tail unit. In addition, its unreliable M-88s were replaced by more powerful M-89s with left-hand rotation, giving 1,300hp (969kW) at take-off and 1,150hp (857 kW) at 19,700ft (6,000m). This machine was designated Ta-3.

In flight tests performed by Yu Stankevitch the aeroplane proved to have quite a good performance, and it was noted that it was easier to handle than a MiG-3 fighter. In a combat turn at 3,300ft (1,000m) the fighter climbed 2,300ft (700m). It would not spin when speed was lost, but simply dropped its nose. The landing speed was perhaps rather high at 87 to 93mph (140 to 150km/h), but this was the inevitable price of high wing loading and a gross weight increased to 13,227lb (6,000kg).

However, there were many problems with the new M-89s. Vibration, metal shards in the oil and other faults constantly delayed the tests. Other deficiencies included large forces on the control column during landing and the unsatisfactory view from the cockpit, especially downward and laterally. In spite of the more powerful powerplant, the maximum speeds obtained at sea level and at 23,300ft (7,100m) were lower than those of the OKO-6bis, being 285 and 360mph (460 and 580 km/h) respectively – the estimated design speed at 23,000ft (7,000m) was 377mph (607km/h). This was mainly due to the poorer manufacturing standards of the Ta-3, rebuilt from the OKO-6, its greatly increased gross take-off weight, the presence of an aerial mast and the increased area of the fins.

The aeroplane's weapon system was unchanged except for the removal of the automatic charger to save weight. The cannon and machine guns of the Ta-3 fired 113 shells per second, with a total mass rate of 13.2lb/sec (6kg/sec). The alternative armament comprised two ShKAS machine guns, two ShVAK guns and a 37mm gun. The possibility of installing M-82 engines in the Ta-3 was considered, but this engine was no more developed than the M-89.

Following the LII NKAP flight tests the conclusion was favourable: 'To recommend the Ta-3 for series production ... with the main role of aeroplane and tank destroyer'.

In the middle of these tests Germany invaded the USSR, and in one month the Soviet Air Force requirements for twin-engine fighters changed. The Ta-3's maximum range of 658 miles (1,060km) at a cruising speed of 274 mph (442km/h) turned out to be insufficient, and it was recommended that it be increased by 100%. This was impossible to do quickly, and series production was again postponed.

The tragic death of Vsevolod Tairov in a catastrophic accident during a flight from Moscow to Kuibyshev decided the issue, for full scale development of the Ta-3 slowed down. In any case it was impossible to introduce into series production an absolutely new aeroplane, with a new and underdeveloped engine, while the aircraft industry was being transferred to the east and production was consequently falling off, as shown by the experience with the Su-2.

Finally, in May 1942 the last version of the Tairov twin-engine fighter, designated Ta-3bis, arrived at the LII for testing. This machine was the result of the reconstruction of the Ta-3. The main design change was the fitting of new outboard wings made entirely of Elektron alloy. Because of the increased dimensions of the outer wings the additional 160 gallon (730 litre) fuel tanks were placed inside them. Before modification the fuel had been contained in one 102 gallon (467 litre) fuselage tank and two 80 gallon (365 litre) tanks in the wing centre section. The increase in fuel capacity gave the aircraft a maximum range of 1,280 miles (2,060km).

To increase manoeuvrability the dihedral was reduced twice, but the increase in gross weight had a detrimental effect on take-off distance, rate of climb and maximum speed and, most significantly, made it neutrally stable longitudinally. This characteristic caused a great deal of pilot fatigue on long flights.

By August 1942 the Ta-3bis had completed its test programme. There were no serious problems with the machine's construction, but continual trouble with its M-89s meant that the aircraft could not be recommended for series production. Replacement of the M-89 with the M-82, sufficiently developed by the end of 1942, seemed a good solution, but it had now become clear that there was no great need for a twin-engined, single-seat fighter. Soviet long range bombers usually flew at night, when escort fighters could not help them very much. The tactical bombers on their short range flights were escorted by single-engined fighters. The Luftwaffe, on the other hand, concentrated on tactical missions, and for this reason its bombers were also escorted by single-engined fighters, which were too dangerous an adversary for twin-engined fighters. This caused a loss of interest in twin-engine fighters in the USSR.

The exceptions were the fighters based on the Pe-2 and Tu-2 bombers, which were used periodically during the war.

*For technical data, see Table A on page 163.*

**Two views of the twin-engined Ta-3 fighter prototype.**

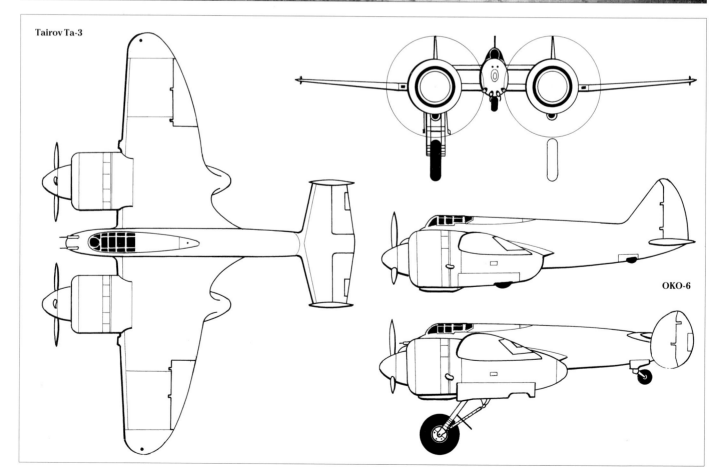

Tairov Ta-3

OKO-6

# Tupolev

In 1944 the Andrei Tupolev OKB developed the Skorostnoi Dnyevnoi Bombardirovsshchik (SDB fast day bomber) with the in-house designation '63'; this is described in detail in the bomber section of this book).

## Tu-1 ('63P')

Using the second SDB prototype as a basis, the Tu-1 ('63P') twin-engined interceptor and long range escort fighter was evolved. Development was initiated during the war and was completed after the war's end. The aircraft was powerfully armed, having two NS-45 45mm cannon in the modified forward fuselage section, two NS-23 23mm guns in the wing centre section and two UBT 12.7mm machine guns. The Tu-1 had PB-1 Gneis-7 radar, and two 1,950hp (1,454kW) Alexander Mikulin AM-43Vs instead of the AM-39Fs used on the SDB bomber.

The Tu-1's flight test programme started in the spring of 1947 and lasted until the autumn, but its performance was only average: maximum speed 398mph (641km/h); service ceiling 36,000ft (11,000m); range 1,398 miles (2,250km); bombload 2,204lb (1,000kg). The new engines gave poor performance and were unreliable. As the war was over, it was decided to cancel the programme.

## Type '104'

The '104' bomber interceptor, based on the series production Tu-2 bomber, was developed in 1944. This aircraft differed from its sister bomber in having a radar installation designed by A Mints and two VYa-23 23mm guns in the lower forward fuselage.

The aircraft undertook its maiden flight on 18th July 1944, piloted by test pilot A Perelyot. Its performance was very similar to that of the Tu-2 bomber, and this precluded Soviet Air Force interest in further development.

*For technical data, see Table A, page 163.*

**The Tu-1, or Type '63P' represented another attempt to rework a bomber into a fighter.**

**The lower nose of the Tu-1 carried two 45mm cannon.**

*Photographs on the opposite page:*

**Two views of the twin-engined Ta-3bis fighter prototype.**

**Four ShVAK guns, mounted within a single unit underneath the nose of the OKO-6.**

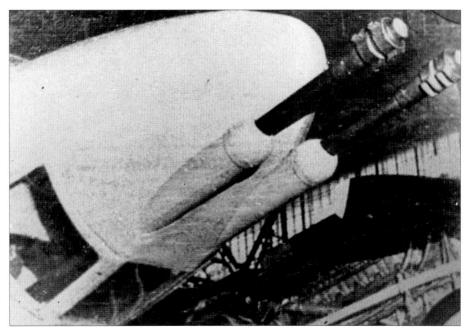

Part Two

# Light Bombers, Attack and Reconnaissance Aircraft

# Bolkhovitinov

## S-2M-103

Victor Bolkhovitinov proposed one of the strangest solutions to the problem of increasing the maximum speed of combat aircraft. A two-seat short range high speed light bomber was designed and built under his guidance. It had two 960hp (716kW) Klimov M-103s arranged in tandem in the fuselage, instead of the conventional wing-mounted installation. The shaft of the rear engine passed through that of the front engine, and the engines drove two contra-rotating propellers, thereby eliminating gyroscopic and torque effects.

The aircraft had several different designations according to the intended role: BBS-1 (blizhny bombardirovschik, skorostnoy, short range bomber, high speed); LB-S (legky bombardirovschik-sparka, light bomber, two-seater); and BB (bolkhovitinov - bomber). At the time it began its state trials, however, it was designated S-2M-103 (skorostnoy, high speed with two M-103 engines), or sometimes simply 'S'.

Flight testing of the S-2M-103 began in the spring of 1940. The prototype proved to have a very high speed for the time, reaching 354mph (570km/h) at 15,400ft (4,700m). The principle behind the project, the installation of the engines in the fuselage, proved to be sound, as the configuration reduced drag considerably, allowing a significant increase in speed, but the first flights showed that the prototype had a poor take-off and landing performance.

The take-off run at the normal take-off weight of 12,455lb (5,650kg) was 3,428ft (1,045m), and for that reason the prototype's gross take-off weight during the flight tests was reduced by 1,102lb (500kg). Even then the take-off run was long at 2,821ft (860m). The landing run was 2,132ft (650m), and the landing speed was high at 102.5mph (165km/h).

The bomber was of all-metal construction. Both the fuselage and wing had a smooth, flush riveted skin. The two-spar torsion box-type wing, of 246.5ft² (22.9m²) area, was equipped with Fowler-type flaps. The fuselage, of elliptical cross-section, consisted of four panels; upper, lower and two side panels. The cockpits for the pilot and navigator were enclosed by a common Plexiglas canopy.

Both engines were installed on a single mounting. The water radiators and primary oil coolers were mounted in an under fuselage tunnel, and additional oil coolers were mounted on each side of the front engine. The landing gear, including the tailwheel was retractable.

On the whole, the aircraft received a positive assessment in the summary of the state trials, which were conducted from late March to early July 1940. The report stated: '...the paired powerplant could be successfully used to produce high speed fighters with pusher propellers and twin-engine bombers'. It was suggested that the designers develop the aircraft, by taking into consideration test pilot remarks and recommendations.

That year the wing was redesigned and given a NACA-230 aerofoil section, and a remote controlled ShKAS machine gun, installed in the rear fuselage, was added to the armament. These changes proved to be advantageous, as the manufacturer's flight tests, conducted during September-December 1940, showed. The tests confirmed that the idea of installing the engines inside the fuselage merited further study and needed to further development. For this reason, work on the design of a single-seat fighter powered by two M-107 engines was included in the 1941 schedule for prototype construction. The fighter was designed, and was designated I-1. Unfortunately development of the bomber, as well as construction of the fighter, was abandoned, and Bolkhovitinov became involved in other work.

*For technical data, see Table D, page 168.*

**The radical twin-engined S-2M-103 high speed short range bomber.**

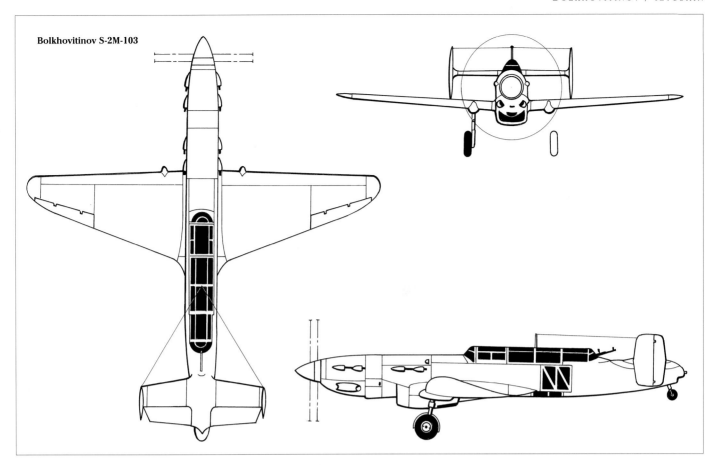

Bolkhovitinov S-2M-103

# Ilyushin

The Il-2 attack aircraft was built in greater numbers than any other aircraft in the history of aviation, more than 35,952 being built. As with the T-34 tank, PPSh machine gun and Katyusha rocket launcher, it was the embodiment of Soviet weaponry. During and after the war the Il-2 was boosted by Soviet propaganda as an invulnerable 'wonder aeroplane', striking terror into the enemy and ostensibly dubbed 'black death' by the Nazis. Recently, several articles have been published asserting that the Il-2 was on the whole an unsuccessful combat aircraft, having caused the loss of a great many pilots. It was asserted that only the Soviet Union could have adopted such an aircraft, because no other nation would have had enough pilots to compensate for the losses. It seems that the truth lies somewhere in the middle.

From 1913 onwards, aircraft designers worldwide tried to design an armoured attack aeroplane capable of flying ground support missions. There were several successful aircraft; both Germany's Junkers J.I and Britain's Sopwith TF.2 Salamander were in production during the First World War and were used operationally. However, in the mid-1930s Sergei Ilyushin became convinced

that the problem could be solved successfully, taking into account the level of development attained by the aircraft industry at that time.

## TsKB-55 and TsKB-57

Sergei Ilyushin's scheme to 'develop and build a special low altitude attack aircraft with powerful attack armament', was included in the plan for experimental aircraft manufacture at the end of 1937.

At that time there was no engine capable of delivering maximum power at sea level, and Ilyushin had to use Alexander Mikulin's AM-34FRN, based on his famous AM-34, as it had the most appropriate performance. However, the AM-34FRN was rated at 960hp (716kW) at sea level and its critical altitude was 11,500ft (3,500m), and neither of these parameters suited Ilyushin's concept.

It should be noted that the many difficulties and shortcomings in the Soviet aero-engine industry precluded modernisation of the USSR's aircraft fleet at the end of the 1930s. The lack of a suitable engine had a significant

effect on the fate of future attack aircraft, and the AM-34FRN was soon phased out. Ilyushin then decided to use the new high altitude 1,350hp (1,007kW) Mikulin AM-35 for his project, designated TsKB-55.

The TsKB-55 was a two-seat cantilever monoplane with a semi-retractable main undercarriage housed in wing fairings. Its most distinctive feature was its streamlined fuselage of high tensile armoured steel, developed at the Vsesoyuzny Institut Aviatsionnykh Materialov (VIAM – All-Union Institute for Aviation Materials) under the guidance of S Kishkin and N Sklyarov. The armoured steel had good impact strength and, most importantly, structural members made from it could be pressed into forms having double curvatures. Moreover, the stamping of such members could be performed in the open air. It was not without difficulty that the industry mastered this new material and its associated technology, but it allowed aircraft to be designed with stressed armoured skins, whereas the earlier Soviet Grigorovich TSh-1 and TSh-3 attack aircraft had been fitted with hinged armour.

The TsKB-55's armoured body contained the vital parts; the engine, crew positions and fuel and oil systems. The water and oil radiators for the cooling and lubrication systems were initially designed so that they could be retracted into the armoured body in the event of intense anti-aircraft fire and extended to provide normal cooling when the danger had passed, but such a system limited the aircraft's time over the battlefield.

An alternative scheme was adopted during the design stage. The radiators were fixed side-by-side behind the engine in the armoured body, and the air intakes were mounted over the engine cowling. This configuration was not as good as the previous one so far as aerodynamics were concerned, and the radiators' effectiveness was reduced, but the aircraft's structure was greatly simplified.

The armoured body was almost entirely included in the fuselage primary structure. It was assembled from stamped sheets of armour of ³⁄₁₆ to ⁵⁄₁₆in (4 to 8mm) thickness, weight reduction being achieved by the optimum distribution of thickness of the armour panels, taking into account both effective resistance to shell splinters and bullets and the loads affecting the armoured body members. Besides, it was considered that at speeds of about 248mph (400km/h) the effectiveness of even the thin armour panels increased.

The first application of K-4 transparent armour was on attack aircraft produced in the USSR, which had the front windshields of their cockpit canopies made from it.

Sergei Ilyushin paid great attention to the survivability of unarmoured structural members. The partial projection of the retracted undercarriage wheels beneath the nacelles allowed the aircraft to land on unprepared surfaces with the gear up, with minimal damage to the airframe.

It was originally planned to arm the attack aircraft with five 7.62mm ShKAS machine guns, four fixed in the wing and one movable. The normal bomb load was 881lb (400kg), the bombs being housed in wing bomb bays.

All of these proposals by Ilyushin were accepted. In January 1939 the preliminary design was presented to the customer and the mock-up was approved. After confirmation of the mock-up commission protocol by Voenno-vozdushniye Sily (VVS – air forces of the USSR) chief A Loktionov, the manufacture of two TsKB-55 prototypes began. They were of mixed construction, with wooden rear fuselages and fins, all-metal wings and tailplanes, and fabric covered elevators.

On 2nd October 1939 test pilot Vladimir Kokkinaki made the maiden flight of the first TsKB-55 prototype. On 30th December that year he flew the second prototype. Manufacturer's tests were conducted until March 1940, and in April the second prototype was moved to the Nauchno Issledovatelyskii Institut (NII – scientific and research institute of

the VVS) for its State Trials, conducted by leading engineer N Kulikov and pilot Major A Dolgov. By that time the aircraft had received the service designation BSh-2 (Bronirovanny Shturmovik, armoured attack aircraft).

It was mentioned in the report of the tests that the aircraft could be used by the VVS as an attack aircraft/short range bomber if its main faults were eliminated. The pilots noted that the BSh-2 was rather simple to fly and had no peculiarities as compared with the R-10 and BB-1. The general conclusion of the military specialists was favourable. In the opinion of military officials it was necessary to manufacture a batch of AM-35-powered BSh-2s and have them undergo service trials to investigate tactical performance and develop combat tactics.

The official tests had revealed some shortcomings. First of all the pilot's forward view was inadequate owing to the single-engined configuration. The low sea level speed of 225mph (362km/h) and under-development of the AM-35 engine were also noted. The engine troubles were caused by the powerful centrifugal high altitude supercharger, allowing an altitude of 14,750ft (4,500m) to be attained, which was completely unnecessary in an attack aircraft flying at low altitude. In low level flight the supercharger was a considerable drain on the engine's power. In response to a request made by Sergei Ilyushin during the manufacturer's trials of the TsKB-55, the Mikulin Design Bureau engineers designed the AM-38, which had no supercharger and was more powerful than the AM-35 at low altitudes but had the same weight and dimensions. The AM-38 was installed in the first prototype TsKB-55 for flight tests. In addition, the aircraft's structure was modified to eliminate shortcomings revealed by the official tests. Longitudinal stability was improved by increasing the tailplane area and moving the cg forward (the BSh-2, which had passed the tests, had an excessively aft cg position, at 31.4% of mean aerodynamic chord).

On Ilyushin's initiative the aircraft was modified with urgency. The ½in (12mm) armoured wall and the fuel tank were installed in the armoured body instead of the gunner's cockpit, as required by the military officials; the armament was unchanged. The first flight of the modified aircraft, now designated TsKB-57, took place on 12th October 1940, with Kokkinaki at the controls. The factory tests performed by him revealed a maximum speed of 262mph (423km/h) at sea level, 38mph (61km/h) higher than that of TsKB-55.

Development work continued. When modifying the second prototype, Ilyushin tried to take into consideration all of the requirements, and the aircraft was prepared as a standard for series production. In an effort to improve the pilot's forward view the AM-35

engine was lowered 6¾in (175mm) and the pilot's seat and canopy were raised 2in (50 mm). Armoured glass and a short transparent cowl were mounted behind the pilot's head to improve his rearward view. These alterations gave it a distinctive 'humped' contour.

On 29th December Kokkinaki flew this aircraft, now redesignated TsKB-55P, for the first time. Very powerful armament distinguished it from its forebear. Two of the four wing-mounted machine guns were replaced by 23mm PTB-6 cannon, and eight cannon were installed under the wing. However, armament trials revealed that the PTB-6s were unsuitable because their recoil was twice as great as calculated by the weapon's designer, Yakov Taubin. Less powerful 20mm ShVAK guns were therefore installed as a matter of urgency, and the aircraft was then sent for its official tests.

Test pilot A Dolgov noted that the new aircraft, designated Il-2, had better controllability than the BSh-2, improved pilot view and could be easily guided on to a target.

It is interesting to compare the performance of two aircraft. The Il-2 had much more powerful attack armament and a third 341lb (155kg) fuel tank in place of the rear cockpit, increasing total fuel capacity to 1,036lb (470kg). However, although the aircraft had been converted to a single-seater its flying weight increased to 11,706lb (5,310kg), compared with the 10,416lb (4,725kg) of the BSh-2. Maximum speeds increased throughout the altitude range, being 260mph (419 km/h), or 269mph (433km/h) with boost and 279mph (450km/h) at the critical altitude of 8,000ft (2,460m). Maximum speed was 262 mph (422km/h) at 17,500ft (5,350m). The rate of climb also improved, especially at low altitude, increasing from 24ft/sec (7.4m/sec) to 33ft/sec (10.3m/sec) at sea level. The difference in performance was the result of the two aircraft being powered by different engines. While the AM-35 produced 1,200hp (895kW) at 14,750ft (4,500m) and 1,350hp 1,007kW) at take-off, the AM-38 produced 1,600hp (1,193 kW) at 5,750ft (1,750m) and 1,665hp (1,242 kW) at take-off. This accounted for the Il-2's improved take-off performance.

The test results showed that the Il-2 was the world's first practical armoured attack aircraft, meeting all modern requirements and capable of flying ground support missions, destroying all kinds of ground targets including armour by the use of bombs, rockets and gunfire. It was therefore decided to put this version of the aircraft into production. Military officials had no objections to the single-seat version of the Il-2 proposed by Ilyushin. The removal of the gunner was a necessary measure, allowing the main shortcomings revealed during the official tests of the BSh-2 to be eliminated.

*Top:* **The first prototype Ilyushin attack aircraft, the TsKB-55 (or BSh-2).**

*Right:* **Detail of the BSh-2 cockpit canopy.**

*Below:* **The single-seat TsKB-57 prototype.**

## Il-2 in Production and Service

Simultaneously with the flight tests, it was decided to introduce the Il-2 into series production. Preparation began in February 1941 at Plant No.16 in Voronezh. On 10th March 1941 the head of the flight test station, Major K Rykov, flew the first production attack aircraft. Despite apprehension that the AM-38 engine recently put into production might not pass its 50 hour flight tests, it operated reliably under all conditions.

By the end of March the second attack aircraft was complete, and in April the rate of production increased. In May 1941 Plant No.18 built 74 aircraft, and in June 159.

By the beginning of the Second World War only 18 Il-2s had been delivered to the units of Western military districts, and not all of them had been mastered by the pilots and tested in flight. No Il-2s engaged in combat with German aircraft on 22nd June 1941.

The 4th Shturmovoy Aviatsionny Polk, (ShAP – Attack Air Regiment), in Voronezh, commanded by Major Getman, was the first to get the new aircraft. Before the outbreak of war the pilots had time for only a few circling flights and evaluation missions, and according to the personnel they had only 17 Il-2s instead of 65.

Nevertheless, on 1st June 1941 the regiment had its baptism of fire at the approaches to Berezina and Bobryusk. Even inexperienced pilots immediately appreciated the Il-2's easy handling, powerful armament and high survivability. The Soviet Army Air Force Command and the leaders of the People's Commissariat of Military Industry quickly appreciated the usefulness of the Il-2, and tried to deliver as many aircraft as possible to the units. From the beginning of the war the rate of production of Il-2s at the Voronezh plant was 10 to 12 aircraft daily. The rate could have been higher, but Plant No.18 continued to build the Yermolayev Yer-2 bomber at the same time. At the end of October 1941 Il-2 production temporarily ceased while the plant was evacuated, and several aircraft assembled at Plant Nos.1 and 381 could not save the situation. At that time the German army began its decisive attacks on Moscow. A total of 144 Il-2s, only half of which could be considered combat-capable, faced the enemy on all fronts, and of this number only 36 attack aircraft fought at the point of the Wehrmacht's main onslaught. Among the Soviet aviation units the pilots of the 215th Fighter Air Regiment, commanded by Major P Reiko, fought especially courageously. In June the pilots relinquished their I-15bis fighters and began to convert to the Il-2.

Unfortunately they had little time for training. In the region of Dukhovshina-Yartsevo the regiment hit the enemy tank and vehicle columns. Usually the leader of each group of attack aircraft flew a Pe-2 bomber, guiding the group on to its target. Upon the leader's command the attack aircraft performed a combat climb then dropped their bombs and launched rockets. They then descended and strafed the enemy with gunfire.

An heroic feat was performed on 3rd October 1941 by Senior Lieutenant A Novikov, who turned his burning aircraft towards a column of enemy troops on a road. For this and other exploits the 215th Regiment was renamed the 6th Guard Regiment in an order of the People's Commissariat of Defence dated 6th December 1941.

The 65th ShAP, commanded by Major A Vitruk, first used the Il-2 to attack hostile bombers. During one encounter the pilots of a group led by Major Vitruk managed to shoot down three Messerschmitts while defending one another. Muscovites who remained in the city remember 11th November 1941, when Lieutenant G Svetlichny of the 312th Attack Air Regiment could not reach Tushino airfield and landed on Gorkii Street near the Belorussian railway station, practically in the centre of Moscow.

By that time the Ilyushin Design Bureau had been evacuated from Moscow. One of the chief designer's last tasks was to enable the Il-2 to operate from snow-covered airfields. In a very short time a retractable ski landing gear was designed; in flight the skis were drawn up against the engine nacelles, thus keeping drag to a minimum. Conversion did not take long, but it was later decided not to use the ski undercarriage.

The main problem at the end of 1941 was the fall in production rates owing to the evacuation of the factories. The Voronezh plant evacuated to Kuibyshev, and for 35 days produced nothing at all. The situation was no better at Plant No.1, which continued to produce MiG-3 fighters. Production of the attack aircraft was organised under harsh conditions at the new location, personnel working in unheated shops in the open air. At that time Shenkman and Tretiakov, the directors of the plants, received a telegram:

'You have let down our country and our Red Army. You have not manufactured Il-2s until now. The Il-2 aircraft are necessary for our Red Army now, like air, like bread. Shenkman produces one Il-2 a day and Tretiakov builds one or two MiG-3s daily. It is a mockery of the country and the Red Army. I ask you not to try the government's patience, and demand that you manufacture more Ils. I warn you for the last time. Stalin'.

The words: 'The Il-2 aircraft are necessary ... like air, like bread' became the motto of the manufacturers, who immediately completed the erection of the shops and initiated the delivery of components. As a result, by the end of January 1942 the leading Plant, No.18, had a daily output of seven Il-2s. In February the newly established Plant No.30 in Moscow began production of the attack aircraft, and in March Plant No.1 was turning out three aircraft per day.

In the winter 1941-42 the first Il-2 operations were assessed. Experience of combat operations with attack aircraft showed that a well trained pilot was able to destroy two tanks at a range of 1,000 to 1,300ft (300 to 400m) after being accurately guided to the target, while an average and satisfactorily trained pilot could destroy one tank. There were instances when German crewmen stopped their tanks and abandoned them for the duration of an attack.

Some Il-2s were armed with more powerful 23mm VYa guns, and although the weapon's rate of fire was lower than that of the ShVAK, they played a significant role. Enemy infantry, motor transport and other targets vulnerable to air attack suffered heavy losses from Il-2 machine gun fire.

## Il-2 M-82

Combat experience revealed the Il-2's vulnerability to attack from behind by enemy fighters. From the very first days of the war, front line pilots realised the necessity for an aft-mounted remote controlled machine gun, rear-firing rockets or a rear gunner's cockpit, as on the TsKB-55 prototype. In a letter to Stalin, Captain E Koval, a navigator in the 243rd Attack Air Regiment, wrote:

'I consider it my duty to request that the designer and the aircraft industry improve our formidable attack aircraft. The main shortcoming of the aircraft is that it is absolutely unprotected against hostile fighters attacking from behind. In most cases the fighter approaches from behind at 10 to 15m [32 to 50ft] and opens fire, trying to damage the engine or kill the pilot. Compensating for this shortcoming by providing fighter protection does not seem to be effective'.

Koval added that attack aircraft operate at low and extremely low altitudes, while their escorting fighters had to fly at 3,300 to 5,000ft (1,000 to 1,500m) over the target. He concluded that a rear gunner was a necessity.

Sergei Ilyushin decided to respond to the wishes of the pilots at the front by modifying the M-82 powered version of the aircraft, and a production Il-2 was used. The section of the armoured body up to the front spar, which formed the engine cowling, was removed, and the double-armoured wall carrying all the load from the welded engine bearer was installed along the front spar of the wing centre section. The engine was not armoured.

Having re-equipped the aircraft, the designer increased the fuel capacity to 1,179lb (535kg) and installed a gunner's cockpit with a UBT machine gun designed by M Berezin. The aircraft was designated Il-2 M-82 (it was sometimes referred to as the Il-4).

On 8th September Vladimir Kokkinaki made the first flight of the new attack aircraft. The manufacturer's tests were quickly completed, and showed that at normal weight of 12,466lb (5,655kg) the Il-2 M-82 was capable of maximum speeds of 237mph (382km/h) at sea level and 261mph (421km/h) at 8,500ft (2,600m). The rate of climb and take-off/landing characteristics had deteriorated, but handling qualities were virtually unchanged. It was Ilyushin's opinion that the new two-seat version should lead single-seat Il-2s and protect them from attack by enemy fighters, but the Il-2 M-82 did not go into production because the process of preparing the factories to build it would have interrupted output.

## Il-2 two-seater

It was suggested to Ilyushin that, instead of introducing the Il-2 M-82 into production, he could design a two-seat Il-2 AM-38 with defensive armament and put it into production without having to halt the line. As a result, a version of the rear gunner's cockpit requiring only minimal changes to the structure of the attack aircraft was developed. The additional cockpit was installed outside the armoured body, and the gunner was protected by additional ¼in (6mm) armour plates. A 12.7mm UBT machine gun was mounted on a semiturret gun mounting, and could be fired at angles of up to 35° upwards, 35° to starboard and 15° to port.

The installation of the gunner's cockpit and armament increased the aircraft's flying weight by 374lb (170kg), so to keep the take-off run approximately the same as that of the single-seat version, the slats were provided with a lock allowing them to be fixed at an angle of 17° for take-off. Increased loading on the tailwheel meant that its attachment point had to be enlarged and reinforced.

At the beginning of March 1942 a two-seat Il-2 with the new gunner's cockpit began manufacturer's tests. These showed that the maximum speed decreased by between 6.2

*From the top:*

**Wind tunnel tests on the Il-2 at TsAGI.**

**Static test loading an Il-2 airframe.**

**Single-seat Il-2s undergoing manufacturer's tests.**

Above: By the start of the Second World War, the Voronezh plant was building ten to twelve Il-2s per day; all being delivered immediately to the front line.

Below: Ilyushin OKB representatives and engineers visited front line units to observe the Il-2 in operational conditions, allowing modifications to be made to aircraft on the line.

and 12.4mph (10 and 20km/h) and that the two-seater was more difficult to handle. It was therefore decided to increase the power of the AM-38 to improve performance and manoeuvrability, and the Mikulin Design Bureau began development work on the engine.

Two other versions of the two-seat Il-2 were developed. One had an entirely armoured gunner's cockpit with a blister which looked very similar to those of the TsKB-55 and Il-2 M-82. Because this cockpit was wider and roomier than the first version, the gunner could not only cover the rear hemisphere but he could also repel attacks from both sides and fire on ground targets as well. However, this modification required significant structural alterations and the bomb bay's capacity was almost halved, and for these reasons it was discontinued.

Likewise, the Il-2 fitted with the MV-3 turret was not widely used. Although this turret provided wide angles of fire, it was too bulky and caused a considerable deterioration in the aircraft's performance. The turret was not introduced into production.

In the summer of 1942 the German army launched a broad offensive in the south of the Soviet-German front. Usually, small groups of Il-2s attacked the enemy columns moving over the steppes, mainly using guns and rockets. Bomb loads seldom exceeded 440lb (200kg), and sometimes bombs were not even carried. An order issued by The People's Commissariat of Defence analysed the shortcomings of combat operations by attack aircraft and provided recommendations for their correct application. The order imposed a minimum bomb load of 881lb (400kg) for Il-2s flying on these missions. First Lieutenant I Pstygo of the 504th ShAP was among the first pilots to fly with a 1,322lb (600kg) bomb load.

Development continued. In January 1943 two-seat attack aircraft powered by updated AM-38F engines giving improved performance for take-off and landing and at low altitudes began to be delivered to the front. The new engine produced 1,700hp (1,268kW) at take-off and its service ceiling was 2,500ft (750m), compared with 5,400ft (1,650m) for the AM-38. Its revolutions were increased from 2,150 to 2,360/min, and the compression ratio was reduced from 6.8 to 6.0, allowing the use of low octane fuel. The design bureau sought to increase engine reliability by changing the inlet configuration, and the installation of an air filter proved helpful.

In accordance with TsAGI recommendations, counterbalance weights were installed in the elevator control system to make it easier to lift the two-seater's tail at take-off and improve longitudinal stability. The aircraft's static longitudinal stability, which had worsened owing to the cg being displaced rearwards by approximately 3.5% of mean aerodynamic chord, improved when the cg was moved forward again by increasing the sweep back of the outer wing panels to 15°. Production of Il-2s with increased sweep back began at the end of 1943.

Increasing the Il-2's attack armament was another way of enhancing its combat capabilities. The ShVAK and VYa guns with which it was equipped were not powerful enough. More powerful guns of larger calibre were necessary if well protected and heavily armoured targets were to be destroyed. Tests conducted in the spring and summer of 1942 revealed that the performance of recently produced single-seat Il-2s had deteriorated compared with aircraft manufactured in the autumn of 1941, not to mention the prototypes, but it was still satisfactory for the air force. At a weight of 12,760lb (5,788kg) the aircraft reached 236 to 246mph (380 to 396 km/h) at sea level (depending on the external stores carried) and 257 to 264mph (414 to 426km/h) at 8,200ft (2,500m), and climbed to 3,300ft (1,000m) in 2.2 minutes.

On 30th October 1942 production Il-2 two-seaters powered by AM-38s were used on the Central Front for the first time when they successfully attacked Smolensk airfield, occupied by the enemy. Their rear guns proved to be an effective means of protection against hostile fighters, and during the service trials alone the gunners shot down seven Bf 109s and repulsed many attacks.

The Soviet Air Force Commander Marshal Alexander Novikov wrote that they had been fully justified in placing principal reliance on the Il-2 during the Battle of Stalingrad: 'The attack aircraft were easier and cheaper to produce than bombers, and made up for the deficit in the bombers at our disposal largely owing to their large numbers and excellent combat qualities'. He also noted that attack aircraft were less susceptible than bombers to the caprices of the weather, flying missions in instrument meteorological conditions. The number of Il-2s at the front gradually increased. By the beginning of the counter-offensive at Stalingrad there were 1,644 attack aircraft in the combat units, and by the start of the Kursk battle 2,817 were operational. In both instances Il-2s comprised almost a third of the Soviet combat aircraft fleet.

Although Il-2s were built at three plants in 1941, the production contribution of these plants was not equal. Voronezh aircraft Plant No.18 delivered the greatest number of Il-2s to the front. After the plant's evacuation from Voronezh to Kuibyshev the aircraft was built there. Plant Nos.1 and 18 were not far from each other, and in late 1942 Plant No.1 manufactured almost as many Il-2s as the leading plant. During late 1942 through to early 1943 Plant No.381, which had been involved in Il-2 production, was converted to the La-5 fighter, while Plant No.30, returned to Moscow, began manufacturing attack aircraft. It the middle of 1944 each plant (Nos.1, 18 and 30) manufactured ten Il-2s a day.

## Il-2-37 with 37mm guns

In late 1941 the bureau began work on an installation of two 37mm Sh-37 guns for the single-seat attack aircraft, designed by a group led by Boris Shpitalny. Because these guns were of large dimensions they were installed in underwing fairings, and the gun was lowered considerably because it was necessary to install a high capacity ammunition box. As a result the gun attachment points became complicated and large fairings had to be installed.

**Single-seat Il-2 ready for take-off. Underneath the wing trailing edge are four RS-82 rockets.**

During tests the aircraft attained 231mph (373km/h) at sea level and 254mph (409km/h) at 7,900ft (2,400m) at a weight of 12,927lb (5,864kg). The rate of climb deteriorated and the take-off run increased. The landing speed was 90mph (146km/h).

Moreover, the Sh-37 proved unreliable, and the low position of the guns relative to the aircraft's centre of mass caused an increase in the nose-down moment when they were fired, a 'pecking' motion of the aircraft, and consequent inaccurate firing.

In March-April 1943 two new, advanced 37mm NS-37 guns designed under the leadership of Nudelman and Suranov were installed in a two-seat AM-38F-powered Il-2. A belt feed to the guns allowed them to be attached directly to the undersurface of the wing, and they were housed in relatively small fairings. Each gun had 50 rounds loaded not in ammunition boxes, but directly into the wing. If necessary, the aircraft could carry up to 440lb (200kg) of bombs in overload.

A small batch of Il-2-37s, as the type was designated, was manufactured at Plant No.30 and underwent service trials with the 208th ShAP during the Kursk battle. In the opinion of the pilots, the handling techniques for the new variant did not differ from those for a fully loaded two-seat Il-2. The fairings and the distribution of large masses in the wing (one gun with ammunition weighed 552lb/237kg) increased the aeroplane's inertia and made it more sluggish to manoeuvre. In addition, the powerful recoil of the guns caused certain difficulties with aiming. It was practically impossible to fire only one gun at a time because it caused the aircraft to yaw violently.

Although the Il-2 with 37mm guns was a formidable weapon system capable of destroying even Tiger tanks, it did not see widespread use.

## Il-2 combat operations during 1943-1944

In the summer of 1944 the Soviet Command decided to use clustered projectiles against the enemy armoured vehicles, and the PTAB 2.5-1.5 'cumulative' aircraft bomb, developed under the leadership of I Larionov, was put into production. The small calibre bombs were loaded directly into the bomb bay and were dropped on the enemy vehicles from altitudes up to 328ft (100m). As each Il-2 could carry up to 192 bombs, a 'fire carpet' 229ft (70m) long and 49ft (15m) wide covered the enemy tanks, giving a high probability of destruction. This was important because the low accuracy of the Il-2's bomb sight was one of its shortcomings.

Pilots of the 291st ShAP were the first to use the PTAB 2.5-1.5 bombs. In one operation on 5th June 1943 six attack aircraft led by Lieutenant Colonel A Vitrook destroyed 15 enemy tanks in one attack, and during five days of the enemy advance the 291st Division pilots destroyed and damaged 422 enemy tanks.

In the Battle for Kursk General V Ryazanov became a master in the use of attack aircraft en masse, developing and improving the tactics of the Il-2 operation in co-ordination with infantry, artillery and armoured troops. Ryazanov was later twice made a Hero of the Soviet Union, and the 1st Attack Aircraft Corps under his command became the first to be awarded a Guard title.

However, the successes of attack aircraft combat operations were accomplished with great losses. The Luftwaffe Command claimed that the Russians lost 6,900 Il-2s in 1943 and 7,300 in the following year. Although these figures exaggerated the losses by a factor of 2 to 2.2, they were substantial nonetheless. In 1943 one loss corresponded to 26 Il-2

sorties, and to even fewer in certain operations. Approximately half of those lost were shot down by enemy fighters, the other half falling to anti-aircraft fire of ground-based guns. Assessing the main reasons for such great losses, the Air Force Commander, A Novikov, considered that poor training of the crews and units was not to blame, but attributed them to flawed tactical procedures in attack aircraft operation. On almost all fronts the pilots adopted a peculiar scheme of approaching the target at 3,300 to 4,900ft (1,000 to 1,500m) altitude without considering its nature, then gliding down and recovering after the attack with a turn to port. The enemy therefore knew the attackers' manoeuvres beforehand, and prepared all of his anti-aircraft defences, taking full advantage of relief features, forest, bushes etc, before their appearance over the battlefield.

The German Bf 109 and Focke-Wulf Fw 190 attacked successfully when the Il-2 gunners were inattentive and the formations were broken up. A damaged and lagging Il-2 often became the victim of fighters. However, attack aircraft pilots could sometimes use skilful defensive tactics, and gunners mastered aggressive fire techniques.

The Il-2's survivability was appraised in the 1st ShAP, and Ilyushin's predictions were confirmed. As a rule the lower armour was not pierced, being hit by low calibre projectiles, and the cockpit also turned out to be effectively armoured. One pilot managed to land his Il-2 with only half of the elevator and rudder and with the port tailplane damaged as a result of anti-aircraft fire, and another landed without any covering on the wing centre section and with no flaps. The rear fuselage, outer wing panels and oil radiators suffered most from anti-aircraft fire. Sometimes the rear fuselage was insufficiently strong, and aircraft with metal outer wing panels appeared to have better chances of survival.

Much attention was paid to eliminating these shortcomings. When deliveries of metal to the aircraft factories became regular, they began to build the aircraft with all-metal wings and to reinforce their rear fuselages with additional lengths of angle extrusions.

*Photograph on this page:*

**Pilots brief in front of a snow camouflaged single-seat Il-2. The slogan on the sides was a popular one, 'Death to the Fascist Occupants'.**

*Photographs on the opposite page:*

**A mix of two-seat and single-seat Il-2s. Hawker Hurricanes to the right.**

**Two views of a two-seat Il-2 with unusual canopy at NII-VVS. Note the RS-82 rockets underwing.**

These features were incorporated in Il-2s manufactured in the second half of 1944.

The results were positive. An analysis of attack aircraft operation in the 3rd Air Army showed that irretrievable losses totalled 2.8% of the number of sorties, and damage was sustained on half of the sorties. The ease with which the Il-2 could be mastered by pilots and technicians promoted its widespread use on all fronts. Pilot A Yefimov, twice Hero of the Soviet Union, remembered: 'It was one of the most easily-mastered aircraft. There were no difficult instrument operations to distract the pilot from aiming at the target. The aircraft forgave the pilot even for flagrant errors. I do not know of a single case when an aircraft went out of control or entered a spin because of a pilot's mistakes'.

The Il-2 was widely used by the Soviet Navy's air arm. An effective method of attack against shipping was to approach at a height of 100ft (30m) at about 250mph (400km/h) and drop the bombs so that they ricocheted off the water and destroyed the target vessel.

Naval People's Commissar N Kuznetsov considered this method, named top-machtovoe bombometanie, or mast-top bombing, to be approximately five times more effective than horizontal bombing. Lieutenant Colonel N Stepanyan was among the best attack aircraft pilots. On 14th December 1944 Stepanyan led 42 Il-2s of the 47th ShAP in an attack

on Libava naval base. Together with Pe-2 bombers, the attack aircraft sank seven freighters and damaged six more. Thirteen Il-2s were shot down, including the one flown by Stepanyan, who was posthumously proclaimed a Hero of the Soviet Union, his second such award.

During the Second World War, 26 attack aircraft pilots flying Ilyushins were twice awarded the title of Hero of the Soviet Union. In conclusion, it is worth quoting the assessment of the Il-2 by the German infantry commander General von Lauken, Commander of the East Prussia Group in the final stages of the war. He wrote: 'The effectiveness of Russian aviation activity in the Danzig region was enormous, and petrified the troops. Neither our air force nor our powerful artillery could oppose this air power'.

## Il-2KR

The Il-2KR was used as an artillery observation and reconnaissance aircraft from the summer of 1943. The RSI-4 radio was replaced by a more powerful unit, and an AFA-I or AFA-IM camera was installed in the rear fuselage. Externally, the Il-2KR differed from the Il-2 in having an aerial mounted on the windscreen.

## Il-2U

The training of attack aircraft pilots was not simple. The 1st Reserve Air Brigade was located in Kuibyshev, and was later awarded the Red Banner Order for its activities. By the beginning of August 1941 eight attack air regiments with 306 Il-2s and 292 trained pilots were transferred to the front. Later, more than a thousand pilots were undergoing training every month, and the deficit of attack aircraft trainers was noticeable.

In 1942 such an aircraft, designated Il-2U, was designed, and production began in 1943. The instructor could correct errors and demonstrate piloting techniques by means of a dual control system. A special version of the Il-2U, armed with two ShKAS machine guns, two RS-82 rockets a 440lb (200kg) bomb load, was used to teach attack aircraft combat techniques.

In 1943 the training of attack aircraft pilots in the 1st Reserve Air Brigade was performed at 13 airfields. Every month in the brigade commanded by A Podolsky up to 20 Attack Air Regiments were formed. This allowed the number of front-line regiments to be increased from 79 in January to 104 in October of that year.

By the end of the war there were 150 Attack Air Regiments, of which 120 were located at the front.

*Photographs on this page:*

*Top and centre:* **The Il-2U operational trainer. Armament was slightly changed.**

*Right:* **Plant No.18 converted to producing Il-2s without interrupting output.**

*Photographs on the opposite page:*

**Three views of the 37mm cannon-equipped Il-2. Note the large fairings for the weapons and barrel length.**

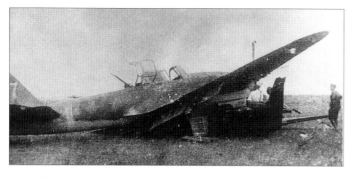

*Above:* Il-2 operational losses were high. It was the destiny of many aircraft to be destroyed, in this case following a ground collision.

*Top right:* A pilot about to board a snow camouflaged Il-2 which is bannered as belonging to the 'Moscow Formation'. Note the rear gunner's canopy is hinged to open to the right.

*Centre:* Battle-worn Il-2 managing to keep its slogan – 'For the Honour of the Guards!' clean.

*Bottom left:* An Il-2 bearing the name and portrait of the famed late 18th century Russian general Alaexander Suvorov.

*Bottom right:* Regiments that operated with considerable valour were awarded the 'Guard' title. The Guard banner on this Il-2 denotes their courage.

*Photographs on page 56, top:* Formation of Il-2s approaching the front line.

*Page 56, lower left:* Close-up of the armoured nose of an Il-2. Note also the typical airfield conditions – these aircraft are operating from a true 'flying field' – there is no runway as such, merely a wide expanse of operating area.

*Page 56, lower right:* A pair of RS-82 rockets under the wing of an Il-2. While the type could carry four on each wing, a shortage of the rockets often meant that they only carried four in total.

**Three views of the M-82-engined Il-2 prototype.**

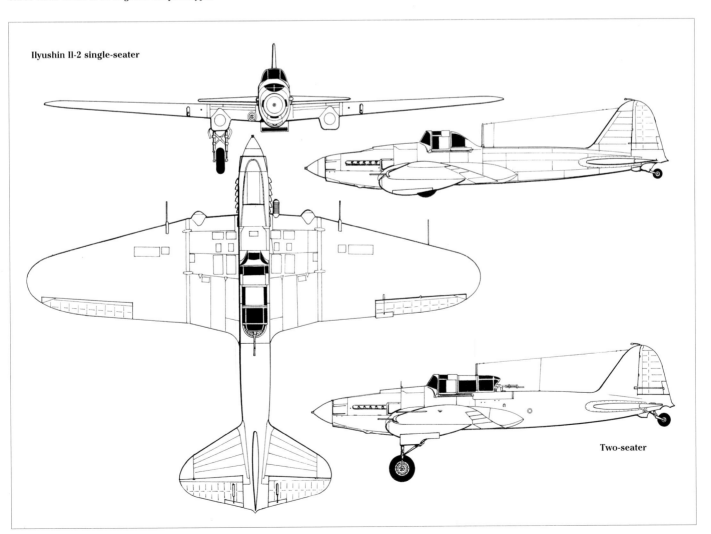

Ilyushin Il-2 single-seater

**Two-seater**

## Il-10 *Best, but at end - note date on next page*

Even before the Il-1 fighter had completed its tests, Sergei Ilyushin realised it had no future, because Soviet aviation was maintaining air superiority in the middle of 1944 and there was no further need for an armoured fighter. He took the initiative to design a two-seat, high speed manoeuvrable armoured attack aircraft based on the Il-1's structure and also designated Il-1. The bureau's work on this project was soon given the highest priority.

As on the TsKB-55 prototype, the armoured fuselage of the new attack aircraft contained not only the engine and pilot's cockpit, but also the gunner's cockpit. As distinct from the Il-2, the gunner, with his 20mm Sh-20 turret-mounted gun, was seated just behind the pilot's armoured backrest. He was protected from the rear by an armoured bulkhead which also served as a member of the fuselage primary structure. This compact cockpit layout avoided a great longitudinal distribu-

tion of mass, thus improving controllability and manoeuvrability. The design team headed by Ilyushin designed a more rational system of armour, which was reinforced in the lower part of the cowling and made thinner along the sides of the pilot's and gunner's cockpits. Taking into account operational experience with the Il-2, it was concluded that there was no need to armour the upper front fuselage sections. These were therefore made of aluminium because, even if the enemy managed to hit the target, the angle of impact of a shell with the skin was assumed to be very small.

The Il-1 had newly developed double armouring of vital structural members, comprising two ⅜in (8mm) armour plates. This protected the crew not only from machine gun fire, but also from 20mm gunfire. In accordance with the design bureau's tradition, the armoured body was integrated into the fuselage primary structure.

The Il-1 two-seat attack aircraft had the same dimensions and structural features as

its single-seat forebear, but its structure was all-metal. Its offensive armament was similar to that of the Il-2, comprising two 23mm VYa guns, each provided with 300 rounds, and two 7.62mm ShKAS machine guns with 1,500 rounds apiece. Like the Il-2 its normal bomb load was 881lb (400kg), while in overload it could carry up to 1,322lb (600kg). The Il-1 had two bomb bays, whereas the Il-2 had four, and they were designed to take bombs of up to 110lb (50kg). External carriers were used to carry two 220 or 550lb (100 or 250kg) bombs. This speeded up the loading of bombs before a flight. The Il-1's defensive armament was considerably increased. An experimental 20mm Sh-20 gun with 150 rounds was installed on a VU-7 mounting, and the tail was protected by a DAG cassette with ten 4.4lb (2kg) aerial grenades.

In April 1944 the aircraft was complete in the Kuibyshev factory's experimental shop. Following the manufacturer's tradition of allocating even type numbers to attack aircraft and bombers, it was designated Il-10.

On 18th April 1944, after the installation of the Mikulin AM-42 prototype engine and the fitting of all on-board systems, the Il-1 made its maiden flight, piloted by test pilot Vladimir Kokkinaki. He completed all of the production tests in a short time, and on 13th May the aircraft was handed over for its state trials. The prototype performed 47 flights, most carried out by Lt Colonel A Dolgov, who was highly appreciative of the aircraft, especially with regard to stability, controllability and performance. He also noted that piloting technique did not differ from the production Il-2.

At a flying weight of 13,966lb (6,335kg) the Il-10 had a maximum speed of 315mph (507 km/h) at sea level and 342mph (551km/h) at 9,000ft (2,800m) – 93mph/150km/h greater than that of a production Il-2 – and it reached 16,400ft (5,000m) in five minutes, compared with eight minutes for the Il-2. Although its range was sufficient and its take-off and landing performance was good, the take-off run was longer than that of its forebear. There were also some deficiencies, most of which were concerned with the unreliability of the new AM-42 engine, which required major modification.

On the whole, the test results proved the soundness of the concept. The optimum combination of powerful offensive and defensive armament in an armoured attack aircraft with high speed and good agility not only allowed effective multiple missions to be flown, but permitted the Il-10 to engage all types of enemy fighters in combat. According to a comparative assessment of three types of attack aircraft powered by the AM-42, the Su-6, Il-8 and Il-10, the Il-10 was the best. In August 1944, in accordance with a decision of the State Defence Committee, series production of the type began. Originally it was planned that 100 Il-10s should be manufactured by the end of 1944.

Aircraft Plants Nos.1 and 18 produced the first 125 Il-10s in January, 1945. The 108th Guard Attack Air Regiment, in the 2nd Air Army moving towards of Berlin, was the first unit to receive these formidable aircraft. Production machines differed slightly from the prototype. In particular, the experimental Shpitalny Sh-20 movable gun was replaced by a 12.7mm Berezin UTB machine gun, and later by the UB-20. The VU-7 turret was replaced by a VU-8 as previously used on the Il-8 attack aircraft, and having similar characteristics.

The first combat mission by Il-10s took place on 12th February 1945, when a squadron of the 108th Guard Attack Air Regiment led by Hero of the Soviet Union F Zhigarin, attacked enemy tanks and motorised infantry in the region of Sprottau airfield, the unit's base. Despite active opposition the Il-10's successfully drove home their attack and returned to base.

During a short lull at the front, Lieutenant Colonel O Tomilin, commander of the 108th Regiment, trained his Il-10 pilots in ground attack. On his initiative a simulated aerial combat was staged to enable them to study air combat tactics. The 'opponent' of the new attack aircraft was an La-5FN fighter from the 5th Guard Fighter Air Regiment, which was also based at Sprottau. The Il-10 was piloted by Captain A Sirotkin and the La-5FN by Hero of the Soviet Union Captain V Popkov, a well known ace with 37 victories to his credit. By the end of the war Popkov's score had increased to 41, and he was awarded with a second Golden Star of a Hero of the Soviet Union.

The mock combat took place at low and medium altitudes, both pilots turning and using complex manoeuvres. Only after sharp and energetic manoeuvring did the fighter manage to get close to the Il-10's tail. Conversely, the La-5FN was centred in the crosshairs of the Il-10 gunner's camera more than once. Immediately after landing Popkov said: 'It is a good attack aircraft, almost a fighter and a deserving rival for the La-5FN'.

It is interesting to compare the Il-10 with the Luftwaffe's Focke-Wulf Fw 190, which was in widespread use as an attack aircraft by the end of the war and had a normal bomb load of 330lb (150kg). All the bombs were carried externally, for the Fw 190 had no internal bomb bays. Its speed at low altitude, where it is best compared with the attack aircraft, was 9.3 to 12.4mph (15 to 20km/h) higher. After its bombs had been dropped the Il-10 was barely inferior to its rival in horizontal manoeuvrability, although it was inferior vertically.

But the Il-10 was a two-seater, and hence better protected. The weight of its armour at 2,226lb (1,010kg) was 15.8% of its normal weight, while the Fw 190's armour weighed only 793lb (360kg), representing 8.2% of its flying weight. The German aircraft also had feebler offensive gunnery and bomb armament. For example, the weight of fire of an Il-10 was 1.61 times greater than that of a production Fw 190 without externally mounted 30mm guns, according to test data. This meant that by the end of the war the Soviet Air Force an had excellent attack aircraft operational.

Service pilots noted several considerable advantages of the Il-10 over the Il-2:

• a wide speed range and improved manoeuvrability improved the fighter's escort abilities and allowed it to engage in air combat;
• the all-round crew armour increased survivability;
• its easy handling in flight and relatively simple maintenance on the ground allowed both air and ground crews to convert to the type in the shortest possible time.

Unfortunately, the defects in the new AM-42 engine noted during the state trials had not been eliminated. In the summer and spring of 1945 many missions had to be abandoned owing to engine failures, and the designers did not manage to eliminate the defects until the war's end.

Meanwhile, the factories were increasing their output of the underdeveloped attack aircraft. During the first four months of 1945 Plant No.18 produced 301 Il-10s and Plant No.1 another 389. This allowed the number of regiments converted to the Il-10 to be increased. By the end of the Second World War, however, only 146 Il-10s remained operational, and only 120 were combat ready. The Il-10 comprised 4% of the total Soviet attack aircraft fleet. The majority of Il-10s had been delivered to the 3rd, 15th, 16th and 8th Air Armies, engaged in active service.

Substantial numbers of Il-10s were involved in the war against Japan. Operating against hostile ships, Il-10 pilots widely practised 'mast-top' bombing in addition to the usual level bombing or shallow dive bombing. On 10th August 1945 six Il-10s led by Captain I Voronin delivered a blow against Japanese vessels in the port of Rasin. In the face of heavy anti-aircraft fire Voronin attacked and sank a torpedo-boat destroyer, and his gunner, A Ivanov, shot down a Japanese fighter which approached the Soviet aircraft. It was also over Rasin that the commander of the 26th Attack Air Regiment of the Pacific Fleet, Major A Nikolayev, became a Hero of the Soviet Union for his achievements. After the end of the war with Japan all of the Soviet Air Force Attack Air Regiments were converted to the Il-10.

The post-war Il-10 had some different features. Instead of two 23mm VYa guns and two 7.62mm ShKAS machine guns, four 23mm NS guns with 150 rounds each were installed in the wing. These newly developed guns were almost half the size of their predecessors and their recoil was 1.6 times less, allowing a simple and light gun mount to be designed. They gave increased weight of fire and improved accuracy because dispersion was decreased to between a half and a third of the former amount. New, powerful PTAB bombs and updated rockets capable of destroying heavy tanks and armoured vehicles were included in the armament.

The Il-10 remained in production until 1948, by which time 4,540 had been manufactured. After development it was redesignated Il-10M. Besides the combat variant, a trainer version designated UIl-10 (Il-10UT) was also manufactured in small quantities. In this aircraft the gunner's position was fitted out as a second cockpit and the offensive armament was slightly simplified. Plant No.1 produced 268 of these aircraft, 227 of them in 1945.

*Photographs on the opposite page:*

*Top and centre:* **Two views of the Il-10 during state trials at NII.**

*Bottom left:* **On the Il-10 the aerial mast was moved slightly forward and the cockpit canopy was more streamlined.**

*Bottom right:* **An Il-10 undergoing static testing.**

*Photographs on this page:*

*Right:* **Il-10s received their baptism of fire in February 1945, three months before the final victory over Germany.**

*Below:* **Production Il-10 displayed at a post-war aviation exhibition.**

**Post-war production standard Il-10.**

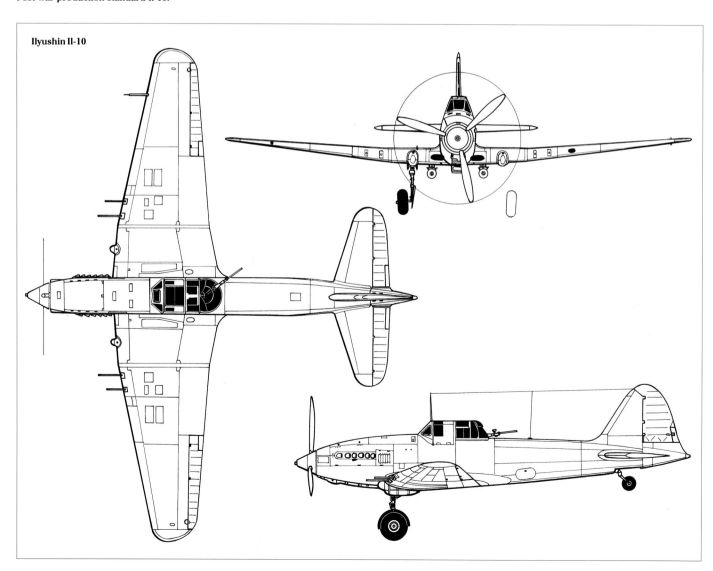

**Ilyushin Il-10**

## Il-8

The Ilyushin Design Bureau had already begun to design an armoured attack aircraft before the Second World War. An all-metal, low wing twin-finned monoplane designated TsKB-60 was developed, to be powered by two AM-38s. It was planned to produce it in two versions, a single-seater and a two-seater with defensive armament. The aircraft was to have powerful offensive armament consisting of a 37mm nose gun and a normal bomb load of 1,322lb (600kg), and a maximum of 2,204lb (1,000kg).

The preliminary design of the aircraft, redesignated Il-6, was approved on the eve of war, but when combat actions began the design bureau and aircraft factories were busy increasing the volume of production and eliminating the defects of the available aircraft, and the Il-2 took priority. Work on the new design was therefore postponed.

*Below:* **While retaining the format of the Il-2, the Il-8 was much enlarged. Here the Il-8 is seen during state acceptance trials.**

In the summer of 1942 Sergei Ilyushin received a request for a proposal for a heavy attack aircraft with a bomb load of up to 2,204lb (1,000kg). Taking combat experience with the Il-2 into consideration, he chose a single-engine configuration which was essentially an oversized Il-2 with reinforced armour, increased range and the same armament. The aircraft had the new Mikulin AM-42, an updated AM-38F rated at 1,770hp (1,320kW) at 5,250ft (1,600m), and providing 2,000hp (1,492 kW) at take-off. (The AM-38F could deliver 1,500hp/1,119kW at 2,500ft/750m and 1,700hp/ 1,268kW at take-off.)

The maiden flight of the prototype, designated Il-8, took place on 10th May 1943. The aircraft was piloted by Vladimir Kokkinaki, who noted that it was simple and easy to handle. At a weight of 15,983lb (7,250kg) it had a maximum speed of 270mph (435km/h) at sea level and 292mph (470km/h) at 7,400ft (2,240m), almost 31mph (50km/h) faster than

a production Il-2. Climb rate increased by 15% and range was almost doubled. Owing to the powerful engine the take-off run was only 1,043ft (318m), while the landing speed was 82mph (132km/h). But the tests were delayed by engine unreliability, and it proved very difficult to eliminate smoke emission and vibration. Nevertheless, in February 1944 the Il-8 underwent state tests and was recommended to be put into production provided all the problems were overcome.

By the end of the tests the Ilyushin Design Bureau was involved in designing the Il-1 (Il-10). Ilyushin himself proposed redesigning the Il-8's engine cooling and lubrication systems, undercarriage and empennage after the style of those in the Il-1 (Il-10), and all the experience gained by the bureau was used to redesign the aircraft. As a result a completely new aircraft was developed under the original designation, Il-8.

Work on the prototype was completed in

the autumn of 1944, and on 13th October the remodelled Il-8 made its first flight with Kokkinaki at the controls. Again the production tests were delayed, this time because the retrofitting of an AV-9L-22B four-bladed propeller was not completed. However, the problem of engine vibration was solved just before the state trials began, just after the end of the war. The new arrangement of the water and oil radiators, the more streamlined shape of the armoured fuselage, which was like that of the Il-10, and other improvements increased speed at sea level to 286mph (461 km/h) and at 9,200ft (2,800m) to 316mph (509 km/h) at a flying weight of 16,776lb (7,610kg). However, a simulated dogfight showed that the Il-8 had no chance of outperforming the Yak-3 fighter in aerial combat.

When the report by leading pilot Colonel A Dolgov and engineer S Frolov on the Il-8's state trials was proposed, the Deputy Commander-in-Chief of the Soviet Air Force wrote: 'Manufacturing the Il-8 is not expedient because the Il-10, which outperforms it, is in production'. Sergei Ilyushin agreed with this decision, but two years later his design bureau designed the Il-20 heavy armoured bomber and attack aircraft, which incorporated the designers' accumulated experience.

*For technical data, see Table B, page 164.*

*Left:* **Second Il-8 prototype.**

*Below:* **The series of Ilyushin attack bombers proved themselves to be a major element in the repulsion of German forces from Soviet soil.**

# Kocherigin

## OPB-5

Sergei Kocherigin's Design Bureau started designing the OPB-5 single-seat dive bomber, powered by the new Shvetsov M-90 air cooled engine, in 1940. It was a single-engined, low wing monoplane with a conventional empennage, but its structure incorporated many innovations. The all-metal wing was of the inverted gull form, permitting the use of a short, light undercarriage and a bomb bay with a wide opening in the lower fuselage, to improve the aircraft's stability.

Thick wing root sections allowed the main wheels to be retracted rearwards into the wing, between the two spars. The leading edges of the outer wing panels had automatic slats, and flaps were mounted on the trailing edges of the wing centre section and outer panels. Air brake flaps, in the upper and lower wing surfaces in front of the flaps, could be

deflected 90°, not only limiting the diving speed but also reducing the landing speed to 76.4mph (123km/h). The aircraft's empty weight was 6,186lb (2,806kg), and its take-off weight was 8,470lb (3,842kg).

The OPB-5's cigar-shaped fuselage contained the cockpit, bomb compartment and fuel tanks. The cowling of the radial engine had a central circular air intake. A number of wind tunnel tests of a Polikarpov I-185 mock-up fitted with an M-90 engine preceded the adoption of this innovation.

The fuselage consisted of an all-metal forward section and a wooden rear section. The armament included two large-calibre BS machine guns and two ShKAS machine guns, installed on both sides of fuselage, and the bomb load comprised a single 1,102lb (500 kg) bomb. With its powerful gun armament the OPB-5 could withstand hostile fighters, because it conceded little to its opponents in

performance and manoeuvrability after it had dropped its bomb. The pilot was protected from rear attacks by an armoured backrest, and the canopy windscreen was made of armoured glass.

Flight testing of the OPB-5 began in 1941, but were not completed because of underdevelopment of the M-90. Difficult conditions during the initial stages of the war obliged the designers to stop development work on the aircraft. The main attention of aircraft industry employees was directed to increasing production of the Pe-2 dive bomber. According to calculations, the M-90 powered OPB-5 could have had a good performance: a maximum speed of about 372mph (600km/h) at 18,700ft (5,700m), a range of 410mph (660km), and a service ceiling of 32,500ft (9,900m).

*For technical data, see Table D, page 168.*

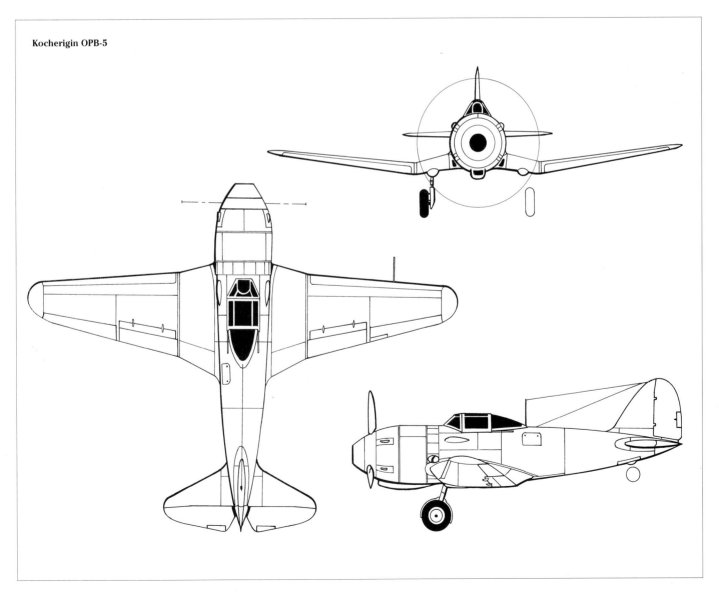

**Kocherigin OPB-5**

# Neman

### KhAI-5

The design group led by the talented young engineer Joseph Neman was established in the early 1930s at the Kharkov Aviation Institute (KhAI). Earlier, Neman worked under Konstantin Kalinin, well known in the Ukraine.

One of Neman's first tasks at the KhAI was to design the KhAI-1 passenger aircraft, the first of its type in Europe to have a retractable undercarriage. The aircraft was put into production, and quickly attracted the attention of the military.

From 1934 the main effort of Neman's team was devoted to the SR (KhAI-5) short-range bomber and reconnaissance aircraft. Simultaneously, the KhAI-6 Skorostnoy Photorazvedchik (SFR – high speed photographic reconnaissance aircraft) was built. The KhAI-5 incorporated advanced ideas such as a retractable undercarriage and a smooth veneer stressed skin, all of which had been introduced and tested on the KhAI-1. In addition, the very successful MV-2 turret designed by I Venevidov and G Mozharovsky (later designated MV-3), fitted with ShKAS machine guns, was first used on the KhAI-5.

Complicated flap and aileron mechanisms, which were tested on the contemporary KhAI-6, were also used on the KhAI-5. It was powered by a 712hp (531kW) American Wright Cyclone F-3 engine. This engine was installed in many Soviet combat aircraft prototypes in the 1930s, even after its Soviet version, the M-25, had gone into production.

Test pilot Boris Kudrin flew the new aircraft for the first time in June 1936, and it surpassed all expectations. Its maximum speed exceeded the top speeds of all operational reconnaissance aircraft of similar type by almost 62mph (100km/h).

The state trials of the KhAI-5, conducted at the Nauchno Issledovatelyskii Institut (NII – scientific and research institute (of the VVS) from 29th August to 24th October 1936, were somewhat unusual. Another reconnaissance aircraft prototype, designated R-9 and built at the Tsentral'nyi Konstruktorskoye Byuro (TsKB – central, ie state, construction/design bureau) of Plant No.1 by S Kocherigin's team, embarked on its flight tests at the same time. The R-9 was an advanced version of the SR high speed, retractable undercarriage reconnaissance aircraft tested in 1935. Although the SR had attained a record speed of 285mph (460km/h), the military had rejected it because of its unsuccessful undercarriage retraction system. In their desire to get the aircraft into production at any price, the TsKB designers reached a compromise which finally ruined the aircraft. The new version, the R-9, had a fixed undercarriage covered by fairings which caused a great deal of drag.

Comparative flight tests of the KhAI-5 and R-9 were conducted by a group of pilots, A Dolgov becoming the leading test pilot for the Kharkov-built machine. At a flying weight of 5,544lb (2,515kg) its maximum speeds were 217mph (350km/h) at sea level and 241mph (388km/h) at 8,200ft (2,500m), and it climbed to 9,850ft (3,000m) in 6.5 minutes, had a service ceiling of 25,250ft (7,700m) and a range of 901 miles (1,450km). The KhAI-5 was significantly faster than the majority of reconnaissance aircraft operational with the Soviet Air Force. The commission recommended that the KhAI-5 be adopted as the main reconnaissance aircraft of the Soviet Air Force in 1937. In the concluding remarks on the results of flight tests, signed by Chief of the Air Force Yakov Alksnis, it was stated that it was necessary to solicit the People's Commissariat for the Defence Industry to put the KhAI-5 into production because of its obvious superiority over current operational reconnaissance aircraft.

### R-10

Production of the KhAI-5, designated R-10, was launched at the Kharkov and Saratov factories. The R-10 was a two-seat low wing monoplane of all-wooden construction except for its empennage and ailerons. It was intended for reconnaissance missions, and also could be used as an attack aircraft and short range bomber. Its fuselage was a semi-monocoque structure of which the wing centre section and fin formed an integral part. From the fourth aircraft the fabric covered rudder and ailerons had Duralumin frames, and from the fourteenth production aircraft the tailplane was Duralumin. Pneumatically operated Shrenk-type flaps reduced the landing run significantly. The landing gear comprised a retractable main undercarriage with braked wheels and a castoring tailwheel.

Initially the R-10 had an M-25A engine, but later the 730hp (544kW) M-25V was installed. From the tenth production aircraft the VISh-6 two-bladed metal propeller was fitted. Fuel was contained in 79 gallon (360 litre) wing tanks. The first 24 aircraft had riveted fuel tanks, but welded and protected tanks were then adopted.

The R-10's standard armament consisted of three ShKAS machine guns; two in the wing and one turret mounted. The bomb bay had cassette-type bomb carriers able to carry 22, 55 and 110lb (10, 25 and 50kg) bombs up to a total weight of 660lb (300kg). Sighting and bomb-dropping was performed by the pilot/observer using an OPB-1M or PAK-1 sight.

During series production the R-10 was constantly improved. The KhAI-5*bis* prototype re-engined with an M-25E reached 264mph (425 km/h) during NII VVS flight tests in 1938. Modified and strengthened production R-10s were powered by the more powerful M-88, M-62 and M-63s, and a trainer version was designed. Some of the aircraft phased out of the air force inventory and given the civil designation PS-5 were used by state airline Aeroflot.

More than 490 R-10s were manufactured. The pilots of the 43rd Air Brigade, commanded by HSU Nikolay Kamanin, were the first to familiarise themselves with the aircraft. The pilots liked the new aircraft, which was easy to fly. The R-10's Service history includes combats over Khalkhin-Gol in the summer of 1939. Partly disassembled aircraft were delivered to their units by railway, and were received in the desert region of Tamtsak-Bulak by brigades of plant assemblers who quickly prepared them for flight.

A few regiments equipped with the R-10 participated in the Finnish War of 1939. Soviet pilots flying there had to endure extremely severe conditions, flying reconnaissance and attack missions over the Mannergaim Line in low cloud, in temperatures down to –50° of frost, and in snow storms and Arctic winds.

In late 1940 the aged R-10s began to be replaced by more up to date aircraft. Nevertheless, at the beginning of the Second World War the they played an active part in the battles of Moscow and Leningrad, flying reconnaissance missions alongside Sukhoi Su-2s and Yakovlev Yak-4s, and were used for close air support. A few remaining R-10s were still operational in 1943.

### KhAI-51 and KhAI-52

An attempt to design an attack aircraft based on the R-10 was undertaken in 1937. As a result there appeared the KhAI-51 and KhAI-52 powered by the 900hp (671kW) M-63 and armed with seven ShKAS machine guns and 880lb (400kg) of bombs. The KhAI-52 was test flown at Kharkov by A Dolgov in August 1937.

In accordance with a government decision the KhAI-52 went into production, and initially a pre-production batch of ten machines was built. However, work on the design of the KhAI-52, which promised to be an advanced aircraft, was interrupted by the unexpected arrest of Neman for false accusation and the destruction of his design bureau.

*Above:* **Prototype KhAI-5 light tactical bomber.**

*Right:* **Operational R-10. Very little is known of their wartime use.**

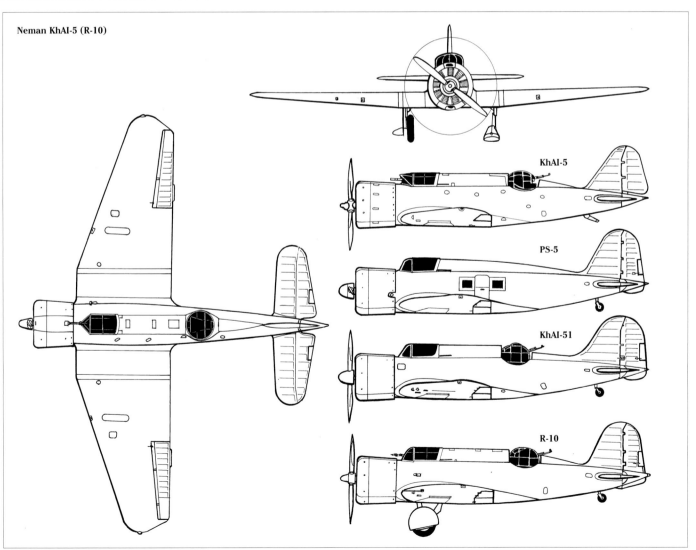

**Neman KhAI-5 (R-10)**

KhAI-5

PS-5

KhAI-51

R-10

# Polikarpov

### R-5

Designed by Nikolay Polikarpov in the late 1920s as a reconnaissance aircraft and built in small series, the R-5 was used during the first years of the Second World War as a light bomber and attack aircraft. It was a classic biplane, principally of wooden construction, and was powered by an M-17F engine delivering 730hp (544kW) at take-off. The flying weight of the reconnaissance version was about 6,525lb (2,960kg), and the light bomber version weighed up to 7,385lb (3,350kg). It carried two crew; a pilot and a gunner who protected the rear hemisphere with a 7.62mm machine gun. Bomb carriers installed beneath the lower wing could carry up to 660lb (300kg) bombs. The R-5 was operational with the Soviet Air Force from 1931 to 1937, and considerable numbers were later used for civil aviation tasks.

After the outbreak of the war many R-5s were converted as a matter of necessity into light bombers, and along with U-2 biplane trainers and UT-1 and UT-2 sports monoplanes were used to bomb hostile targets in the enemy's rear at night. The R-5 was operational at the front until 1944, serving as a liaison, ambulance and transport aircraft.

**Polikarpov R-5 in tactical camouflage and carrying external fuel tanks.**

# VIT-1 and VIT-2

In addition to producing fighters, Nikolay Polikarpov conducted a great deal of work on the development of a twin-engined multi-purpose aircraft. In 1937 the three-seat VIT-1 was handed over for tests. The initials VIT stood for vozdushny istrebitel tankov, or anti-tank fighter, but the aircraft could also be used as a dive bomber or a fighter. The VIT-1 had an all-metal structure with a low set wing, and was powered by two 960hp (716kW) Klimov M-103 engines driving three-bladed propellers. The main undercarriage wheels retracted into the engine nacelles but the tailwheel was non-retractable. Armament consisted of two 37mm guns mounted in the wing centre section, one 20mm ShVAK with 10° range of movement in the nose, and one 7.62mm ShKAS machine gun in a rear turret. A bomb load of up to 1,322lb (600kg) could be carried internally in the fuselage bomb bay, plus two 1,102lb (500kg) bombs externally. It was intended that the VIT-1 would use this weaponry to destroy tanks. The navigator/gunner sat in the glazed nose, from where he could direct attacking fire, while a second radio operator/gunner defended the aeroplane's rear hemisphere.

The VIT-1 first flew in the summer of 1937. Following the test flights, in which the aircraft showed a speed of more than 279mph (450km/h) and a range of about 620 miles (1,000km), it was decided to modify its structure and install more powerful engines.

On 11th May 1938 well known Soviet test pilot Valery Chkalov undertook the maiden flight of the new VIT-1, with 1,050hp (783kW) M-105s and a twin-finned empennage. The landing gear wheels were faired to improve aerodynamics during take-off and landing, and in flight they were retracted into the rear of the engine nacelles. The cockpits of the navigator/gunner, pilot and radio operator/gunner were generously glazed. Armament consisted of a 20mm movable ShVAK gun in the nose, a ShVAK gun in the rear turret, two 37mm and two 20mm ShVAK guns in the wing centre section and two 7.62mm ShKAS machine guns on an underfuselage mounting to protect the lower hemisphere. The bomb load was the same as that of the VIT-1.

Production tests of the VIT-2 were conducted by test pilot Boris Kudrin, and state trials by Peotr Stephanovsky. The maximum speed at 14,750ft (4,500m) was 318mph (513km/h). The commission recommended that the aircraft be introduced into series production as a high speed dive bomber, but that some of the armament be removed to increase the speed.

**Rare illustrations of the VIT-2 anti-tank fighter.**

# SPB(D)

Using the experience gained in the development and testing of the VIT-1 and VIT-2, the Polikarpov Design Bureau produced another version of the Skoroostinoi Pikiriyuschii Bombardirovshchik (SPB – fast dive bomber) high speed dive bomber powered by two M-105 engines, designated 'D'. Externally similar to the VIT-2, it had smaller dimensions and structural differences. The first prototype made its maiden flight on 18th February 1940, with Boris Kudrin at the controls. Its flying weight was 15,101lb (6,850kg), and the armament consisted of a nose-mounted 7.62mm ShKAS machine gun, a 12.7mm UB turret-mounted machine gun to protect the aircraft's rear hemisphere, and a ShKAS hatch-mounted machine gun to guard the lower hemisphere. The bomb bay could hold an 1,763lb (800kg) bomb load, and an additional 1,543lb (700kg) of bombs could be carried externally.

After the first prototype, an initial batch of five aircraft was produced. In tests a maximum speed of 323mph (520km/h) was reached, which was better than most of the Soviet fighters of the time. But the SPB suffered a sad fate. After dozens of flights by the production aircraft, several disasters occurred. Test pilot P Golovin was killed on 27th April 1940 while flying the first prototype, but the cause of the disaster was not determined. Then M Lipkin died in the second prototype when wing flutter developed during a dive and the aircraft disintegrated. Investigation revealed that the balance weights in the leading edges of the ailerons had apparently been omitted. B Kudrin managed to land the third prototype SPB after the rudder trimmer broke in flight, but he refused to fly the fourth prototype. To determine the cause of the disasters a model of the aircraft was carefully tested in a Tsentral'nyi Aerogidrodynamichesky Institut (TsAGI – Central Aerodynamic and Hydrodynamic Institute wind tunnel, but these tests were later discontinued owing to the successful flights of another twin-engined fighter prototype designed by Vladimir Petlyakov, designated '100', which could fulfil all the intended functions of the SPB.

*Above and left:* **The high speed SPB undergoing wind tunnel tests at TsAGI.**

*Below:* **Polikarpov SPB during production testing.**

Polikarpov SPB(D)

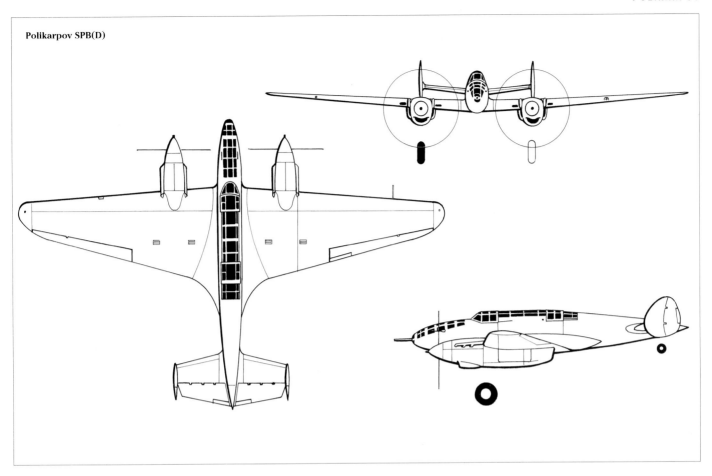

## U-2VS

Designed in the late 1920s by Nikolay Polikarpov's team, the U-2 training and agricultural biplane, which had also performed the roles of passenger and ambulance aircraft, saw unusual service in the Second World War. In the early 1930s it was proposed that the U-2 be used as combat aircraft. Its take-off and landing performance and manoeuvrability could be very useful in combat conditions, and a so-called 'armed version' was built in 1933. A PV-1 machine gun was installed on the port side of the forward fuselage, a DA machine gun mounting was fitted to the rear cockpit and four carriers able to carry up to 440lb (200kg) of bombs were fixed under the wings. In this configuration the aircraft's flying weight was 2,308lb (1,047kg) without a bomb load.

The aircraft underwent tests at the NII VVS during February and March 1933. Although its performance had deteriorated slightly owing to the increases in weight and drag, stability and controllability were almost unchanged. Later, four more armed U-2s were built. Fitted with the same armament, they underwent flight tests at the Borisoglebsk Flying School during June and July 1933, and proved to have a maximum speed of 80.7mph (130km/h) and a service ceiling of 10,250ft (3,120m) at a flying weight of 2,383lb (1,081kg). Naturally the climb rate was reduced and the take-off

and landing runs were longer, but again the stability and controllability of the armed aircraft differed little from those of the basic version. Although the flight test report concluded that it would be expedient to use the armed U-2 as a combat trainer and communication aircraft, it was not put into production. The outbreak of the Second World War forced the designers to reconsider the idea.

During the defence of Odessa in September 1941 the U-2 was used as a reconnaissance aircraft and as a light, short range bomber. The bombs, dropped from a civil aircraft piloted by Peter Bevz, were the first to fall on enemy artillery positions.

Nikolay Polikarpov supported the project, and under his leadership the U-2VS VS (Voiskovaya Seriya – military series) was created. This was a light night bomber, fitted with bomb carriers beneath the lower wing to carry 110 or 220lb (50 or 100kg) bombs up to a total weight of 771lb (350kg) and armed with ShKAS or DA machine guns in the observer's cockpit. Series production of this version started in 1942. The enemy soon became aware of the threat posed by the U-2, and Luftwaffe pilots were given special instructions for engagement with the aircraft, which they nicknamed Rusfaner, or 'Russian [Venetian] Blind'. German pilots considered a hunt for a U-2 as important as an air combat, and this forced Soviet pilots to fly mainly at night.

The defensive armament also had to be improved, so the U-2VS prototype fitted with a new mount carrying a DT machine gun underwent flight test at the NII VVS in 1943 and again in early 1944. The avionics were also improved, a radio with an engine-driven generator being installed in the reconnaissance version of the aircraft.

The U-2VS inspired fear in the enemy, suddenly appearing over his positions and dropping bombs. A number of units operated the U-2VS, including the famous women's 46th Guard Night Bomber Regiment.

The U-2NAK (Nochnoi Artilleriiskiy Korrectirovshchik – night artillery observation) aircraft, with the bombing gear removed and equipped to direct artillery fire, was based upon the U-2VS. Its engine was fitted with a flame-damping exhaust and a silencer.

The unchanged U-2 served as a communications aircraft, and was also used to drop leaflets over the front line, while the U-2GN (Golos Neba – literally voice from the sky, psychological warfare) was equipped with a powerful loudspeaker.

*For technical data, see Table D, page 168.*

*Photographs on the opposite page:*

*Top:* **A U-2VS in winter camouflage and on skis, during tests as the NII VVS.**

*Centre left and right:* **Two views of the rear gun**

mounting on the U-2VS. It could be used to fire rearwards during ground operations, or for self defence.

*Bottom right:* **Readying a camouflaged U-2VS for a night raid.**

*Bottom left:* **The U-2VS was capable of carrying up to eight 132mm RS-132 rockets.**

*This page above:* **U-2NAK night observation aircraft.**

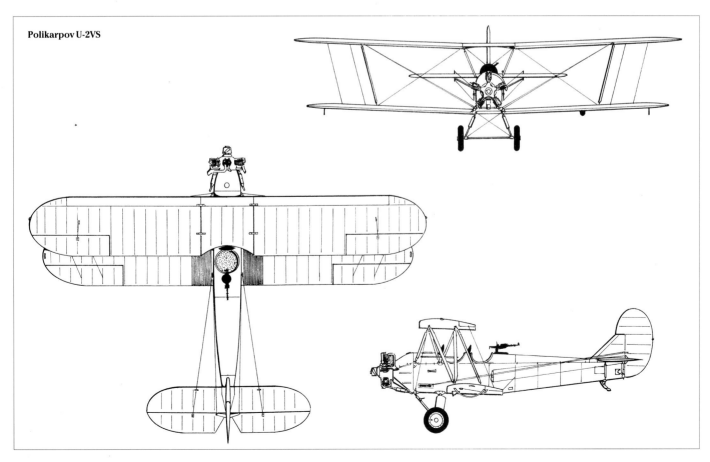

**Polikarpov U-2VS**

# Sukhoi

## 'Ivanov' (SZ)

In the mid-1930s the development of a modern multi-purpose tactical aircraft became an urgent task for the Soviet industry. From September 1935 team No.3 at the Tsentral'nyi Aerogidrodynamichesky Institut (TsAGI – Central Aerodynamic and Hydrodynamic Institute) headed by Pavel Sukhoi, was involved in the design and development of a new multi-purpose aircraft designated SZ (Stalinskoye Zadaniye, or Stalin's Assignment).

The request for proposals for the development of the 'Ivanov' multi-purpose aeroplane was issued in early 1936. The nickname 'Ivanov' originated from Stalin's formulation of the task, which stated: 'The aircraft should be designed for simple tooling, allowing the production of as many aircraft as the number of people named Ivanov living in our country'. Among the competitors were the TsAGI, chief designer Andrei Tupolev, the Tsentral'nyi Konstruktorskoye Byuro (TsKB – central, ie state, design bureau), chief designer Nikolay Polikarpov, the Kharkovski Aviatsionny Institut (KhAI – Kharkov Aviation Institute), chief designer Joseph Neman and two other teams headed by Dmitry Grigorovich and Sergei Kocherigin. The specification required the TsAGI aircraft to be of all-metal construction, those of Nikolay Polikarpov, Dmitry Grig-

orovich and Sergei Kocherigin to be of mixed construction, and that of Joseph Neman to have all-wooden construction.

In July 1936, Andrey Tupolev was appointed chief designer of the Glavnoye Upravleniye Aviatsionnoi Promyshlennosti (GUAP – Chief Directorate of the Aircraft Industry) in accordance with a government directive. Upon his return from a long fact-finding mission to the USA, Vladimir Petlyakov, on Tupolev's recommendation, was appointed chief of the design division of Prototype Aircraft Plant 156, and Pavel Sukhoi became his deputy. Further work on the project was being carried out in this design division.

By February 1937 the VVS had worked out the specification for the 'Ivanov' aeroplane, which was to be a multi-purpose aircraft combining the capabilities of a high speed long range ground attack aircraft, a high speed long range reconnaissance aircraft, a short range bomber and an escort aircraft for high speed bombers. It was to have a maximum speed of 260 to 267mph (420 to 430 km/h) and a ceiling of 29,500ft (9,000m).

Only an up-to-date, highly efficient aircraft could meet such challenging requirements. When designing the aircraft, Pavel Sukhoi paid special attention to the use of new materials and technologies. High strength aluminium alloys were widely employed in the

construction of components, which were made as mouldings, cold extrusions and castings. The design team minimised the amount of welding, the quality of which was difficult to control. An innovation for the Soviet aircraft industry was the use of the loft and template technique, which provided interchangeability of structural members and simplified the assembly process. These innovations facilitated the mechanisation of manufacturing processes and the adaptation of assembly lines to mass production.

The decision to develop a dual control aeroplane ensured certain advantages. It ruled out the need for a specialised trainer, and in a combat environment the navigator could always take over the controls.

The SZ-1 was a low wing cantilever monoplane of all-metal construction with a retractable undercarriage. Instead of using the Mikulin M-34FRN engine originally selected, in March 1937 it was decided to adapt the airframe to take Arkadi Shvetsov's M-62, which had already been chosen to power Nikolay Polikarpov's 'Ivanov'. This experimental nine-cylinder radial, which provided 830hp (619 kW) at sea level, was fitted with a metal two-bladed variable-pitch 9ft 2in (2.8m) diameter VISh propeller.

The monocoque fuselage had a thick skin and incorporated 22 frames. Amidships there was a high and spacious cockpit for a pilot and a navigator who also served as gunner and radio operator. The bomb bay, with stowage for a 440lb (200kg) load, was located under the cockpit between the wing centre section spars. Forward of the cockpit and in the outer wing panels were three self-sealing fuel tanks of 204 gallons (930 litres) total capacity, representing an innovation in Soviet aircraft technology at that time.

The cantilever tapered wing was of two-spar construction with a stressed skin, and comprised a centre section integral with the fuselage and two detachable outer wing panels. The aerofoil had a thickness ratio of 17.6% at the centreline, 15.25% at the wing attachment point and 8% at the wingtip rib. The wing-fuselage joint was sealed by aluminium tape. The wing had 6° dihedral on the lower surface. The skinning of the leading edge and the upper surface up to the second spar was flush riveted, while the remainder of the skinning was attached with round-headed rivets.

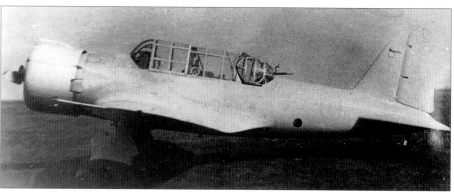

ANT-51 (or 'Ivanov') fitted with an MV-5 turret.

M-87-powered 'Ivanov' during manufacturer's tests.

Frise-type ailerons were fitted to the outer panels. The wings also had deflectable Shrenk-type flaps inboard of the ailerons and beneath the fuselage. The ailerons, rudder and elevators were Duralumin framed and fabric covered.

Armament comprised four ShKAS machine guns with 750 rounds per gun, installed in pairs in the outer wing panels. Defence of the rear hemisphere was provided by a movable machine gun on a dorsal gun ring and a rear hatch gun, both operated by the navigator. Each gun had 500 rounds of ammunition. When stowed, the dorsal gun was enclosed in an unconventional removable fairing. The total bomb load was 881lb (400kg).

On 25th August 1937 the first SZ-1 prototype, which had received the TsAGI designation ANT-51, made its first flight, with TsAGI chief pilot Mikhail Gromov at the controls. According to Gromov the aircraft displayed good stability and handled well.

The second prototype, SZ-2, again powered by the M-62, was completed in December 1937 and went to Yevpatoriya for its state joint trials, where it made its first test flight on 29th January 1938. However, the aircraft crashed on 3rd August 1938. The M-62 engine appeared to be unreliable, and flight tests of the ANT-51 were abandoned in late 1938.

On 17th September 1938 the third 'Ivanov' prototype (SZ-3), powered by an M-87 engine, was rolled out. It was of similar construction to its predecessors. The M-87 was later replaced by a production M-87A fitted with a VISh-23 propeller. According to the report written by test pilot A Chernavsky, who carried out the development flight tests, the SZ-3 had a number of advantages over the SZ-1, having a shorter take-off run, an increased glidepath and greater speed. In addition, the weight of the ailerons was reduced, and the ammunition for the wing machine guns was increased to 850 rounds per gun.

On 27th January 1939 the NII VVS began the aircraft's state trials in Yevpatoriya. These were conducted by pilots Stefanovsky and Pokrovsky, with Tretyakov as navigator, and the prototype was flight tested in both the ground attack and bomber configurations. The normal bomb load for the bomber version was 880lb (400kg), and for the ground attack variant it was 440lb (200kg). The maximum bomb load was 2,204lb (1,000kg). In the resulting report it was recorded:

'The "Ivanov" M-87A aircraft, designed by comrade P Sukhoi, passed the State Trials satisfactorily ... The "Ivanov" should be recommended to enter service as a light bomber, while providing the opportunity to be used in the ground attack and short range reconnaissance roles as well. It should be of mixed construction (wooden fuselage and metal wings), adapted to take the M-87A and

M-88 engines'.

A modified version of the SZ-3 with an M-87B engine, submitted for state acceptance trials in mid-1939, had practically the same performance as the M-87 powered version. It was tested in the reconnaissance role with two wing-mounted 7.62mm ShKAS machine guns and a similar turret-mounted gun. The hatch gun was abandoned. Later the SZ-3 prototype was fitted with an M-88 engine rated at 1,100hp (820kW), the armament being the same as that of the M-87B-powered aircraft. The performance characteristics remained virtually unchanged, but the powerplant was found to be under-developed.

Another 'Ivanov' prototype, developed by the Nikolay Polikarpov team and flown for the first time in late 1938, was marginally inferior in speed compared with the J Neman multipurpose R-10 then in production, but outclassed it in armament and range.

The 'Ivanov' aircraft being developed by Dmitry Grigorovich was unfinished owing to the death of the chief designer. The outcome of the competition was that the Sukhoi aircraft appeared to be the best.

## BB-1 (Su-2)

In accordance with a directive issued by the People's Commissar for the Aircraft Industry on 7th July 1939, the Sukhoi design team was assigned to production Plant No.135 in the town of Kharkov. Here, on 4th August, the Tumanskii M-87A-engined 'Ivanov' was put into series production under the designation BB-1 (Blizhny Bombardirovshick-1, or short range bomber No.1) instead of the Joseph Neman R-10 (this project had been abandoned by the KhAI in October 1939). In September Pavel Sukhoi was appointed chief designer of aircraft Plant No.135 and Design Bureau No.29 (KB-29).

A small number of BB-1s powered by the M-87A were produced. The aircraft was of mixed construction, with a wooden fuselage and fin and metal wings and tailplane.

In April 1940 the state trials of the M-88-engined production BB-1 were successfully completed by test pilot A Dolgov. In this year, in addition to Plant No.135 in Kharkov, production of the M-88 powered BB-1 (soon redesignated Su-2) was initiated at Plant No.31 in Taganrog and Plant No.207 near Moscow. Some aircraft (mainly produced in Plant No.207) were converted to the artillery observation role.

However, the Su-2 was soon withdrawn from the assembly line at Taganrog in favour of the LAGG-3 fighter, after some dozens of Su-2s had been produced. In February 1941 a modified Su-2 with a 1,000hp (746kW) M-88B

engine completed state acceptance trials. Refinements introduced in the aircraft's structure included rearrangement of the exhaust pipes to provide an increase of thrust, and replacement of the MV-5 turret by a TSS-1. Flight tests revealed increases in the maximum level speed, ceiling and range of the modified aircraft. The normal bomb load of 1,322lb (600kg) comprised up to 880lb (400kg) of bombs ranging from 17 to 220lb (8 to 100kg) in the fuselage bomb bay, supplemented by two 220lb (100kg) or even 550lb (250kg) bombs carried externally.

When the M-88-powered BB-1 entered series production the hatch gun and the navigator's armour protection were removed to save weight. Because this enhanced the aircraft's performance at the cost of weakened defensive capabilities, it was necessary for BB-1 formations to be escorted by fighters.

The delivery tempo at the Kharkov factory built up rapidly, and had reached three BB-1s (Su-2s) per day by the start of the Wehrmacht assault. Owing to enormous attrition during the first days of the war, fighter escorts for bombers become a luxury that the VVS could ill afford. The Su-2's vulnerability forced Sukhoi to form a special team to restore the aircraft's defensive capabilities, including the navigator's armour protection and the hatch gun. The task was accomplished in several days, and from July 1941 the armament and armour was reinstated in series production aircraft.

In the mid-July 1941 the Commandant of Soviet Army South-West Front, Semyon Budyonny, visited the Kharkov plant and appealed to the staff to double their output of Su-2s. The factory was put on non-stop production, which increased daily output to six aircraft.

In August 1941 Su-2s were being assembled on the Kharkov line amid intensified Luftwaffe bombing attacks, and the flying units being formed nearby were immediately sent into action. The Wehrmacht offensive forced the evacuation of Plant No.135 to Molotov (later renamed Perm). The 110 Su-2s rolled off the Kharkov production line in 1940 were supplemented by 525 delivered in 1941, exceeding the annual production plan by 5%. Some production Su-2s were adapted to carry six, eight or ten RS-82 or RS-132 rocket projectiles, and 30 Molotov-built M-82-powered Su-2s were also fitted to carry eight RS-82s or RS-132s beneath their wings.

In all its forms the Su-2 displayed extraordinary survivability. Its sturdy construction enabled the aircraft to absorb considerable battle damage and still remain airworthy. Examples of this robustness included flying with only half of the rudder and tailplane and yet returning to base. Filling the void in the self-sealing fuel tanks with exhaust gases greatly reduced the risk of fire.

*Above:* **Two views of a production BB-1, powered by the Tumanskii M-87.**

*Below:* **The bulk of Su-2 production featured the M-88B engine. Prototypes undergoing flight trials.**

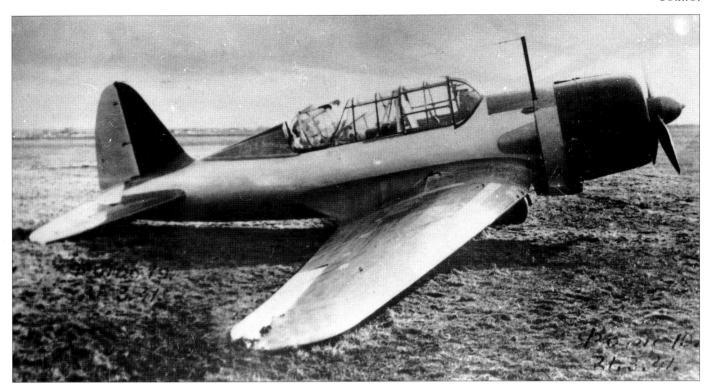

*Top:* **Only a few Su-2s were built at the Taganrog Plant, No.31. One crashed on landing during production tests.**

*Centre left:* **The BB-1/Su-2 was equipped with the advanced MV-5 turret, designed by Mozharovsky and Venevidov, and fitted with a pair of 7.62mm ShKAS machine guns.**

*Centre right:* **While the Su-2 did not have a great performance, it was of great importance during the conflict against Germany.**

*Right:* **An Su-2 at the moment of release of small calibre bombs.**

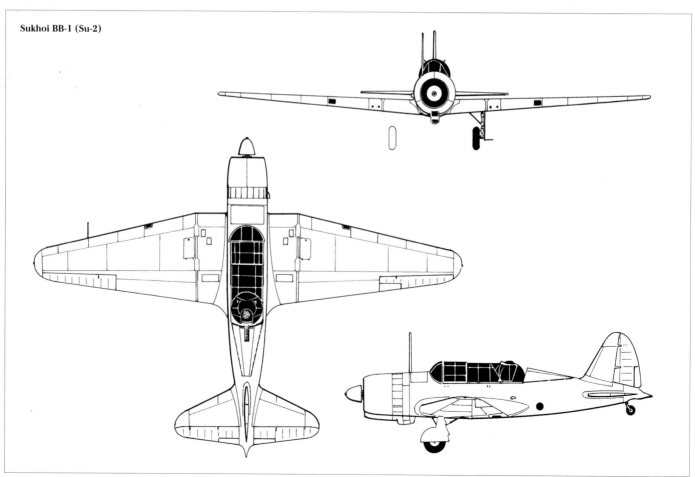

**Sukhoi BB-1 (Su-2)**

*Opposite page:* **BB-1 captured by the Germans and undergoing a thorough inspection.**

*Above:* **Modified BB-1 armament comprised ten underwing RS-82 launchers.**

## Su-2 M-82 (Su-4)

Owing to severe bombing of the railways, not all of the trains carrying equipment and Su-2 parts from the evacuated Kharkov plant reached Molotov. Consequently only 40 Su-2 airframes were assembled at the new location at the beginning of 1942. Most of these aircraft were fitted with the 1,540hp (1,148 kW) Shvetsov M-82 14-cylinder air-cooled radial engine produced by Plant No.19, also in Molotov.

The aircraft designated Su-4 successfully underwent its state acceptance trials between 25th February and 23rd April 1942, flown by test pilot Korobov. It featured enhanced armour protection for the navigator: the TSS-1 turret was fitted with ⅜in (10mm) armour plate to protect his breast, two ⅜in (10mm) armour plates were installed vertically outside the TSS-1 turret, and one similar inclined plate was provided to protect the hatch gun position. The floor of the navigator's compartment was fitted with ³⁄₁₆in (4mm) armour plate. The M-82 engine, which could run even with several cylinders damaged, provided effective forward protection for the pilot, whose cockpit was fitted with ⁵⁄₁₆in (8.5mm) back armour.

The Su-4 seemed to be a promising aircraft with potential for development and improvement owing to its high powered air-cooled engine. Indeed, the evolutionary line of Sukhoi attack aircraft, starting with the 'Ivanov' and passing through the ShB prototype and the Su-2 (Su-4) production aircraft, was crowned by the Su-6 prototype of 1942,

for which Pavel Sukhoi received the coveted title of Stalin Prize Laureate.

A total of 889 production Su-2s and Su-4s had been delivered by March 1942, when the plant in Molotov was disbanded and its personnel distributed among other factories. So the line of Sukhoi production aircraft was discontinued, to be re-established only after Stalin's death.

Like all of the aircraft created by the Sukhoi Design Bureau, the Su-2 (Su-4) was notable for its designer's consideration for the crewmembers. Besides the external radio communication provided by the RSB radio in navigator's compartment, the aircraft was equipped with an SPU-2 internal communication system. Indirect lighting of the instrument panel and warm air heating of the crew positions were innovations in Soviet production aircraft of the time. In case of failure of the electro-hydraulic system, the undercarriage could be extended manually by the navigator, using an emergency cable transmission. Moreover, this dual control aircraft was extremely airworthy, its high survivability being revealed when it was operated under conditions of Luftwaffe supremacy.

By the beginning of the German assault on the Soviet Union 13 bomber regiments had been fully or partly equipped with Su-2s. In the first month of the war, the most dramatic period for the VVS, these regiments were assigned to the western, south western and southern sectors of the front, and their losses were therefore not as great as those of the bomber regiments equipped with the Tupolev SB and Ilyushin DB-3. At the beginning of the war Su-2's comprised 14% of the total bomber force deployed on the Soviet Army's western sector of the front, while by 10th July 1941 this had increased to 21%. By 4th October 1941, 116 of the 174 operational daylight bombers on the South Western Front were Su-2s. The 135th Bomber Air Regiment operated successfully in that area, complet-

ing 630 sorties without loss and destroying 217 tanks and up to 400 infantry vehicles. In May-June 1942 Su-2s comprised 55% of the daylight bombers in service on the South Western Front. On 12th September 1941 female pilot Yekaterina Zelenko rammed a Messerschmitt Bf 109 near the town of Sumy while flying a burning Su-2. This was the only ramming attack performed by a woman in the history of air combat.

Sukhoi Su-2s were flown by pilots of 15 VVS regiments and two separate squadrons. The aircraft participated in combat operations near Lvov, Kiev, Moscow and Stalingrad, and also in the battles of Orel and Kursk. The bomber played a significant role in the fight for Stalingrad. During the Stalingrad defensive operations in 1942 the 8th Air Army lost eight Su-2s in air combats. On average, an Su-2 of the 270th Bomber Air Regiment made 80 sorties before it was shot down, while the 221st Bomber Air Regiment, operating Douglas Bostons, lost one aircraft for every 19 sorties. A similar figure, 20 sorties, was typical for the Pe-2 until its turret mounted 7.6mm ShkAS was replaced by the 12.7mm UB gun, which increased the average number of sorties before being shot down to 54. The Il-2, proclaimed by the Soviet propaganda machine as an outstanding attack aircraft while it was being operated as a single-seater in 1941 and most of 1942, completed an average of 13 sorties before being shot down, this figure being improved two-fold after it was converted to a two-seater. However, because of the poor protection afforded the gunner and his lack of firm support while firing the 12.7mm gun (he sat on a canvas belt in the rear cockpit), gunners had to be changed, on average, every seven sorties. Whether there was any justification in putting the Il-2 on a pedestal in the light of such costs awaits investigation.

Indeed, the 270th Bomber Air Regiment was formed with highly experienced crews, but its ability to retain its personnel and thus accumulate combat experience can be traced to the exceptional survivability of the Su-2. Sometimes, to enhance the aircraft's defensive capabilities on daylight missions, its crew was increased to three.

The pilots of the 288th Bomber Air Regiment, commanded by I Gorokhov, managed to fly their Su-2s overloaded with two externally mounted 551lb (250kg) bombs, which significantly enhanced the effectiveness of bombing attacks. The rear defensive armament of the DB-3 and Pe-2 had proved inadequate, and this was also the case with the Su-2. Replacement of the turret mounted 7.6mm ShKAS with the larger calibre UB gun seemed inevitable.

## ShB

Work on designing a special attack aircraft began in May 1938, and the aircraft began its flight tests in the summer of 1940. The concept of the special attack aircraft was not sufficiently clear for the designers, and the new aircraft was designed and built on the basis of the 950hp (708kW) M-88A powered 'Ivanov' aircraft. The majority of the accessories and structural members of the new aircraft, designated BB-2, were similar to those of the basic aircraft. Its main undercarriage retracted rearwards and the wheels turned through 90°, the only time this structural feature was applied to a Sukhoi Design Bureau aircraft,

and the armour beneath the cockpit was increased. The aircraft had powerful armament consisting of six high-rate-of-fire ShKAS machine guns, and at normal take-off weight it could carry up to 1,322lb (600kg) of bombs. According to calculations the ShB had a maximum speed at sea level of 217mph (350 km/h), a range of about 497 miles (800km) and a ceiling of 26,250ft (8,000m). It did not go into production because production of the Il-2 attack aircraft had already started.

*Most successful version of the BB 'family' was the Su-4, an M-82-powered Su-2. Illustrated is an Su-4 undergoing flight testing of a ski undercarriage.*

Main difference from the prototype ShB and the Su-2 was the new arrangement for the main undercarriage (evident in these views) and extra armour for the cockpit area.

## Su-6 and Su-8

The design and manufacture of the Su-6(A) single-seat attack aircraft by the Sukhoi Design Bureau started in 1940, after the bureau was given the manufacturing base in Podlipki. This work was conducted simultaneously with the testing of the Su-1 prototype and other extensive work on the development of various Su-2 versions. The aircraft, which was intended for operation against ground troops and enemy airfields, was powered by the new Shvetsov M-71 air cooled radial engine being developed at the same time.

The first Su-6(A) prototype was ready by the beginning of 1941, and it underwent its state trials from 28th August to 17th September. It was a single-seat monoplane of mixed construction. The main wing panels, wing centre section and empennage were metal, while the unarmoured fuselage rear section was a wooden semi-monocoque structure covered with veneer. The control surfaces had metal frames and were covered with fabric. Vital elements such as the cockpit and fuel tank were armoured. To improve manoeuvrability and stability at high angles of attack, the wing was fitted with automatic slats.

All of the gun armament, consisting of four 7.62mm high-rate-of-fire ShKAS machine guns and two 23mm VYa guns, was installed in the outer wing panels. The aircraft could carry up to 881lb (400kg) bombs in its internal bomb bays, and small calibre bombs could be stowed in bulk in the bays without carriers,

greatly accelerating pre-flight preparation. Up to ten RS-82 or RS-132 rocket projectiles could be carried on external hardpoints.

The summary of the state tests, signed by the pilot, Major Dolgov, made the following points:

• The Su-6 with the M-71 is faster in horizontal flight than the Il-2 powered by the AM-38;

• without bombs and RS-82 rockets the Su-6 has a maximum speed of [300mph] 483km/h for 10 minutes in boosted mode. This makes the aircraft difficult to catch for enemy fighters with only a small speed advantage;

• it is expedient to consider the manufacture of a small series of Su-6 aircraft powered by the M-71; they are of interest because of their comparatively high maximum horizontal speed and powerful gun and rocket armament.

## Su-6(SA)

The Su-6(SA) back-up aircraft was manufactured with some modification and underwent flight testing at Molotov during February 1942. The new series of five aircraft for service trials were to be manufactured there as well.

The Su-6(SA) was powered by an M-71F enclosed in a NACA-type cowling. Its fuel tank was protected beneath, behind and at the sides by armour plate, and its void was filled by inert gas. The cockpit was protected by armour of ³⁄₁₆ to ⁵⁄₈in (4 to 15mm) thickness.

The tapered wing had a TsAGI 'B' aerofoil section of 15% thickness/chord ratio at the root and 9% at the tip, and was fitted with slats and Schrenk-type flaps. The wing centre section was all metal, while the outer wing panels were wooden with metal spars.

Six RU-235 launchers for RS-82 rocket projectiles were installed beneath the outer wing panels, and two 110 to 551lb (50 to 250kg) bombs could be carried under the wings. The normal bomb load was 440lb (200kg), while in overload the aircraft could carry up to 881lb (400kg) of bombs. Two 37mm OKB-16 guns with 40 rounds each and two 7.62mm ShKAS machine guns with 675 rounds apiece were installed in the roots of the outer wing panels. Cast iron counterbalances were mounted in the outer wing leading edges to delay the onset of wing flutter.

The controls were equipped with balances and aerodynamic compensation. The control system was duplicated, while the Frise-type aileron control was single, using rods. Rudder control was through duplicated cables, and the elevator control used duplicated rods.

## Su-6(S2A)

Wartime operational experience made it clear that attack aircraft needed rear gun mountings to protect them from hostile fighters. In 1942, therefore, the Su-6(S2A) two-seat armoured attack aircraft was built on the basis of the Su-6(SA) single-seater, and was completed in December of that year. It was powered by a 2,200hp (1,641kW) M-71F air cooled radial driving a three-blade AV-5-4A propeller, replaced during testing by a four blade AV-9-4A unit.

Armament comprised two OKB-16 guns with 45 rounds, two ShKAS machine guns with 700 rounds per gun and a BLUB blister gun mounting with a UBT machine gun with 196 rounds. The aircraft had the VV-1 sight, which consisted of a ring on the armoured windshield and a fore sight on the engine cowling.

State tests were carried out from 19th June to 30th August 1943, and Colonel A Kabanov noted in his report dated 4th September 1943: 'On the whole the aircraft creates a good impression, and would be a formidable weapon in engagements against ground troops and with enemy bombers...'. Colonel Pyotr Stefanovsky, the pilot who performed the flight tests, wrote in his report of 6th September 1943: 'This two-seat attack aircraft... could replace the Il-2 because its armour is more effective and its performance is better'.

The report also stated: 'The Su-6 two-seat aircraft was tested in aerial combat with the enemy's Bf 109G-2 fighter without underwing guns, and with the He 111H-11 bomber under daytime conditions... Enemy bombers such

as the He 111, Fw 200 and Ju 87 could evade the Su-6 by climbing. Conclusions: In concert with the use of active, manoeuvring defence during the repulsing of enemy fighters attacks, the Su-6 is capable of higher horizontal speed than the Il-2 and its tail protection, using fire from the rear gun mounting, allows it to resist the enemy fighters while maintaining flight at maximum speed, especially at low altitude, and to turn to allow the gunner to fire from the rear mounting... Owing to the combination of high speed and powerful armament the Su-6 could effectively engage enemy bombers (such as He 111, Fw 200 and Ju 87), as well as the transports ...'.

Sukhoi was awarded the Stalin Prize, First Degree, for the development of this aircraft. Unfortunately the lack of production M-71Fs decided its fate.

## AM-42 -powered Su-6(S2A)

The Su-6 was converted to have a liquid cooled engine at Plant No.284, and then went for state trials, conducted from 28th April to 2nd July 1944. Only basic flight performance data were gathered during these tests, and the programme was not completed because a serious defect was discovered in the AM-42 engine with its AV-9L-172 variable-pitch propeller; this was the burning of the mixture in all of the branch pipes.

On this machine the slats were removed and the compensation between the controls and ailerons was increased. The tailwheel was enlarged, a new hydraulically actuated undercarriage with a piston of larger diameter was installed, and the undercarriage attachment points were reinforced. A standard fighter-type control column was fitted in the cockpit, and the oil cooler output ducts were positioned under the wing. The wing area was increased to compensate for the higher gross weight due to the heavier engine; the wings were now of all-metal construction. During the test flights the OKB-16 guns were replaced by lighter Volkov and Yartsev VYa weapons, allowing 1,322lb (600kg) of bombs to be carried at the same take-off weight.

The Su-6 with the AM-42 was not put into production because the contemporary Il-10 attack aircraft was better and had superior performance. The Il-10, being similar to the Il-2 in its construction, was therefore introduced into the inventory.

**Two-seat Su-6(S2A), powered by the M-71 engine, successfully passed through state trials but was not introduced into service.**

**Front view of the Su-6(S2A) showing its twin 37mm guns.**

The Su-6(S2A) powered by the water-cooled AM-42, providing a very different nose profile.

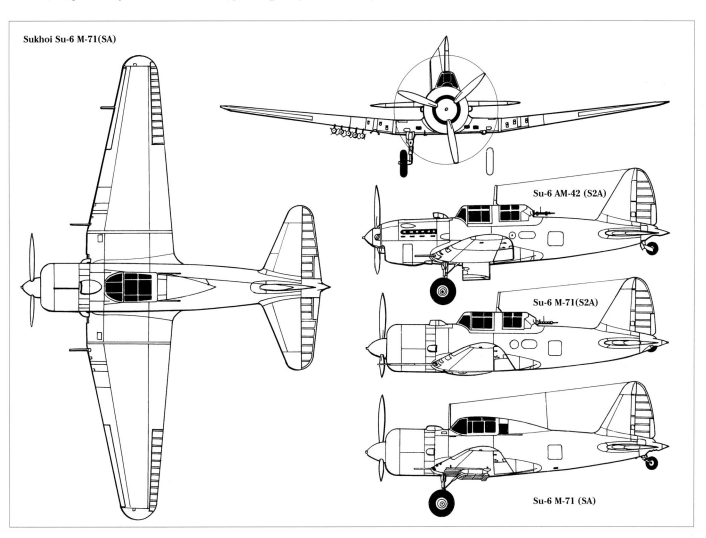

Sukhoi Su-6 M-71(SA)

Su-6 AM-42 (S2A)

Su-6 M-71(S2A)

Su-6 M-71 (SA)

## Su-8 (DDBSh)

Combat operations during the first years of the Second World War revealed the need for a special aircraft to support ground troops distant from base airfields and to strafe communications far in the enemy's rear. The single-engined attack aircraft serving with the VVS had armament of inadequate power and lacked the required range. Not only was powerful armament needed, but the crew's safety was important and they had to be well protected against enemy fighter attacks.

Design of the aircraft began in 1942 in the Urals (Molotov city), at Plant No.79 (the Arkady Shvetsov engine manufacturing plant), where the design bureau and production base had been evacuated. Next year the Su-8 (DDBSh – Dvukhmotornyi Dalny Bronirovannyi Shturmovik – twin engined, long range armoured attacker) two-seater, powered by two 2,200hp (1,641kW) Shvetsov M-71F air-cooled engines, was completed. As the bureau was then returning to Moscow's Tushino airfield, the dismantled aircraft was loaded on a barge and towed there along the Kama, Volga and Moscow rivers. After it had been reassembled at Tushino airfield the tests began there and were continued at the LII, with Nikolay Fikson as pilot.

The Su-8 had extremely powerful gun and bomb armament. Four 45mm OKB-16 cannon with 50 rounds each were installed as a central battery under the fuselage. The cannon were intended for suppressing the forces of German armour, which had the most up-to-date vehicles in their inventory. For use against infantry there were four 7.62mm ShKAS machine guns in each outer wing panel, with 2,400 rounds for each pair. To pro-

tect the aircraft from attacks from the rear, a similar machine gun with 500 rounds was mounted in the gunner/radio operator's LU-100 movable hatch, and a 12.7mm UBT machine gun was mounted in the upper UTK-1 turret. The bombs were attached to carriers in six centre-wing bays. Each bay contained one bomb of 330lb (150kg) or a few of lighter weight, the maximum load being 1,984lb (900 kg). In overload the aircraft could carry three bombs weighing a total of 1,102lb (500kg) externally under the fuselage, bringing the maximum bomb load to 3,086lb (1,400kg).

At a normal take-off weight of 27,365lb (12,413kg) the operational range was 372 miles (600km), and the maximum range was 932 miles (1,500km). The Su-8 had a rather high maximum speed for such a heavy aircraft; 310mph (500km/h) at sea level and 341mph (550km/h) at altitude. Its service ceiling was 29,500ft (9,000m).

The aircraft had a composite structure. Its forward fuselage was made entirely of armoured steel of $\frac{3}{16}$ to $\frac{9}{10}$ in (4 to 15mm) thickness, and the cockpit windshield and the headrest were made of 2½ in (64mm) thick armoured glass. The central fuselage section was made of Duralumin, with armour protection for the gunner/radio operator. The tail section was a semi-monocoque structure comprising a plywood covered wooden frame. The armour, which weighed 3,703lb (1,680 kg) in total, protected the crew, engines, fuel tanks, oil tanks, oil coolers and propeller cylinders from the fire of the large calibre guns. The single-spar wing, of 645ft² (60m²) area and NACA-230 aerofoil section, and having a high thickness/chord ratio, consisted of an all-metal centre section including the engine nacelles and two detachable outer

panels with metal spars, wooden ribs and plywood covering.

The outer panels were attached to the engine nacelles with 7° dihedral. In addition to the main spar, the wing had a metal web carrying attachment points for the four-section flaps and the ailerons. The port aileron had an adjustable trim tab. To enhance slow speed controllability the designers provided automatic slats along the outer wing leading edges. The empennage consisted of an all-metal tailplane with fabric covered elevators and endplate fins. The rudders were horn balanced, and an adjustable trim tab was fitted to the port rudder. The aircraft had the simplest possible undercarriage which retracted hydraulically into the engine nacelles.

Once the design of the DDBSh was completed and building of the first prototypes had begun, the Sukhoi Design Bureau began to develop the Su-6. Minimal changes, such as removal of the cannon battery and engine armour, and the introduction of a third crew member, enabled medium bomber and high altitude reconnaissance versions of the aircraft to be considered. At that time (1944) the DDBSh had successfully undergone its manufacturer's and state tests, but it was decided not to put it into production. There was no longer any need for the attack aircraft because the war was now being waged close to Germany's borders, and Hitler's defeat was close and inevitable.

*For technical data, see Table C, page 165.*

**The Su-8 twin-engined attack aircraft.**

# Tomashevich

## Pegas

Several versions of the innovative Pegas (Pegasus) light attack aircraft were designed under the leadership of Dmitri Tomashevitch. According to performance requirements, the new aircraft had to occupy an intermediate position between the Po-2 light night bomber and the Il-2 attack aircraft.

Two versions were designed simultaneously, a monoplane and a biplane. Both had the same armament; a 37mm gun (or two 23mm VYa guns), a 12.7mm UBK machine gun and bombs to a total weight of 1,102lb (500kg) mounted under the wing centre section. The biplane was to have been a 'slip-wing' with a jettisonable upper wing. This configuration was never flown. Four prototypes were built, from late 1942.

The primary materials used in the Pegas's structure were wood, steel and fabric, and its powerplant comprised two Shvetsov M-11F water-cooled engines rated at 140hp (104 kW) each. Because of the high reliability of the engines, which had been known to take direct hits and continue to function, it was considered unnecessary to protect them with armour plate. The propellers were the same as those fitted to the Po-2. The oil tanks were located under the wing at the junction of the centre section and the outer wing panels, and the unprotected, 41 gallon (190 litre) main fuel tanks were located to the rear of the engine cowlings.

*For technical data, see Table D, page 168.*

*Top left:* **First prototype Pegas attack aircraft. in monoplane form**

*Centre and bottom:* **Two views of third Pegas prototype.**

*This column below:* **Details of the forward fuselage of the fourth Pegas prototype.**

**Rare illustration of a Pegas in flight.**

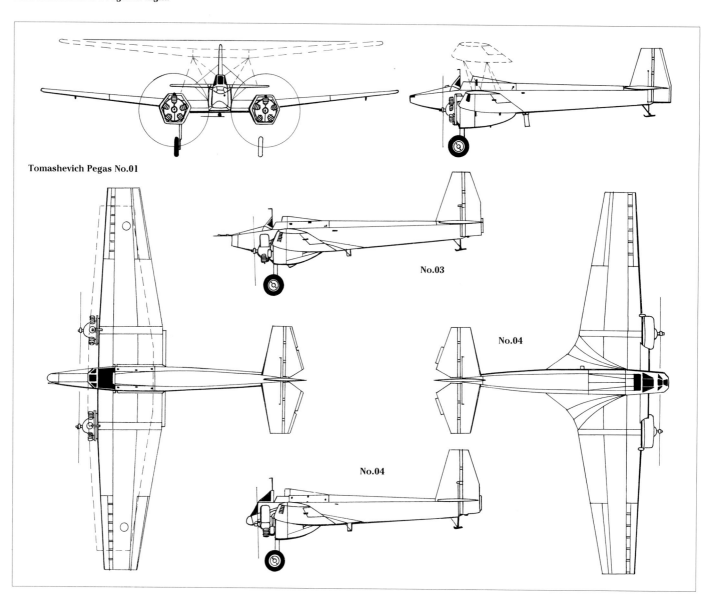

Tomashevich Pegas No.01

No.03

No.04

No.04

# Yakovlev

## BB-22 (Yak-2)

A new twin-engined monoplane appeared on the test airfield near Moscow in the spring of 1939. Its red and white camouflage scheme and streamlined contours attracted everybody's attention, and it was clear that the aircraft could have an exceptional performance. In fact it had already attained 347mph (560km/h) during its first test flights, which was faster than the majority of fighters of the time. This high speed reconnaissance bomber was the first military aircraft to emerge from the Yakovlev Design Bureau, hitherto involved only in the design and construction of light aircraft.

The new aircraft was given the code No.22 and later BB-22 (Blizhnii Bombardirovshchik – short range bomber). Its factory test programme was led by the chief test pilot of the bureau, Yulian Piontkovsky, who demonstrated it to Yakov Smushkeviche, Chief of the Soviet Air Force and a hero of the Spanish Civil War, who appreciated its capabilities.

The No.22 quickly attracted the attention of the General Secretary, who was impressed by its speed. After participation in the May Day flypast over the Red Square, the aircraft was submitted to the Nauchno Issledovatelyskii Institut (NII – scientific and research institute of the VVS) for testing. Leading engineer Holopov, pilot Shevarev and navigator Tretyakov were the team members involved in the flight tests. Aircraft No.22 reached a maximum speed of 352mph (567km/h) at 32,500ft (9,900m) and took 5.75 minutes to reach 16,400ft (5,000m). Such a performance met the technical requirements of 1935 and made the aircraft one of the best in its class in the USSR, as well as abroad, comparing favourably with the Italian Breda 88, French Breguet 690 and other foreign aircraft. The BB-22 surpassed the performance of a production Tupolev SB powered by the same engines by almost 62mph (100km/h), but it was pointed out that this was not its top speed, and that it would be possible to reach 372mph (600km/h) if engine cooling was improved, the exhaust system was changed and advanced propellers were fitted.

The aircraft was of composite structure. Its one-piece wooden wing had two spars and was covered by veneer, and the wooden centre fuselage section was integral with the wing. The forward fuselage was made of Duralumin, while the detachable rear fuselage had a welded steel tube frame with fabric skinning.

Several deficiencies were pointed out in the flight test report. The engine cooling system was inadequate, and the engines overheated, especially in the climb. Consequently, although it was estimated that the aircraft would take 8.7 minutes to climb to 23,000ft (7,000m), it actually took 34 minutes because the pilot had to level out several times to allow the engines to cool. In addition, the structure of the wheel brakes was underdeveloped and the fuel system was not sufficiently reliable.

We now know from the recollections of Aleksandr Yakovlev that on 17th August 1939, soon after the end of Aircraft No.22's state trials, Stalin summoned the designer to the Kremlin. The leader was very surprised that such a speed could be achieved using the same M-103 engines that powered the SB.

In his book *The Aim of Life* Yakovlev wrote: 'Stalin was still walking round the office in a state of surprise, saying: "A miracle, quite a miracle; this is a revolution in aviation".' In fact, although the BB-22 was much faster than other Soviet and foreign bombers, as well as many fighters, it was soon forgotten, and even the specialists of the design bureau recalled it with reluctance. This was mainly because the great hopes pinned upon it in the Second World War proved unjustified.

In particular, the aircraft gained speed at the cost of some other qualities. As pointed out in the report on the state tests, it was unarmoured. Moreover, the narrowness of the cockpit hampered the pilot and made emergency escape practically impossible, and to transform Aircraft No.22 into a short range bomber, guns, bombs, radio equipment and a reconnaissance camera had to be carried.

So, there were no 'miracles' for such Soviet specialists as Tupolev, Petlyakov and Myasishchev. According to test pilot Igor Shelest: '... the ideas of A Yakovlev provided a stimulus for the majority of Soviet aircraft designers to develop new high-speed aircraft. The result was the development of the "100" (Pe-2) and later the "103" (Tu-2).

'These aircraft had approximately the same speed as the BB-22, but they also had powerful armament comprising cannon and large calibre machine guns, armour, and adequate range and endurance'.

The true facts were unknown in the summer of 1939 and, simultaneously with the state testing of the BB-22, the Mock-up Commission was working at Plant No.115, where the plans for converting the aircraft to a bomber were discussed in the presence of designers and representatives of the NII VVS. A new arrangement of navigator's cockpit, providing better view and allowing 'direct communication' with the pilot, was adopted. The problems concerning bomb and gun armament and navigational equipment were also discussed. At the same time, preparation for series production of the aircraft was under way. In March-April 1939, before the BB-22's test programme had begun, Yakovlev had already started transferring photographic copies of the drawings to Plant No.1, where it was intended to manufacture the bomber. A special KB-70 (Konstruktorskoe Byuro, Design Bureau) involved in introducing the aircraft into production was established. The first aircraft, completed on 31st December 1939, was flown the following February.

A service batch was soon built, and underwent tests in March-April 1940. As often happened, the production aircraft were of inferior quality. Despite a reduction in fuel capacity from 2,204 to 1,322lb (1,000 to 600kg), the flying weight increased from the 11,073lb (5,023kg) of the BB-22 as tested to 11,860lb (5,380kg). But the service aircraft had greater firepower and a widened range of firing angles, and the bomb load was increased from 264 to 881lb (120 to 400kg). There was a marked drop in maximum speed, which, at 320mph (515km/h) at 16,400ft (5,000m), was 32mph (52km/h) lower than that achieved by the test aircraft.

The service test programme results led to the conclusion that the powerplant and undercarriage were underdeveloped. Vibration of the empennage had interrupted the tests at the outset.

Careful work began on reinforcing the structure and determining its weak points. Although the production BB-22 (soon to be designated Yak-2, acknowledging the name of its chief designer) passed its test programme in November 1940, it became apparent that the elimination of one problem gave rise to others. So an undercarriage with paired wheels was installed, the cylinders for the undercarriage and flap hydraulic system were enlarged, and the wings and fuselage were covered with fabric.

The BB-22 had unsatisfactory longitudinal and lateral stability within the cg range and with its undercarriage up. This made it suitable only for well trained pilots. Moreover, the engines often overheated during the climb, and water emitted from the system. Further deterioration in performance was noticed. At a weight of 12,477lb (5,660kg) the BB-22 could manage only 247mph (399km/h) at sea level, whereas the test aircraft reached 282 mph (455km/h) at sea level and 297mph (478 km/h) at 15,000ft (4,600m), and time to climb to 16,400ft (5,000m) was 9.5 minutes. The service ceiling was 26,500ft (8,100m), 8,800ft (2,700m) lower than that of the test aircraft. It can be said with certainty that the BB-22 did not outclass the SB, built two years earlier.

In the concluding remarks of the test programme report it was stated that the aircraft was not combat capable and reliable, and that even flights with a 881lb (400kg) bomb load could be dangerous to the crew. It was therefore not surprising that production of the Yak-2 at Plant No.1 soon ceased, work concerning the aircraft's development being concentrated at Moscow Aircraft Factory No.81. The aircraft produced there proved to be somewhat better. In the first place this was due to the production technology; the qualities of surface finish were higher, and engine cowlings and doors were fitted with greater care. This gave an increase in maximum speed of 6.2 to 12.4mph (10 to 20km/h) compared with production aircraft built at Plant No.1. Test flights of the aircraft in overload condition showed that take-off with short term supercharging, carrying a 881lb (400kg) internal bomb load and two externally mounted 220lb (100kg) bombs, was improved, as were combat capabilities. Defects of the gun and bomb armament and inadequate stability were not overcome.

## BPB-22

Besides upgrading the production aircraft, Plant No.81 was involved in converting the BB-22 into a dive bomber. Engineer Curbala headed this programme, and the aircraft was designated Izdelie 31 or BPB-22. It was powered by new M-105 engines with two-stage turbosuperchargers, each rated at 1,050hp (783kW) at 13,100ft (4,000m), and was fitted with air brake panels and an automatic dive entry/recovery control system. At a weight of 13,143lb (5,962kg) the aircraft had a speed 331mph (533km/h) at 16,700ft (5,100m), and 346mph (558km/h) less external bomb load.

At the end of October 1940 Lapkin conducted the first flight, and further tests were conducted at Ramenskoe by Y Paul. This highly experienced test pilot managed to prevent a catastrophe when the fuel suddenly ran out and the engines cut in quick succession. Paul managed to turn the aircraft steeply towards the airfield without allowing it to snap into a spin. He said that with its engines inoperative the aircraft fell like a stone, and a few metres of altitude were insufficient to prevent a crash landing. This incident delayed the aircraft's development.

The attractive BB-22 with integrated cockpit for the pilot and gunner.

The BB-22 with separated cockpits.

Two views of the developed Yak-2 under test at NII VVS in December 1940.

# Yak-4

The version of the reconnaissance and bomber aircraft designated Yak-4 was powered by M-105 engines and had two additional fuel tanks in the outer wing panels, giving a total capacity of 39.5 gallons (180 litres). Maximum speed increased to 284mph (458km/h) at sea level and 331mph (533km/h) at 16,500ft (5,050m), and the rate of climb and service ceiling were improved. Nevertheless, in assessing the aircraft, A Filin, chief of the NII VVS, considered it 'necessary to cease production of the Yak-4 because it did not meet air force requirements', owing to its still unsatisfactory stability, short range and underdeveloped powerplant. So, although it was put into series production at two factories, the BB-22 remained undeveloped. The Yakovlev Design Bureau was heavily involved in I-26 (Yak-1) fighter development, and was unable to devote much time to the bomber before series production ended.

**A Yak-4 under test at the NII VVS, January 1941.**

The last 22 Yak-4s were delivered in April 1941, the total number built being 201, not 600 as Yakovlev wrote in the book *Soviet Aircraft*.

By the beginning of the Second World War 73 Yak-2s and 24 Yak-4s were operational in western military districts near the Soviet border. They were delivered to Nos.314 and 316 Reconnaissance Air Regiments and No.136 Bomber Air Regiment of the Kiev military district. The well trained pilots of 314 Reconnaissance Air Regiment, based at Baranovichi, carried out strategic reconnaissance of the German troops on the eve of the invasion, Yak-4s being used for this purpose because of their high speed compared with other Soviet-built long range aircraft. On several occasions Messerschmitt Bf109Es were scrambled to intercept the Yaks, but failed owing to the speed of the Soviet aircraft. In general, however, the regiment's pilots were unaccustomed to the Yak-4 because the aircraft had been delivered in April 1941 and only six pilots had managed to familiarise themselves with its complicated handling. A total of 127 missions had been flown by 10th June, after which only six or seven airworthy aircraft remained at the command's disposal. More

than ten additional Yak-4s intended for the regiment were not delivered because of the general confusion at the beginning of the war.

The pilots of the 207th Bomber Air Regiment of the 3rd Long-Range Bomber Air Corps tried to familiarise themselves with the aircraft, and the regiment's commander, Colonel G Titiv, used the Yak-4s alongside Ilyushin DB-3Fs in a raid on the bridge across the Berezina River. Records reveal that Yak-2 and Yak-4 reconnaissance bombers had disappeared from the VVS of the Western Front by the end of June, but were fighting the enemy again in the middle of July, thanks to the delivery of reserves. Seven or eight provided defence in the western area until approximately September 1941.

Aircraft of the 136th Bomber Air Regiment of the 19th Bomber Air Division went to war from their airfield at Nehworosch, near the city of Belaya Tserkov Summaries of operations mention that five squadrons of the regiment flew sorties against hostile troops, attacking from an altitude of 3,300 to 5,000ft (1,000 to 1,500m). The Yak-2 was not well known to Soviet fighter pilots, and one was shot down by the pilot of an I-153 on 28th

June. Fortunately the crew managed to escape from their stricken aircraft. The 136th Regiment suffered heavy losses on the ground as well as in the air at the beginning of July 1941, losing most of its aircraft.

The regiment's members never forgot the events of 18th July. The weather in the vicinity of the airfield was cloudy and rainy, and one aircraft returning from a mission snapped into a spin and crashed, while another two were damaged on landing. Only one crew managed to land safely, and theirs was the only airworthy Yak-2 capable of flying combat missions for several days thereafter. Up to 100 Yakovlev bombers, a third of which were powered by M-105s, were operational in the south west area at the beginning of October 1941, but information regarding operations and losses in 1942 has not been traced. In addition to the units mentioned above, Yak-2s and Yak-4s served with the 10th, 44th, 48th and 53th Medium-range Bomber Air Regiments and the 225th Short Range Bomber Air Regiment. According to eyewitnesses, one Yak-4 of the 118th Reconnaissance Air Regiment remained operational until 1945.

*For technical data, see TableD, page 168.*

**Yak-2 undergoing state trials.**

**Very rare photograph of a Yak-2 in flight.**

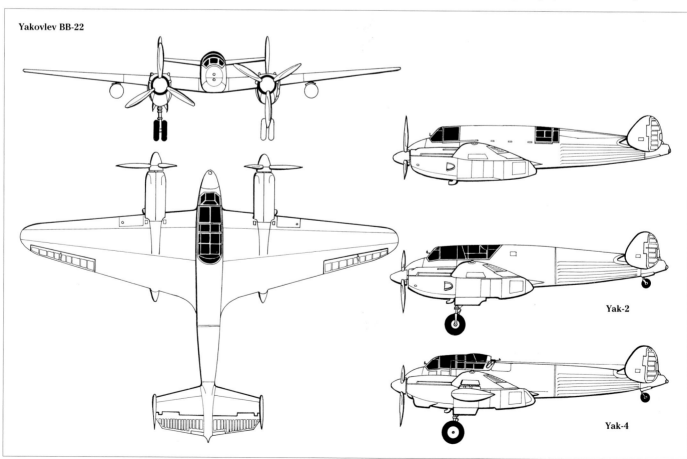

Yakovlev BB-22

Yak-2

Yak-4

## UT-1 and UT-2

Designed in the 1930s by Alexander Yakovlev, the single-seat UT-1 and two-seat UT-2 trainers were used as light attack aircraft during the Second World War. The attack version of the UT-2 was tested at the NII VVS shortly before the beginning of the war, but at that time there was no need to use the trainer in combat operations.

Some aircraft from the UT-1 and UT-2 fleet were transferred from flying clubs to the front at the war's outbreak, and were used as communication aircraft owing to the shortage of combat aircraft. Most of these were destroyed during the first months of war, but it soon became necessary to use such aircraft for combat missions. For this purpose RS-82 rocket launchers were fitted beneath each wing, and two 7.62mm ShKAS machine guns were installed on the upper surface of the wings. Such armament was rather unusual for these trainers, which were among the smallest types to see combat in the Second World War.

Several squadrons and regiments operated UT-1s and UT-2s converted into attack aircraft, and the Germans nicknamed them 'Russian Mosquito Aviation'. One such unit, the 46th Aircraft Regiment of the Black Sea Navy, entered into combat in the summer of 1942, participating in battle for the Caucasus. The UTs terrorised the enemy each night with surprise air raids, after which the Germans searched for the 'Mosquito Aviation' airfields the following morning; its 'bites' were proving too painful.

The regiment achieved a significant success near Novorossiysk. On 31st August Nazi troops broke through to the Black Sea coast

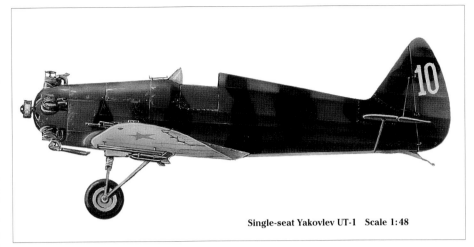

**Single-seat Yakovlev UT-1   Scale 1:48**

on the left flank of the 47th Army of the North Caucasian Front, occupied Anapa and cut off the naval infantry units from the army at the Tamansky Peninsula, threatening to encircle them. It was practically impossible for bomber regiments, with their heavy aircraft, to bomb German tank columns moving along gorges at night, so this difficult but important mission was entrusted to the 46th Regiment. General S Zhavoronkov, Head of Naval Aviation, arrived at the airfield to co-ordinate the operation, and he himself organised day and night bombing of the hostile troops. The regiment's pilots were working like mice in a wheel, flying without respite for three days to attack the enemy tank columns. During that time the artillery co-operated with the pilots, and by their joint efforts the threat to the naval infantry was removed.

The persevering UTs made a significant contribution to the destruction of the Nazi forces near Stalingrad in February 1943, but a month later their combat activity came to an

end with the wide scale deliveries of Il-2 attack aircraft to the front. Because the aircraft of the 'Mosquito Aviation' units flew only at night as a rule, they were painted in a black camouflage scheme. Their tactics were peculiar. An obsolete I-5 fighter flew ahead of the group at medium altitude to serve as bait, circling above the enemy positions. After making unsuccessful attempts to catch the aircraft in their searchlight beams, the Germans would direct random fire at the sound of the engine in the night sky. The UTs then began to attack as if from an ambush, dropping bombs and grenades on the anti-aircraft guns which had betrayed their own positions.

**Yakovlev UT-1 trainers were impressed as light attack aircraft, fitted with RS-82 rocket launchers beneath each wing and two 7.62mm ShKAS machine guns on the upper surface of the wings.**

**Yakovlev UT-2 aerobatic aircraft were converted for combat service at the NII VVS, with three bombs under the centre section.**

Part Three

# Bombers

---

# Bartini / Yermolayev

## Yer-2

The Yer-2 long range bomber has an unusual history. For example, it was put into production twice, in 1941 and 1944. According to the initial design the aircraft was to be powered by Klimov M-106s, but the M-105, Mikulin AM-37, M-40F and, finally, the Charomskii ACh-30B were actually used.

The Yer-2 was based on a civil aircraft called the Stal-7, designed under the leadership of Italian-born Roberto Bartini. This was a twin-engined low wing aircraft with cranked wings similar to those of the German Junkers Ju 87 and a fuselage cross section of flattened pear-shaped form. Notable features of the Stal-7 were its wing-mounted M-100 engines and short undercarriage.

Bartini began designing aircraft at the Scientific Research Institute of the Civil Air Fleet at the end of 1933. His object was to design a 12-seat passenger aeroplane with speed of 248mph (400km/h). This project progressed well, and in the autumn of 1936 the new aircraft was rolled off the assembly line. The Stal-7's fuselage was an all-Duralumin semi-monocoque structure, and the structure and shape of its two-spar wing were developed by Bartini himself. He also allowed for the development of a bomber version of the aeroplane by providing a bomb hatch in the fuselage.

The airliner proved to have an excellent performance. In spite of its low rated, low altitude engines it reached a speed of 279mph (450km/h) at 10,000ft (3,000m), and it had a landing speed of 56mph (90km/h) and a service ceiling of 32,800ft (10,000m). Even on one engine it could reach an altitude of 14,750ft (4,500km). In overload, with a gross take-off weight of 24,250lb (11,000kg) its payload was 13,668lb (6,200kg), demonstrating its very high efficiency.

The Stal-7's tests proceeded well and it was prepared for a very long range flight, being fitted with 27 fuel tanks with a total capacity of 1,627 gallons (7,400 litres) and additional equipment. The flight was made on 28th August 1939, when pilots N Shebanov and A Matveev covered a distance of 3,149 miles (5,068km) at an average speed of 251mph

(405km/h), establishing a new world record. Shortly after this event the idea of a high speed bomber based on the Stal-7 was the subject of powerful lobbying from many proponents. It was put into practice in Bartini's absence, for by that time the scientist/designer had been arrested by the Narodny Komissariat Vnutrennikh Del (NKVD - People's Commissariat of Internal Affairs, forerunner of the KGB) as the result of an absurd charge alleging that he was connected with the Nazi secret service.

Assigned to work in the Soviet Union in 1924, in accordance with a decision of the Central Committee of the Italian Communist Party, Bartini took part in the design of many aircraft, but the Stal-7 was one of his most successful creations. It is now difficult to explain why the commercial transport version of this aircraft did not enter series production, as there was a definite demand in the USSR for aircraft of this type. When it was demonstrated at the Paris Air Show of 1936 the Stal-7 made a great impression on industry experts owing to its clean lines and original design.

---

## DB-240

Following Bartini's arrest in February 1938, the designer's team, which also believed in the potential of a bomber version, continued the design work. A notable member of this group was Vladimir Yermolaev, a young and energetic engineer, who became the team's new leader. Bartini had praised his talent on more than one occasion, and nobody was surprised at his nomination by the chief designer, even though he was only 30 years old.

At the beginning of 1939 the preliminary design of the long range bomber was finally completed. The team was called Experimental Design Bureau 240, and was eventually reinforced by designers from the Civil Air Fleet.

In July 1939 the production of two aircraft with the designation DB-240 (DB – dalny bombardirovshcik, long range bomber) and fitted with M-106 engines was begun at the plant. Although the aerodynamic configuration of

the Stal-7 was retained, the structure of the future bomber was completely redesigned. The aircraft had a crew of four. A navigator was seated forward in a glazed cockpit, a single-seat pilot's cockpit was offset to port, and a gunner and a radio operator were housed in the central fuselage. The aircraft was provided with dual controls for pilot and navigator.

A ShKAS machine gun was mounted in the forward position. A machine gun ring which could be stowed inside the fuselage was positioned on the fuselage and carried a large calibre UBT machine gun, and there was a ShKAS machine gun mounted in an underside hatch. The bomb bay could accommodate a bomb load of up to 4,409lb (2,000kg), and two 1,102lb (500kg) bombs could be attached to external carriers. The fuel tanks held 8,708lb (3,950kg) of fuel, and it was possible to fit an additional tank holding another 1,432lb (650kg) of fuel.

Unfortunately the M-106 engines were not ready on time. It was therefore necessary to use less powerful M-105s which lacked high altitude capabilities, and this had an adverse effect on the aircraft's performance.

On 14th May 1940, N Shebanov, who had carried out the Stal-7's development tests, took off from Moscow Central Aerodrome to make the DB-240's maiden flight. On 27th September that year the aircraft was moved to the Nauchno Issledovatelyskii Institut (NII – scientific and research institute (of the VVS) for its state acceptance trials. The flight tests revealed that the aircraft's maximum speed was 276mph (445km/h) at 14,000ft (4,250m) instead of the anticipated 310mph (500km/h) at 19,700ft (6,000m), and that the maximum ceiling was 25,250ft (7,700m) instead of 36,000ft (11,000m), owing to insufficiently powerful engines. Other shortcomings included a long take-off run, powerplant defects and poor defensive armament.

At the same time, however, there were a number of positive characteristics, such as the large bomb load, good fuel reserves and range – 2,547miles (4,100km) with a 2,204lb (1,000kg) bomb load – excellent fields of view for the pilot and navigator, and a good configuration for defensive fire.

*Top and above:* **Two views of the DB-240 long range bomber, June 1940.**

**View of the DB-240 during state and production tests, October 1940. This view well illustrates the offset pilot's cockpit.**

Soon after the tests the State Commissariat of Defence decided that the aircraft would go into production as the Yer-2 at Plant No.18 in Voronezh. Simultaneously the DB-240 was transferred from the NII VVS.

## Yer-2

Serial production of the Yer-2 began in March 1941, and in April the first seven were delivered to the air force. Production bombers differed from the prototype in some respects, and the maximum speed was reduced by 3 to 5mph (5 to 8km/h) and normal flying weight was increased from 24,911lb (11,300kg) to 27,601lb (12,520kg).

At the beginning of the Second World War two Yer-2 bomber units, the 420th and 421st Long Range Bomber Air Regiments, were established. Not until late in the summer of 1941 did these units undertake operational flights.

In the autumn of 1941 all the Yer-2s that were in good condition were formed into the 81st Bomber Air Division. By the beginning of the German advance upon Moscow only 34 out of 63 of the long range bombers were in good repair. It was not possible to strengthen the division with new aircraft, because Plant No.18 had stopped producing Yermolayev's aircraft in August 1941 in order to concentrate on the manufacture of Il-2 low level attack aircraft. Using all the Yer-2s available, the 748th Long Range Bomber Air Regiment (later renamed the 2nd Guard Long Range Bomber Air Regiment) was formed, with Colonel N Novodranov as its commander.

The Yer-2 played a significant part in countering the November offensive by German forces against Moscow. Day by day the Soviet Air Force destroyed enemy military equipment on the battlefield and in the rear, and also bombed trains in Vyas'ma, Mtsensk and Sukhinichi. Among the aviators distinguishing themselves were A Krasnukhin, S Dan'shin and A Molodchy. But the attrition rate of the Yer-2s, operating without cover and at low altitude, was high. Three were brought down during a single day in November.

The Yermolayev Design Bureau attempted to improve the bomber, and in July 1941 a Yer-2 with powerful AM-37 high altitude engines and large calibre guns instead of the ShKAS weapons was rolled out. In addition the undercarriage wheels were reinforced and the navigator's and radio operator/gunner's seats were armoured.

After the first flights had been made by the well known Arctic pilot and Hero of the Soviet Union A Alekseyev, the aircraft was transferred to the NII VVS to undergo flight testing. At a flying weight of 28,659lb (13,000kg) it attained a speed of 313mph (505km/h) at 19,700ft (6,000m), but the range was slightly reduced at 2,174 miles (3,500km) with fuel reserve and a 2,204 (1,000kg) bomb load. One of the principal shortcomings of the AM-37 powered Yer-2 was its excessively long take-off run; at a gross take-off weight of 28,659lb 13,000kg the run was 2,500ft (760m), and for an overweight aircraft (33,068lb/15,000kg) it was more than 3,280ft (1,000m). This hampered operation from grass airfields.

At the height of the summer of 1942, as the Soviet long range aircraft became firmly established, the Yer-2 began to give way to new aircraft. On 1st July the eight remaining operational Yer-2s of the 747th Regiment were phased out of action. Somewhat later some were used by the 45th Air Division.

## Diesel Yer-2

It seemed that the Yer-2 had no prospects, but it soon began a second existence. This came about when attempts were made to install diesel engines in bombers. Some engines of this type were developed in the USSR in the early the 1940s, and Yermolayev realised their performance potential and decided to fit a pair of M-40Fs, designed by Aleksei Charomskii, on his bomber.

One of the great merits of diesel engines was their high fuel efficiency, their fuel consumption being 40% less than benzine engines of the same power rating. In addition, with diesels there was no danger of detonation, and it was therefore possible to use inexpensive tractor kerosene instead of standard aero-engine fuels, and this was less volatile and less likely to ignite. This was important under field conditions. As the aircraft's gross take-off weight increased to 29,761lb (13,500 kg), it was necessary to increase its wing area and reinforce its undercarriage. The radiators also had to be changed. The re-engined aircraft attained a speed of 267mph (430km/h) at 19,900ft (6,050m).

Although a production line was set up for the M-40F, the engine suffered from two fundamental defects; it was complicated to control and impossible to restart at high or even medium altitudes.

The M-30B diesel engine (later redesignated ACh-30B), which was also used to power the Yer-2, was more reliable and refined. In the conclusions of the test report for the prototype ACh-30B powered Yer-2 it was noted that the aircraft was simple to handle, suitable for pilots of average abilities, and could be successfully used as a long range aircraft.

The Yer-2 with ACh-30Bs went into production at the end of 1943 at Plant No.39 in Irkutsk, and the first production aircraft went for state acceptance trials in February 1944. Compared with the prototype it had a widened cockpit for two pilots, and a wing and tailplane of increased area. Furthermore, the armament was more powerful, the aircraft being equipped with an electrically operated machine gun ring for a 20mm ShVAK gun. Fuel capacity was increased to 12,037lb (5,460kg).

This variant of the Yer-2 was in service with the VVS after the war, right up to the appearance of four-engined long range bombers. At the end of the Yer-2's life it underwent another metamorphosis when the Yermolayev Design Bureau converted the bomber into a special purpose passenger carrier, the Yer-2ON (Osoboyo Naznacheniya – personal assignment or special use). It had finally become a transport aircraft again, like its forebear, the Stal-7.

*For technical data, see Table F, page 172.*

*Opposite page:* **View of the M-105P engine installation on the Yer-2.**

*Photographs on this page:*

*Right:* **Close-up of the M-105P engines and nose section of a production Yer-2.**

*Below and bottom:* **Two views of an AM-37-powered Yer-2 under test at NII VVS.**

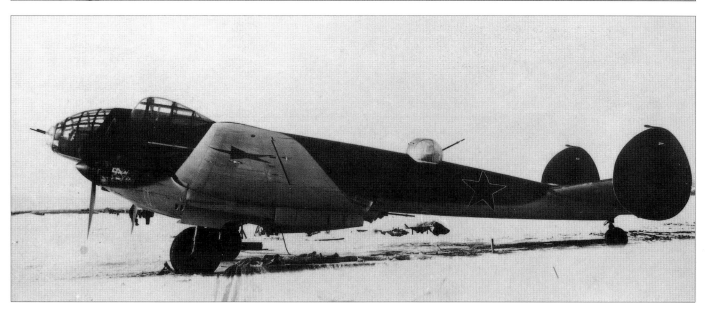

Along with the Pe-8 and Il-4, Yer-2s formed the basis of Soviet long range aviation.

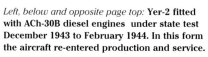

*Left, below and opposite page top:* **Yer-2 fitted with ACh-30B diesel engines under state test December 1943 to February 1944. In this form the aircraft re-entered production and service.**

*Right:* **Rare view of a Yer-2 in flight.**

**Yermolayev Yer-2**

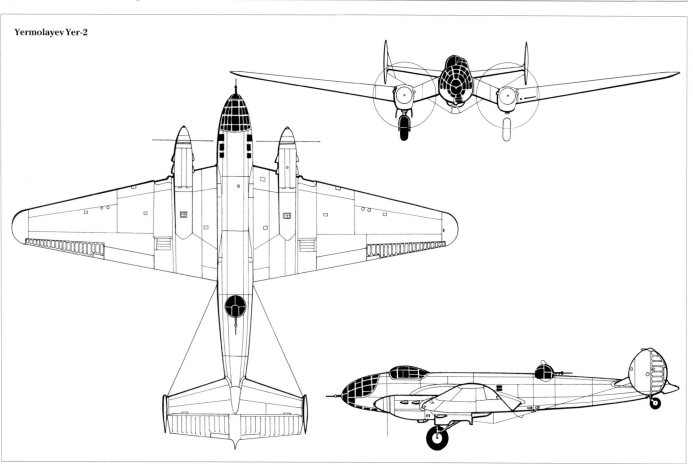

# Belyayev

## DB-LK

Engineer V Belyayev, who managed a small team of designers, designed and built a peculiar long range bomber of flying wing configuration, the DB-LK. The aircraft was very different in shape from all other aircraft of a similar role adopted in the Soviet Union. It was semi-tailless with a 'butterfly'-like wing having marked forward sweep and backswept tips. The crew of pilot, navigator, gunner/radio operator and gunner, all of the bomb load and a small amount of the fuel were housed in the large engine nacelles, which were, in effect, twin fuselages. The empennage was located behind the wing centre section. A large underfin was located beneath the centre section, and carried the tailwheel, and the tailplane and elevators were mounted at the top of the fin. The centre section had a movable trailing edge which served as an additional elevator.

The aircraft's unconventional configuration, without the traditional fuselage, reduced overall drag and airframe weight and gave an increase in speed and range. Simultaneously, the designers largely succeeded in overcoming the difficulties of crew arrangement and bomb stowage posed by this layout.

The DB-LK's powerplant consisted of two 950hp (708kW) Turmanskii M-87B radial engines (it was planned to install two 1,100hp/ 820kW M-88s driving three-blade VISh-23D propellers at a later stage). The main undercarriage units retracted into special compartments close to the bomb hatches.

The tail section of each engine gondola ended in a revolving unit containing a mounting for two ShKAS machine guns. These units rotated around the longitudinal axis of the gondolas, being driven by electric motors. Extensive Plexiglas glazing gave the gunner (in the port gondola) and the gunner/radio operator (in the starboard gondola) an excellent view. In addition to the four rear-firing machine guns, the bomber had twin machine guns mounted in the leading edge of the five-spar centre section. The main bomb load, up to 2,204lb (1,000kg), was carried internally in the nacelles, but external racks could carry bombs of 1,102lb (500kg) or even 2,204lb (1,000kg) if necessary. The bomber had a normal take-off weight of 19,975lb (9,061kg), the maximum being 23,527lb (10,672kg).

The flight tests, which were conducted by M Nuikhtikov, generally confirmed the designer's predictions. The bomber attained a speed of 245mph (395km/h) at sea level and 303mph (488km/h) at 16,400ft (5,000m). Take-off run and landing roll were 2,034ft (620m), the service ceiling was 28,000ft (8,500m), and

the range with a 2,204lb (1,000kg) bomb load and maximum fuel and oil was 1,802 miles (2,900km).

More than 100 flights were made during the flight test programme, and there was no difference in handling between the DB-LK and aircraft of conventional design. Test pilots who flew the DB-LK considered the obviously inadequate view from the pilot's and navigator's cockpits to be a serious shortcoming, as good visibility was a vital necessity, especially when the bomber was leaving its target area.

The design team agreed with the remarks of the test pilots, and a number of changes were introduced on a projected modified version of DB-LK with more powerful M-71 engines.

There was no possibility of continuing work on this prospective aircraft during the difficult early period of the war. The aircraft industry was putting all its effort into series production of the already familiar Il-4 bomber, which was slightly inferior to the DB-LK in speed and bomb load.

*For technical data, see Table F, page 172.*

**Belyayev DB-LK**

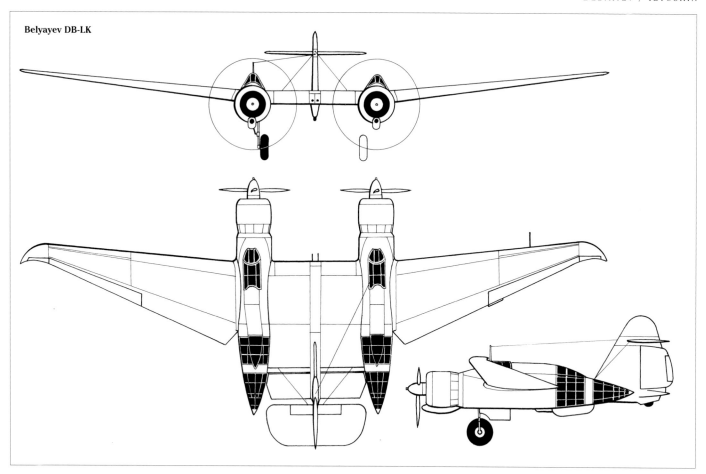

*Photographs on the opposite page:*

*Top:* **Belyayev DB-LK, showing its radical format.**

*Second from top:* **The DB-LK from the side showing the extensive rear glazing and the babochka (butterfly) type wing.**

*Third from top and bottom:* **Rare illustrations showing the DB-LK following a crash-landing during tests.**

# Ilyushin

In the early 1930s the backbone of the Soviet long range bomber force comprised TB-3 heavy bombers designed by Andrei Tupolev. With a normal bomb load of 2,204lb (1,000kg) these aircraft had a range of 1,367 miles (2,200km) at a cruising speed of 112 to 124mph (180 to 200km/h). Five movable machine guns protected the TB-3 from attack by enemy fighters. At the time of its introduction into the air force's inventory the TB-3's performance was sufficiently high, but rapid development of the aircraft industry, the increasing speeds of combat aircraft (and of fighters in particular), and the general increase in the efficiency of air defence made it necessary in 1932-1933 to begin designing a new long range bomber to replace the TB-3 in the second half of the 1930s. The operational requirements for such an aircraft included a range of 1,864 miles (3,000km) with a 2,204lb (1,000kg) bomb load, and a maximum speed of no less than 217mph (350km/h) at optimum altitude. Andrei Tupolev set about de-

signing the DB-2 to meet these requirements.

Sergei Ilyushin had rather different ideas regarding the new generation long range bomber. Having begun his design activity in the aircraft industry in 1931, he had been appointed head of the design bureau at Plant No.39, where he was also led one design section. For the first time in his career he was involved in the development of a long range bomber. After studying the problem he concluded that a bomber having the specified maximum speed would be useless for bombing targets deep in the enemy's rear, owing to the increasing speeds of promising new fighters, which were capable of 248 to 279mph (400 to 450km/h).

Ilyushin's proposal was the result of his investigations into long-range bombers and the study of various general arrangements including the flying wing. He defined the optimum parameters for his bomber and calculated the required engine power. The research showed that a high-speed long-range bomber could take the form of a twin-engined, low-wing cantilever monoplane powered by relatively light and fuel-efficient

engines and high aerodynamic and weight efficiency.

The task was complicated by the lack of suitable engines. The water cooled Mikulin M-34 then being produced in the Soviet Union for such aircraft had an excessively high specific fuel consumption. For that reason a licence was acquired for production of the French Gnome-Rhône K14 Mistral Major air-cooled radial. This promising engine produced 800hp (596kW) at 12,600ft (3,850m), weighed only 1,322lb (600kg), had a small mid-section and was quite economical. In 1934 it was placed into series production in the USSR as the M-85, its updating being conducted under the leadership of A Nazarov. It was planned to install this engine in the future long range bomber.

## TsKB-26 and TsKB-30

The long range bombers developed in the first half of the 1930s had wings with low loading and high aspect ratio, giving a reduction in

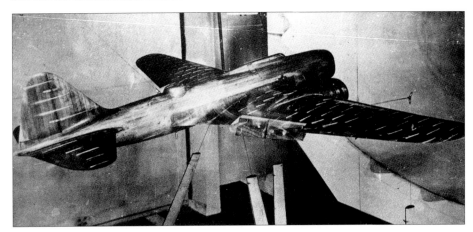

Photographs on this page:

Wind tunnel tests at TsAGI on a model of the DB-3.

The second prototype DB-3, the TsKB-30, performed long range flights during 1938 and 1939.

Photographs on the opposite page:

One of the DB-3 prototypes during testing.

Ground-running the long range record breaking DB-3 Ukraina.

induced drag and an increase in range. Sergei Ilyushin considered that long range could also be attained by a high speed aircraft having a wing of medium aspect ratio with a thin biconvex aerofoil section and reduced area, owing to the increased wing loading. He therefore designed for his bomber a special wing with a low aspect ratio of 7, a high loading of 28.5lb/ft$^2$ (140kg/m$^2$) and a low thickness ratio. To improve take-off and landing performance special TsAP-type control surfaces were used. High aerodynamic efficiency was achieved by having a small fuselage mid-section, an internally housed bomb load, smooth wing/fuselage junction, retractable undercarriage, smooth airframe skinning and improved cowling for the engines.

The resulting bomber, designated DB-3, represented the acme of aircraft design in the Soviet Union on the eve of the introduction of the pattern manufacturing technique in the aircraft industry.

The DB-3's structure was similar to that of the Tupolev SB, but the spar tubes were made of chrome/molybdenum steel. Each wing panel spar consisted of four parts riveted together to make the complete spar, and their production was a difficult process. The quali-

ty of welding was controlled by X-rays, and these revealed a number of defective spars. The internal riveting small-diameter tubes was also a very difficult and slow process.

The wing had a complex structure, but was rigid and sufficiently light. The fuselage was simpler but used frames of varying profiles. Many small welded units were required. The well-designed bomb bay was located behind the pilots cockpit and was fitted to carry ten 220lb (100kg) bombs. External bomb racks could take large-calibre bombs of 1,102lb (500kg) and 2,204lb (1,000kg). This allowed the aircraft to be used as a short range bomber in its overloaded form, with a bomb load of 5,511lb (2,500kg), a record for twin-engined aircraft at that time. In accordance with the operational requirements the aeroplane was designed as three-seater.

Defensive armament comprised three movable 7.62mm ShKAS machine guns providing the heaviest rates of fire in the world at that time. The navigator's gun, protecting the front hemisphere, was placed in the fuselage nose, and the rear hemispheres were defended by the gunner in the rear cabin using machine guns in a mid-upper turret and a ventral hatch.

Sergei Ilyushin's project for a high speed long range bomber was accepted late in 1933, and in the middle of 1934 production of the prototype, designated TsKB-26 Tsentral'noye Konstruktorskoye Byuro – central, ie state, design bureau, began. This aircraft was not a long range prototype, however, but an experimental version of the aircraft for demonstration and validation of the concept it embodied. To produce the TsKB-26 as quickly as possible it was given a composite structure; a wooden fuselage and fin, and a metal wing and tailplane.

Test pilot Vladimir Kokkinaki performed its maiden flight in the summer of 1935. The test flights proved that the aircraft had a high performance, especially with regard to speed, compared with the DB-2 (ANT-37) prototype, which was suffering flutter and buffet problems. The TsKB-26 differed also in having good stability and controllability. It could fly on one engine, and was highly manoeuvrable (the first loop by a twin-engined airplane in the Soviet Union was performed by Kokkinaki in the TsKB-26). This was possible because of the high strength of the aircraft's primary structure, which Sergei Ilyushin had designed to take high 'g' loads, foreseeing an inevitable growth in flying weight owing to increases in defensive armament and the installation of additional equipment. The TsKB-26 was demonstrated to People's Commissars Klim Voroshilov (defence) and Sergo Ordzhonikidze (heavy industry) late in the summer of 1935. They appraised the aeroplane highly, and urged Ilyushin to hand over the second prototype, the all-metal TsKB-30, for official state tests as quickly as possible, because it met the Soviet VVS requirements completely.

Development of the TsKB-26 was rather protracted. On 1st May 1936 it was flown over Moscow's Red Square, and preparations to attempt record breaking flights, initiated by

Stalin himself, soon began. The Soviet Union had joined the Fédération Aéronautique Internationale at that time, and was seeking world records. On 17th June 1936 Kokkinaki reached an altitude of 37,053ft (11,294m) carrying a 1,102lb (500kg) payload, thereby gaining the USSR's first aviation world record. Kokkinaki beat the previous record, held by the French pilot Signerin, by 919m. By August 1938 Kokkinaki had taken five more world records for payloads from 1,102lb (500kg) to 4,409lb (2,000kg) and speed over a 16,400ft (5,000km) closed-circuit route.

In March 1936 the second prototype, the TsKB-30, was rolled out. It differed from the

TsKB-26 in having a longer, all-metal fuselage and improved cowlings for its M-85 engines, and was fully armed and equipped. When tested by Kokkinaki it proved to have a high performance. At a flying weight of 14,109lb (6,400kg) it reached 208mph (335km/h) at sea level and 257mph (415km/h) at 15,750ft (4,800m), while its landing speed was 68mph (110km/h). It took 12.8 minutes to climb to 16,400ft (5,000m), and had a service ceiling of 29,750ft (9,060m). The aircraft successfully underwent its state tests, and in August 1936 was introduced into inventory of the Red Army VVS, designated DB-3 (Dalny Bombardirovshcik - long range bomber).

# DB-3

The DB-3 went into production at Plant No.39 in Moscow and Plant No.18 in Voronezh. To perfect the bomber during series production, Plant No.39's experimental workshop was transformed into a design bureau, with Sergei Ilyushin as chief designer. This was simply a formality, because by that time the Ilyushin OKB had already been formed as a united team of designers capable of solving different problems concerning the development and updating of advanced combat aircraft.

From May to October 1937 pre-production DB-3 No.3039002 underwent state tests at the Nauchno Issledovatelyskii Institut (NII – scientific and research institute of the VVS). Its performance proved to be slightly inferior to that of the prototype. At a weight of 14,550lb (6,600kg) it had a sea level speed of 201mph (325km/h), attained 242mph (390km/h) at 16,400ft (5,000m) and reached its service ceiling in 46 minutes. With such a performance the DB-3 considerably outperformed Germany's Junkers Ju 86D and even the new Heinkel He 111B then under test at Rechlin. The He 111B was 6.2 to 12.4mph (10 to 20km/h) slower at all altitudes and its service ceiling was 4,600ft (1,400m) lower, while its armament was the same and controllability and stability were better.

Not only were the DB-3's aerodynamics excellent, but its fuel and oil capacity were equal to one-third of its maximum take-off weight. As a result it had ranges of 2,485 miles (4,000km) with a 1,102lb (500kg) bomb load and 1,926 miles (3,100km) with a bomb load of 2,204lb (1,000kg), while the He 111B managed 1,031 miles (1,660km) with 1,653lb (750kg) and 565 miles (910km) with 3,306lb (1,500kg). Early in its successful life the DB-3 gained the high appreciation of its pilots. Particularly notable were its ease to take-off, rapid climb, good stability without any suggestion of yaw, steady level flight (which made it a good bombing platform), tight turns with 40° to 60° of bank, and easy landing approach. It had no dangerous tendencies such as rapid loss of speed, wing stall and arbitrary ballooning during landing. The DB-3 also had good single-engine capabilities, and at a normal flying weight of 15,432lb (7,000kg) could climb and turn in both directions on one engine. However, pilots noted a lack of longitudinal stability owing to the generally accepted aft cg position.

In 1937, with the help of a number of Ilyushin Design Bureau designers including A Belov, V Biryulin, M Yefimenko and A Levin, the two plants manufactured 45 DB-3s, and that year the bomber was introduced into the inventory of the Soviet VVS. It considerably outperformed similar bombers built in Germany, England, France and the USA.

Its high performance, especially with regard to range, was proved during two long range flights made by the modified TsKB-30, now named Moskva, during 1938-1939. On one of these, flown on 28/29th April 1939, pilot V Kokkinaki and navigator M Gordienko covered 4,971 miles 8,000km (4,048 miles/ 6,515km in a straight line) non-stop at an average speed of 216mph (348km/h). This was a significant achievement for Soviet aviation at that time. The Moskva's long distance flights greatly influenced the development of the DB-3's airframe, engines and equipment. Moreover, flights by Kokkinaki and many other Soviet pilots enabled piloting techniques for long range flights to be developed and revealed the crew fatigue limits. These aspects also promoted efficient weather survey and communication services.

All of this elevated the combat capabilities of Soviet long range aviation, based at that time on different variants of the DB-3, which was constantly being improved. In 1938 the M-85 engine was replaced by the M-86 with an augmented rating of 950hp (708kW). This allowed the DB-3's good take-off performance to be retained in spite of increased weight. The maximum speeds at an various altitudes remained the same. From 1938 the bomber's speed was increased by the installation of M-87As and the use of VISh-3 variable-pitch propellers instead of fixed-pitch units, which meant that engine power was used to best advantage during different phases of flight. The M-87A, which had the same take-off power as the M-86, provided 800hp (596kW) at an altitude of 15,500ft (4,700m).

During tests at the NII VVS early in 1939, two bombers produced at Plants Nos.18 and 39 demonstrated improved performance. At a flying weight of 15,873 to 17,195lb (7,200 to 7,800kg) their sea level speeds were equal to 265 to 270mph (428 to 436km/h) at a critical altitude of 16,300ft (4,960m). The service ceiling had increased to 30,200 to 30,500ft (9,200 to 9,300m), and the time to climb to 16,400ft (5,000m) was 10.7 minutes. The take-off run was 1,148 to 1,312ft (350 to 400m) and the maximum overloaded weight had risen to 21,375lb (9,696kg). In the final test report it was noted that the aeroplanes produced by Plant No.39 were of higher quality. In 1938 another factory, No.126 in Komsomolsk, was also converted to DB-3 production, increasing output by 400 aircraft.

## DB-3T and DB-3TP

The Ilyushin Design Bureau constantly extended the applications of the DB-3, and the DB-3T variant of 1937 was used as a naval torpedo bomber. By virtue of special external attachment points it could carry a 45-36 type torpedo (the first number denoted the torpedo's calibre in centimetres, the second its year of introduction into the inventory) with a 440lb (200kg) warhead and a total weight of 2,072lb (940kg). The DB-3T (T – torpedonosyets, torpedo) was equipped to enable the missile to be dropped using either low or high torpedo bombing methods. In the first case the 45-36 AN low altitude aerial torpedo was dropped from 100ft (30m) at a speed of 198mph (320km/h). It was forbidden to drop the torpedo lower or higher because its casing could be cracked when it hit the water or it could sink too deep. Although low altitude torpedo bombing offered the highest probability of destroying the target, it demanded a high degree of piloting skill and good aircraft handling and manoeuvrability. In high altitude torpedo bombing the DB-3T dropped the torpedo from 1,000ft (300m). The missile was parachuted down, and when it touched the water it began to travel in a circle on the target's course. In addition to its torpedo, the DB-3T could carry the usual bomb load, and could be used as a bomber or for dropping mines. It could also serve as a long range naval reconnaissance aircraft.

Introduced into the USSR Naval Aviation inventory, the DB-3T became the first mass produced Soviet torpedo-bomber, fully meeting the operational requirements. On its technical basis a new aspect of Naval Aviation, Torpedo Aviation, was born in 1939-1940 for the destruction of enemy vessels by torpedoes and bombs, and also for mining enemy seaways and exits from naval bases.

However, the DB-3T could take off only from land bases, and sometimes these were not readily available, especially in the areas covered by the Northern Fleet. In 1938, therefore, a new version, the DB-3TP (Torpedonosyets Poplavkovyi – torpedo floatplane) was designed. The floats, taken from the Tupolev TB-1P, naturally reduced the torpedo-bomber's performance. During tests in the summer of 1938 at a normal flying weight of 16,644lb (7,550kg) and carrying a torpedo, the DB-3TP reached a speed of 213mph (343 km/h) at 13,100ft (4,000m), and its climb rate and service ceiling were also reduced. Even this performance met estimated requirements and was better than the Beriev MDR-5 and Chyetverikov MDR-6 flying-boats. The DB-3TP retained the type's good handling.

Test pilot Sukhomlin assessed the seaplane thus: 'The aircraft is well-produced as a torpedo-bomber and naval high speed bomber. It is fully suited to these roles'. Nevertheless, the DB-3TP was not put into series production owing to operational complications. It was very difficult to load bombs, attach torpedoes and service the engines while the aircraft was on the water.

## TsKB-54

There were other versions of the DB-3. In March 1938 it was submitted for state tests as an escort for long range bombers. The new variant had powerful armament consisting of a nose mounting with a ShVAK gun, an upper turret with a ShVAK gun, and an under fuselage mounting for a remotely-controlled ShKAS machine gun, installed on the pivoting fairing of a remote pylon underneath the fuselage centre section.

It was intended that by including the escort in a DB-3 formation it could use its guns to defend the bombers from attacks by enemy fighters. The aircraft did not go into production because it could not fulfil all the functions of the escort fighter.

## DB-3F

In 1938, continuing their work on perfecting the DB-3, improving its technical features and performance and reducing the labour intensity of series production, the bureau's team of designers began to develop a new version, the DB-3F (known as the Il-4 from March 1942, acknowledging its chief designer).

The aeroplane had smoother lines to its forward fuselage, considerably improving the navigator's working conditions. The most important changes concerned the airframe; mainly the wing, which was increased in area by 118ft² (11m²) and made a little thinner, though its aerofoil section was unchanged. Alterations were also made to the fuel system and undercarriage. These major changes meant that almost the entire manufacturing process had to be altered. The DB-3 was designed in accordance with the manufacturing standards of the early 1930s, but by the end of the decade it was already impossible to build an aeroplane using the so-called 'cut-and-fit' method. Much labour consuming work was required, demanding the manipulation of multiple component steel structures, the bending of sheet metal components and the welding of small joints. In the modified aircraft the wing spars were based on T-beams, and open double-sided riveting was widely used. As a result the quality of the airframe was improved. The fuel system was simplified by reducing the number of fuel tanks from ten to six. It was provided with a neutral

gas system fed from a carbon dioxide bottle. The undercarriage retraction mechanisms were simplified and the shock absorber stroke was increased, improving taxying capabilities.

On 21st May 1939 test pilot Vladimir Kokkinaki performed the maiden flight of the DB-3F (Forsirovannii, literally forced, or intensive as in production-enhanced). After it had successfully completed its production flight test programme, its state tests started on 31st August the same year. The DB-3F had a normal flying weight of 16,887lb (7,660kg), including a 2,204lb (1,000kg) bomb load in the bomb bay and full defensive armament. Powered by M-87B engines with a nominal power rating of 950hp (708kW), the experimental aircraft had a maximum speed of 276mph (445km/h) at 17,700ft (5,400m), and its maximum range at a total weight of 21,560lb (9,780kg) with a standard 2,204lb (1,000kg) bomb load was 2,174 miles (3,500km). Take-off and landing performance was considerably improved. The glidepath was steeper, shock absorption was softer and braking was more effective, thus improving taxying. In the resulting report on the state tests it was noted that the DB-3F was considerably better than the DB-3 for bombing missions. The newly-

developed canopy ensured excellent working conditions for the navigator, facilitating target location and defensive fire.

Series production of the DB-3F had already begun, using the newly-developed M-88 engine. The main feature of this engine was the use of a two-speed supercharger, which allowed it to attain 1,000hp (746kW) at 19,700ft (6,000m). The first flights of the new variant which was already in series production, demonstrated that there was insufficient space inside the old cowlings for the new engines, and new cowlings with increased air inlet area were designed. However, the engines were not fully developed and had many defects, and consequently suffered frequent failures. Their pistons constantly burned and oil consumption was excessive, causing an abnormal amount of exhaust smoke. It was a long time before even the modernised M-88B was cleared of faults.

An important step was taken to increase the DB-3F's defensive armament. Instead of the old type guns, newly-developed weapons designed by G Mozharovski and I Venevidov were installed. They had excellent manoeuvring properties in both the horizontal and vertical planes, ensuring rapid aiming. The new MB installation reduced the aircraft's

A production DB-3 undergoing state trials at the NII VVS.

A TsKB-54 escort with ski undercarriage.

DB-3S bomber prototype with three bombs mounted externally under the centre section.

speed by about 9.3mph (15km/h), and the DB-3F now had a maximum speed of 213mph (343km/h) at sea level and 254mph (410 km/h) at 21,650ft (6,600m). At a flying weight of 17,636lb (8,000kg) it reached 16,400ft (5,000m) in 13.6 minutes, and its service ceiling of 30,200ft (9,200m) could be reached in 40.5 minutes. In the final DB-3F test report the commander of the NII VVS, General Filin, suggested that some of the earlier production aircraft might be rearmed with the new weapons.

The introduction of advanced working practices proceeded with difficulty during series production. In 1939-1940 the total annual output of all of the factories was 1,000 aircraft, but in the first half of 1941 the rate decreased slightly. Even so, DB-3 and DB-3F bombers comprised 86% of the Soviet Long Range Aviation force on the eve of war.

## DB-3s in action

DB-3 regiments were used in combat missions against Nazi troops during the offence against Moscow, performing mostly tactical tasks. Crews of the 751st BAR (from the complement of the 1st Heavy Bomber Air Division) distinguished themselves considerably, and the regiment was soon promoted to the 8th Guard Bomber Air Regiment. Their DB-3Fs bombed the enemy in the regions of Maloyaroslavets, Rzhev, Vyazma and Yartsevo.

By 22nd October 1941 there were 439 bombers in Soviet Long Range Aviation units, of which 310 were DB-3s. By 15th December 1941 the figures had fallen to 273 and 182 respectively. The regiments continued to score successes, attacking enemy troop concentrations on roads and at railway junctions. As a result of a government resolution issued on 5th March 1942 the DB-3 regiments were reorganised. The units and regiments of long range bombers were re-formed into the Aviatsiya Dal'nevo Deisviya (ADD – Long Range Air Arm), headed by General Headquarters under the command of General A Golovanov.

Work on the DB-3F continued in two basic directions; improving combat capability and increasing the quantity. In the 3rd BAR some versions of the Il-4 had their defensive weaponry bolstered by the installation of movable large calibre machine guns, which were successfully tested. In May-June 1942 an updated UTK-1 turret with a UBT machine

**Performance of the DB-3 was improved following the fitment of M-87A engines from 1938.**

**Production DB-3s participating in exercises just prior to the outbreak of the Second World War.**

gun designed by I Shebanov had been fitted to production aircraft. The lower turret used on Petlyakov Pe-2 bombers could not be fitted because it upset the aircraft's cg. The gunners compartments were equipped with armoured shields. To retain the range, the normal flying weight of the four-seat version of the Il-4 was increased to 20,877lb (9,470kg), and the fuel capacity was increased by 1,157lb (525kg) by the use of two external tanks suspended on the bomb rack mountings. The maximum speed decreased at all altitudes by 3.1 to 6.2mph (5 to 10km/h), the rate of climb dropped by 40% and the service ceiling by 3,600ft (1,100m) – all of these figures were compared with the prototype, built in 1940. This performance was regarded as satisfactory for night flights, and, moreover, the aircraft's range according to the tests proved to be 2,361 miles (3,800km). However, this figure corresponds not to the cruising speed of the DB-3F, but to economical speed.

During the Second World War the production aircraft were fitted with M-88Bs, which had the same power as the earlier M-88 used before but were more reliable for long range missions. The engines had a service life of some 150 hours.

The evacuation of Engine Plant No.29, which was producing M-88Bs, and some difficulties connected with their production at a new location, made it necessary to use engines of other types. At the aircraft factory in Komsomolsk-on-Amur test pilot Galitsky spent a long time testing a production Il-4 powered by M-82s, which were more powerful and, consequently, heavier. The aircraft's weight increased to 19,510lb (8,850kg), 1,801lb (817kg) heavier than the prototype, built in 1940, under the same loading conditions. Its maximum sea level speed was 235mph (379km/h), and its speed at altitude was 271mph (437km/h). The rate of climb and service ceiling increased as well, but cruising range fell to 1,578 miles (2,540km). However, all the difficulties with M-88B production were eventually overcome, and series production was resumed. This engine was more reliable than the M-82, M-89 and M-90 (though there were attempts to power the Il-4 with these engines).

Ilyushin bombers had suffered no losses on the ground because the Luftwaffe made no raids on airfields in the Soviet rear. In the morning of 22nd June 1941 VVS Commander-in-Chief of the Red Army General P Zhigarev set the 3rd Bomber Air Corps the task of annihilating the enemy troops in the region of the Suvalkin salient. The first bombers to take off belonged to the 207th BAR, led by their commander, Lieutenant-Colonel G Titov. On the next day the DB-3s had to attack Königsberg, Danzig and Warsaw.

Subsequently, ADD's main forces were

used against the enemy's motorised infantry, which had penetrated the front line. The DB-3s fought hard, but suffered heavy losses. For example, on 26th June 1941 43 DB-3F crews failed to return from their missions, mainly owing to bad planning and organisation of the raid. The bombers had no escort fighters at all, and were therefore obliged to fly at low altitudes, where the anti-aircraft fire was intense. The German command noted that the DB-3 was almost as fast as the SB but was harder to shoot down. The pilot was protected by an armoured backrest and the fuel tanks were similarly protected, and the aircraft had a more robust structure and was more fire-resistant. Attention was also drawn to the fact that all of the bombers had lower-hatch machine guns and could carry a crew of four. The additional gunner increased the DB-3's defences.

An important task assigned to the DB-3 was the bombing of Berlin. The newspaper *Pravda* reported at the time: 'On the night of 7th/8th August a group of our bombers performed a reconnaissance flight over German territory and dropped incendiary and high explosive bombs on military objectives near Berlin. As a result of the bombing some fires were started and explosions were seen. All of our bombers returned safely'.

It subsequently transpired that the air raid was performed by DB-3Ts of the 1st Mine-Torpedo Regiment of the VVS Krasnoznamyonny Baltiiski Flot (KBf– Red Banner Baltic Fleet) under the command of Colonel E Preobrazhensky. From August, 12 DB-3Fs of a long range aviation group commanded by Major V Schelkunov began flying missions to Berlin. An attempt was made to increase the bomb load (the total bomb load during the first flights was 1,763lb/800kg) by suspending two FAB-500 or FAB-1000 bombs externally, but the short take-off strip of the grass airfield in Kogul and the aeroplanes' worn-out engines resulted in disaster. All subsequent flights were made with the standard 1,763lb (800kg) load. On 12th August 1941 the enemy detected the Soviet airfields and started bombing them. In addition, instruction No.34 issued by Hitler that same day proclaimed, in particular: 'As far as conditions allow, our aircraft must annihilate the military air bases on Dago and Esel islands. It is very important to destroy these airfields, which enable air raids to be made on Berlin'.

That order demonstrated once again the great psychological importance attached to the DB-3 and DB-3F missions. By that time long range aviation crews had started to fly at night, at high altitudes. From 10th July until 30th September 1941 DB-3Fs flown by Baltic Fleet and Black Sea Fleet crews delivered blows against objectives in Königsberg, Danzig, Helsinki, Warsaw and Konstanza, among other targets. As a direct result of the 4th Bomber Air Corps' attacks, the output of Rumania's oil industry decreased by 30%.

One cause of alarm was the fact that the Soviet aircraft industry produced only 757 DB-3s and DB-3Fs during the whole of 1941. The production capacity of Plant No.126 was totally inadequate, because as a result of its evacuation to Siberia there was nowhere to build the aircraft. Therefore, in March 1942, following a government decision, Il-4 production was organised at a factory in Fili (the plant was returned from Siberia and designated Aircraft Plant No.23). The next responsible decision was to stop Pe-2 production in Irkutsk in favour of the Il-4. As a result, 858 aircraft had been built by the end of this year of great changes.

From the beginning of the autumn of 1941 a wooden navigator's cabin, cockpit floor and tail fairing were installed on production aircraft owing to a shortage of Duralumin. The fourth crew member and the armoured protection for the gunner considerably displaced the aeroplane's cg, upsetting longitudinal static stability and controllability. This was rectified in the machines built from the summer of 1942, which had a newly-developed detachable wing section with an 'arrow' along the leading edge which moved the cg. forward relative to the mean aerodynamic chord. The detachable part of the wing with the 'arrow' had a new aerodynamic profile which in-creased the relative thickness by 10%, and a composite structure of metal spars with wooden ribs and skin. The thicker detachable wing profile and the displacement of the lower ribs outside the skin (this structure formed a so-called 'rib-skin') permitted the installation inside the cantilevers of three protected fuel tanks instead of one, increasing the total weight of fuel by 2,502lb (1,135kg) compared with the production DB-3F. The aircraft's flying weight also increased, being 26,741lb (12,130kg) in overloaded configuration, but the performance was sufficiently high. At a normal flying weight of 22,167lb (10,055kg) its maximum speed was 251mph (404km/h) at 22,000ft (6,650m). Because of the high fuel capacity, range increased considerably. With a normal internal bomb load of 2,204lb (1,000kg) the aircraft had a range of 2,227 miles (3,585km) at 211mph (340km/h), and this could be increased to 2,650 miles (4,265km) if the speed was reduced to 155 mph (250km/h). A 21.5ft$^2$ (2m$^2$) increase in flap area meant that the aircraft was still able to operate from front line airfields despite the considerable increase in weight. Newly-developed AV-5F-158 propellers of greater diameter also contributed to this ability.

Thanks to the new wing aerodynamics, controllability and manoeuvrability were greatly improved. According to pilot assessments, handling with the 'arrow' seemed to be easier. The DB-3F had one very good fea-ture; it could perform a long flight on one engine at a flying weight of up to 20,767lb (9,420kg). DB-3Fs of the structure described above were in action until the war's end. To 1,528 DB-3s were added 5,256 DB-3Fs and Il-4s, the last 160 of which were produced after the war. Until the day of victory Il-4s formed the basis of the Soviet ADD, reorganised in 1945 into the 18th Air Army.

The most distinguished ADD pilots who flew DB-3s and Il-4s were rewarded during the war with the highest military decorations, and S Kretov, A Molodchy, E Fedokov, V Osipov and P Taran were made Heroes of the Soviet Union. Navigators and radio operator/gunners were seldom given awards in the Soviet VVS, but an Il-4 navigator, V Senko, was twice made Hero of the Soviet Union.

*Below:* **Loading a DB-3T torpedo-bomber of Soviet Naval Aviation.**

*Photographs on the opposite page:*

**Only one prototype of the DB-3TP floatplane was built.**

**The improved DB-3F had a much more streamlined nose section.**

**Side aspect of a DB-3F. Note the modified MV turret.**

*Left:* **A DB-3F undertaking testing of ski 'shoes'. The wooden skis were used for take-off only and stayed on the ground after the bomber had taken off.**

*Centre and bottom:* **From the autumn of 1941, as Duralumin stocks dwindled, more and more of the DB-3F's structure was made of wood. This example, seen at NII VVS, has wooden wing skinning.**

*Top left:* **Modified MV turret on a DB-3F.**

*Top right:* **Il-4s on the production line.**

*Centre:* **DB-3F with branches to break up its outline on an operational airfield.**

*Left:* **Loading FAB-100 into the internal bomb bay of an Il-4.**

*Top left:* **An Il-4 with its cowling removed, revealing its M-88 engine.**

*Top right:* **While a naval Il-4 torpedo-bomber is readied for a mission, Soviet airmen and an airwoman break for food.**

*Centre:* **Torpedoes ready for loading into Il-4s.**

*Left:* **Torpedo-loaded Il-4 on the way it its target.**

*Top:* **A snow-camouflaged Il-4 is pulled into position by a tracked vehicle.**

*Centre:* **Il-4 en route to Berlin.**

*Right:* **Il-4s operating from a front line airfield.**

Above: **As well as Berlin, Il-4s hit targets as far afield as Warsaw.**

Left: **Il-4 prototype fitted with a pressurised cockpit.**

**Ilyushin Il-4 (DB-3F)**

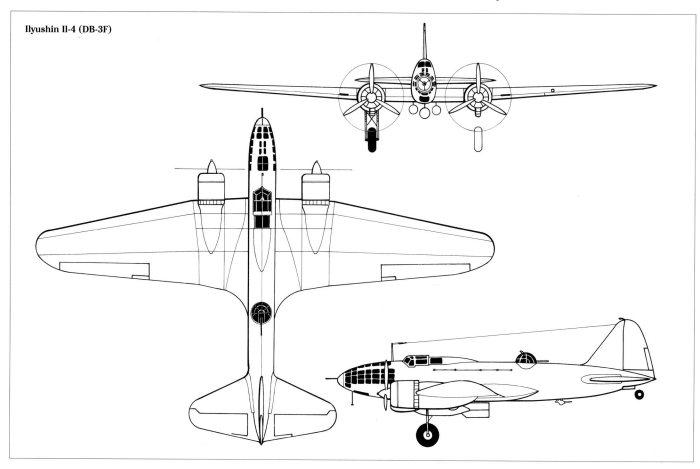

## Il-6 long range bomber

The Il-6 bomber was of similar configuration to the Il-4, differing by slightly greater overall dimensions. New Charomskii ACh-30B diesels rated at 1,250 to 1,500hp (932 to 1,119kW), had it cruising at 217 to 236mph (350 to 380 km/h) with a range of 3,106 miles (5,000km).

Only two prototypes were built, and flight testing began on 7th August 1943. The tests were conducted by Vladimir Kokkinaki at the plant and later by Alexey Grinchik and Nikolay Rybko at the NII VVS. The bomber's development was cancelled owing to weaknesses in the airframe and engines.

*For technical data, see Table F, page 172.*

**ACh-30B diesel engines powered the Il-6 – the last version of the Il-4 bomber series.**

# Myasishchev

## DVB-102

Although he was innocent, Vladimir Myasishchev was charged with crimes against the state at the beginning of 1938. Like many other Soviet aviation specialists, designers and scientists repressed in the late 1930s, he was imprisoned in the special TsKB-29 design bureau attached to the Narodny Komissariat Vnutrennikh Del (NKVD – People's Commissariat of Internal Affairs, forerunner of the KGB). In parallel with his work on Project '100' in the Petlyakov team, Myasishchev developed a preliminary design for a long range, high altitude twin-engined bomber of modern configuration. The aircraft was designed around the newly-developed Klimov M-120 TK engine, which afforded 1,800hp (1,342kW) for take-off.

The project's revolutionary nature stemmed from the bomber having a performance that made it invulnerable to fighters. According to estimates the aircraft would have a maximum speed in excess of 310mph (500km/h), a service ceiling of 32,800ft (10,000m), a normal bomb load of 8,818lb (4,000kg) and range of 2,485 miles (4,000km) at cruising speed.

The project promised to be a breakthrough for the Soviet aircraft industry. Designated '102', the ambitious undertaking received the approval of the NKVD authorities, and Myasishchev was encouraged to establish his own design team.

Indeed, such a performance needed innovative technologies and solutions to design problems. According to the preliminary design, the DVB-102 (Dalny Vysotny Bombardirovshick – long range, high altitude bomber) was to be an all-metal, high wing cantilever monoplane with a twin-finned empennage and a retractable undercarriage. It had an extremely thin, high aspect ratio wing for such a heavy aeroplane, the wing's maximum thickness ranging from 16 to 10%. The wing's centre section was built up on three spars, while its outer panels had two spars and integral fuel tanks. Four electrically operated landing flaps were provided.

A 4,409lb (2,000kg) bomb could be housed in a 22ft 11½in (7m) long bomb bay fitted with hydraulically operated doors which retracted inside when opened. To ensure sufficient rigidness the bomb bay section was built on a robust frame. Besides the interior bombs, the DVB-102 could carry external rack-mounted bombs. Armament comprised a movable ShVAK-20 cannon with 176 rounds in the nose, and two (upper and lower) machine gun mountings to defend the rear hemisphere. The upper installation consisted of twin 12.7mm UBK and 7.62mm ShKAS guns, with 700 and 1,500 rounds respectively, while the lower comprised a single UBK gun with 300 rounds. The aircraft was also to have an RSB*bis* radio and an AFA-6 camera.

Among the principal innovations in the bomber's construction were two pressurised crew compartments to provide normal working conditions without oxygen masks at any altitude. The forward compartment housed the pilot and navigator, while the aft one accommodated the gunners. At high altitude the pressure inside the compartments was equivalent to that at 6,500 to 10,000ft (2,000 to 3,000m). The decision to have pressurised crew compartments inevitably led to the need for remotely controlled defensive armament, and this proved to be a challenging technical problem at the end of 1930s.

The use of a nosewheel undercarriage was another advantage of the DVB-102, facilitating its taxying, take-off and landing. The nose gear retracted into the fuselage, while the main undercarriage members retracted into the engine nacelles.

Construction of a prototype was initiated in May 1940. On 25th July 1940 Petlyakov, Myasishchev and other imprisoned specialists engaged in Project '100' were released following the successful completion of the conversion of the newly-developed '100' high altitude twin-engined fighter into the light dive bomber later known as the Pe-2. In 1941 the work on the DVB-102 prototype was interrupted owing to the evacuation of Myasishchev's team to Omsk. Here, in local Civil Air Fleet repair shops hastily adapted to suit the needs of development work, construction of the new bomber was resumed.

On 17th February 1942 test pilot V Zhdanov made the first flight on the DVB-102 prototype. The joint development/acceptance test flights, undertaken by test pilot F Opadchy, were conducted both with and without the turbo-superchargers operating. The trials were completed on 2nd September. Only eleven flights were performed at the normal flying weight of 33,068lb (15,000kg), while 19 were made with the machine in a lightened configuration. About 80% of the trial period was spent developing and modifying the aircraft. The tests were complicated by the unreliable M-120 engines, the service life of which appeared to be limited to only 25 hours.

At the end of June the engines were replaced by new units of the same type, and the unsatisfactory turbosuperchargers were replaced by conventional superchargers providing an increase in take-off power. These and other modifications ensured satisfactory engine operation up to 26,250ft (8,000m). In the test report it was noted that the aeroplane had a greater maximum speed than contemporary Soviet and other long range bombers, and was almost as fast as the short range bombers.

Although the DVB-102's performance met the specified requirements, its unsatisfactory M-120 engines had to be rejected in favour of the M-71 air-cooled engines newly developed by A Shvetsov and affording 2,100hp (1,566kW) at take-off.

Adapting the airframe to take the radial engines demanded much additional work. Initially the aircraft was equipped with engines having conventional superchargers, and then TK-3 turbo-superchargers were installed.

Flight tests of the re-engined aircraft began in May 1943. At that time, owing to the successful progress being made with the DVB-102 programme, Myasishchev received a message from Stalin, thanking him: '... for his concern with long range aviation'.

However, some weeks later Myasishchev accepted Stalin's offer to take charge of the design department of Plant No.22 at Kazan, where Pe-2s were being manufactured.

Following Petlyakov's death in a crash on 12th January 1942, his former deputies A Izakson and, six months later, A Putilov, had been in charge of maintaining and improving Pe-2 production standards. Despite this, standards fell and the aircraft's performance deteriorated. A State Commission headed by Pavel Sukhoi revealed the causes, and in a month the aircraft had regained its agility. When Stalin offered Sukhoi leadership of the design department of Plant No.22, the designer answered that he needed to think about it. Stalin, accustomed to immediate acceptance of his proposals, therefore offered the post to Myasishchev. Sukhoi's colleagues maintain that it was because of this episode that no aircraft developed by the Sukhoi Design Bureau was placed into series production until after Stalin's death, and that it was also the reason behind the bureau's disbandment in 1949.

Thus, before flight testing of the M-71-powered prototype, the Myasishchev bureau had been split into two parts, one in Kazan headed by the chief designer, and the other moved to Moscow. In August 1943, while being ferried on the Omsk-Kazan-Moscow route with test pilot V Zhdanov at the controls, the DVB-102 demonstrated its promising performance.

When they were resumed in Moscow, the tests suffered from numerous troubles with the M-71, which was later replaced by its boosted version, the M-71F, fitted with a TK-3 turbo-supercharger. Test flights continued in to 1946, mainly owing to the unreliability of the powerplant and the TK-3 in particular. (Polikarpov faced similar problems during the flight tests of his I-185 fighter prototype.) At a normal flying weight of 34,200ft (15,500kg) the DVB-102 powered by M-71Fs with TK-3 turbosuperchargers attained a maximum speed of 354mph (570km/h) at 28,000ft (8,500m) and had a service ceiling of 35,250ft (10,750m). In overload condition with maximum fuel its range was 2,323 miles (3,740km).

At Stalin's behest, in 1946 the promising development work on this unique Soviet strategic high altitude bomber was halted and the Myasishchev Design Bureau was disbanded. The real reasons behind this decision have nothing to do with the 'official' explanation linking it to the lack of suitable engines and Stalin's under-estimation of strategic aviation. It was widely proclaimed that Stalin's concern for strategic aviation had been heightened by Hiroshima and resulted in the unprecedented national programme to produce a Soviet version of the Boeing B-29 (the Tu-4). It is absolutely impossible even to imagine that this programme, launched in June 1946 and headed by Andrei Tupolev, could have been abandoned owing to engine problems.

*Above:* **The M-120-powered DVB-102 prototype.**

*Below:* **DVB-102 with M-71 engines.**

**Myasishchev DVB-102**

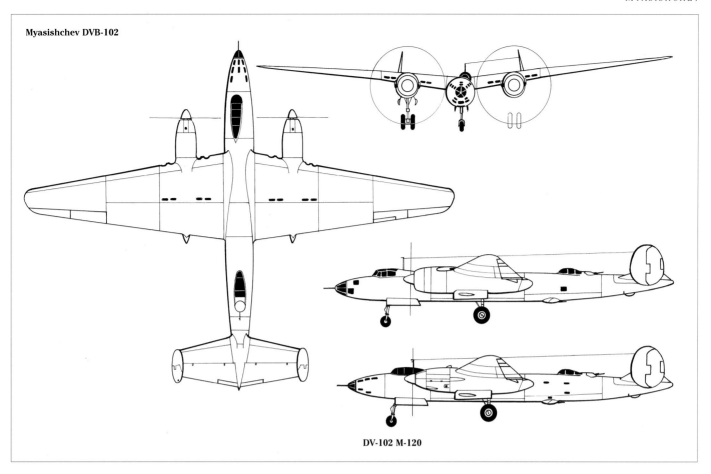

**DV-102 M-120**

## DB-2VK-108

In the summer of 1944 the Myasishchev Design Bureau launched the parallel development of a family of three high speed daylight bombers in under the designations VM-16 (two-seater), VM-17 (three-seater) and VM-18 (four-seater). All three versions, officially designated DB-2 VK-108, were to be built around Klimov's new VK-108 12-cylinder liquid-cooled engine providing 1,800hp (1,342kW) for take-off. The engine was to drive a new VISh-108LO four-bladed variable-pitch propeller with a diameter of 10ft 2in (3.1m).

The wing and twin-finned empennage were the same for all versions. The aircraft spanned 58ft 5in (17.8m) and had a wing area of some 462.8ft² (43.0m²), and its tailplane spanned 16ft 3in (4.95m). Its all-metal fuselage was well suited to series production, and the cockpit and armament housing had special features. The main undercarriage legs retracted rearwards into the engine nacelles, and there was a retractable tailwheel.

All three versions could be readily converted into long range escort fighters with their bomb bays accommodating two additional 37mm or 45mm cannon. Fuselage and wing tanks provided capacity for 2,204lb (1,000kg) of fuel, and in overload condition up to 3,924lb (1,780kg) of fuel could be carried. All three had armour protection for the crew,

and provision was made for RSB-3bis radio as well as AFA-3, NAFA-3, and AFA-IM camera installations.

The VM-16 (VM denoting V Myasishchev) was designed to have a crew of two accommodated in a single cockpit. A clear view downwards was provided by a glazed lower nose that distinguished the VM-16 from other variants of the DB-2VK108 family. The navigator doubled as gunner, and had a swivelling seat to allow him to operate the remotely controlled rearward-firing 20mm B-20 cannon with 100 rounds, located in the tail. A similar fixed weapon in the nose was provided with 150 rounds.

A bomb bay in the fuselage mid-section just behind the cockpit carried a normal bomb load of 2,204lb (1,000kg). In overload condition it was possible to carry up to 6,613lb (3,000kg) of bombs, including one 4,409lb (2,000kg) bomb in the bomb bay. The estimated range with such a load, with a take-off weight of 25,132lb (11,400kg) and fuel weighing 2,204lb (1,000kg), was 590 miles (950km). At the normal loaded weight, with 3,946lb (1,790kg) of fuel and a take-off weight of 22,599lb (10,251kg), the bomber was expected to have a range of 1,553 miles (2,500km).

Initiated in August 1944, development of the prototype was finished in December, and in June 1945 the development flight tests had been completed. With a take-off weight of 20,723lb (9,400kg) the aircraft attained a max-

imum speed at sea level of 357mph (575 km/h), while at 19,700ft (6,000m) the maximum speed rose to 434mph (700km/h). Estimated service ceiling was 33,000ft (10,000m).

As a result of the war ending, there was no need to put such a bomber into series production, and the VM-16 was not submitted for state trials.

The three-seat VM-17 bomber featured an enhanced defensive armament. Besides the fixed B-20 cannon with 150 rounds in its nose it had a dorsal ring-mounted B-20 cannon with 200 rounds behind the pilot's seat, and the third member of the crew, a gunner, was provided with a dorsal turret-mounted 12.7 mm UB gun and an LUS-20 mid-lower ventral mounting with B-20 cannon and 200 rounds. With the same bomb load as the VM-16 a normal take-off run could be accomplished with assistance from solid-propellant rocket boosters.

In June 1945 the VM-17's development tests were initiated. Its performance was slightly inferior to that of the VM-16 owing to the installation of airbrake grids and its greater take-off weight, and it had a maximum speed of 338mph (545km/h) at sea level and 416mph (670km/h) at 19,700ft (6,000m). The service ceiling was 33,000ft (10,000m). With a normal bomb load of 2,204lb (1,000kg) and 3,946lb (1,790kg) of fuel, giving a take-off weight of 23,699lb (10,750kg), the VM-17 had a range of some 1,367 miles (2,200km), while with a 6,613lb (3,000kg) bomb load and 2,204lb (1,000kg) of fuel (take-off weight 26,432lb/11,990kg) its range was 528 miles (850km). The fate of the VM-17 was the same as that of the VM-16.

The four-seat VM-18 prototype was also built in June 1945. Compared with other two prototypes it had a longer nose with a navigator's compartment and lacked the the lower nose glazing. The armament and its arrangement were the same as for the VM-17 with the exception of the fixed nose cannon, which was installed beneath the pilot's seat and moved to the port side.

In overload condition the total bomb load was increased to 8,818lb (4,000kg), including 4,409lb (2,000kg) in the bomb bay. Provision was made for the VM-18 to be converted into a long range escort fighter, in which configuration the bomb bay could be fitted with twin 37mm or 45mm NS cannon with a total of 90 rounds.

At a normal take-off weight of 23,214lb (10,530kg) the VM-18's estimated maximum speed was 336mph (542km/h) at sea level, 410mph (660km/h) at 19,000ft (5,800m) and 354mph (570km/h) at 28,000ft (8,520m). Estimated performance included a climb to 16,400ft (5,000m) in 6.3 minutes, a service ceiling of 33,000ft (10,000m) and a range of 1,180 miles (1,900km) in overload condition (27,215lb/12,345kg) with 4,409lb (2,000kg) bomb load and 3,946lb (1,790kg) of fuel.

To give greater range while retaining the bomb load, provision was made for the fitting of alternative outer wing panels which increased the span from 58ft 6in to 67ft 6in (17.8m to 20.6m) and the wing area from 462 to 516ft² (43 to 48m²). No information survives about the testing of the VM-18.

Just before the war's end the DB-2VK-108 family of bomber prototypes was augmented by a high altitude two-seater designated VM-19. The prototype was powered by two Klimov VK-109 liquid-cooled engines with multi-speed turbosuperchargers. The VK-109's maximum power was 1,530hp (1,141kW) at 26,250ft (8,000m) and 1,800hp (1,342kW) at 21,500ft (6,500m), with 2,075hp (1,547kW) available for take-off.

The engines drove VISh-108LO three-bladed variable-pitch propellers of 10ft 9in (3.3m) diameter. The airframe structure and principal dimensions were similar to those of the previous DB-2VK-108 prototypes.

Defensive armament was reduced to a fixed nose mounted B-20 cannon with 150 rounds and a movable rear-firing B-20 cannon with 100 rounds, remotely controlled by a navigator who doubled as a gunner. The crew of two was accommodated in a pressurised cockpit. Normal bomb load of 2,204lb (1,000kg) was housed in a bomb bay similar to that of the VM-16. In overload condition up to 4,409lb (2,000kg) of bombs in the bomb bay could be supplemented by two 1,102lb (500kg) bombs carried externally beneath the wings.

The VM-19's equipment included an RSB-3bis radio, Sch-3 radar, AFA-3 and AFA-IM cameras positioned behind the bomb bay and a KPA-12m oxygen system.

According to the estimated performance figures the VM-19 would attain 369mph (595 km/h) at sea level, 428mph (690km/h) at 16,400ft (5,000m) and 447mph (720km/h) at 26,250ft (8,000m), and climb to a height of 16,400ft (5,000m) in six minutes. At a take-off weight of 23,677lb (10,740kg), including a 2,204lb (1,000kg) bomb load and 3,835lb (1,740kg) of fuel, it had an estimated ceiling of 41,000ft (12,500m) and a range of 1,367 miles (2,200km), and at a take-off weight of 26,234lb (11,900kg), including a bomb load of 6,613lb (3,000kg) and 1,984lb (900kg) of fuel, its range was 528 miles (850km).

On 5th March 1945 the bomber's mock-up was approved and tooling-up for the prototype was begun. There is no information about its testing.

*For technical data, see Table F, page 172.*

**Externally, the DB-2VK-108 looked very much like the Pe-2. Inside, it represented considerable refinement and redevelopment.**

# Petlyakov

## PB-100

By the spring of 1940 the test programme of the '100' high altitude fighter, created under the leadership of Vladimir Petlyakov in the Special Design Bureau of the NKVD (the aviation specialists arrested by the KGB-forerunner were working in this bureau), had made quite significant progress, and had convincingly demonstrated the new aircraft's qualities. In February the People's Commissar of Internal Affairs, Lavrenty Beriya, wrote to Molotov, president of the USSR's Parliament, proposing that a small series of '100' fighters be built. 'This new design of aircraft is different from others, both existing and projected,' he wrote, adding that the '100' could be used not only as a fighter but also as a dive bomber, thanks to the bombing apparatus with which it was equipped. At the beginning of March the Committee of Defence decided to build a series of ten '100' fighters at the Plant No.18.

However, the events of spring 1940 caused an early reversal of this decision. The VVS leadership realised that the expectations concerning Nikolay Polikarpov's SPB dive bomber, a further development of the VIT series, were unjustified. Failures were dogging the aircraft, two accidents and a number of incidents having occurred over a short period. In the opinion of the Soviet Air Force Commander-in-Chief, Yakov Smushkevich: 'Production of the SPB, and any work in connection with it, should cease'.

He was also quite pessimistic about Alexander Arkhangelsky's conversion of the SB bomber into a dive bomber. 'The SB is unlikely to be upgraded later,' he wrote to Alexey Shakhurin, People's Commissar of the Aircraft Industry, 'and it is quite unknown if it will prove suitable as a dive bomber.'

The Soviet Air Force had no single-engined dive bombers like the Luftwaffe's Junkers Ju 87 or Japan's Aichi D3A1 Navy Type 99. When Sergei Ilyushin's BSh-2 was used as a test aircraft, the lack of an aircraft capable of destroying small targets, and especially armoured vehicles, became evident.

Meanwhile, at the end of spring and the beginning of summer 1940 the combat aircraft purchased in Germany, including the twin-engined Junkers Ju 88 dive bomber, began to arrive in the USSR. This very large aircraft, carrying a crew of four, equipped with dive-brake flaps and automatic dive recovery and capable of carrying a heavy bomb load, must have impressed Soviet specialists. The successful combat operations of the Ju 88 in France, in support of the German armed forces, was an additional factor worthy of acknowledgement. The leaders of the VVS and

the People's Commissariat of the Aviation Industry came to the common conclusion that there was an urgent need for a similar aircraft to be designed in the USSR. It should be noted that Andrei Tupolev's '103' was almost completed but would not fly until January 1941, whereas the '100' was already flying. Consequently the decision to 'reprofile' the '100' high altitude fighter as a dive bomber was finally taken by a council in Alexey Shakhurin's office on 4th June 1940. On the same day it was decided to recommend that Ilyushin's BSh-2 armoured attack aircraft and Vsevolod Tairov's OKO-6 armoured fighter be put into series production. The Committee of Defence then adopted a decision to launch the dive bomber variant of the '100' into series production at two Moscow Plants, Nos.22 and 39. The principal performance parameters of the new aircraft were determined by this decision, and the production of 30 new dive bombers at Plant No.39 and 50 at Plant No.22 was schemed for 1940. At the same time the decision to build ten '100' high-altitude fighters at Plant No.39 remained in force.

A total of 45 days were allotted to Vladimir Petlyakov and his team for this major conversion, which entailed designing and testing a new fuselage and the brake flaps and their control system, radical revision of the crew arrangement, and changes to the powerplant. Sets of working drawings for the new bomber were to be provided to both factories by 1st August 1940. However, even that exhausting rate of work, which was peculiar to the Special Design Bureau during the period of the '100' fighter's development, was considered insufficient.

A further 100 specialist designers and engineers apiece from the Yakovlev, Ilyushin and Arkhangelsky bureaux were shared out among the design team of the 'prisoners' bureau (though Petlyakov was released in the summer of 1940 and appointed chief designer of Plant No.39 in October). An additional meal break was introduced at 2200 hours, followed by two or three more hours of work. This extra concentration of effort produced results, and all of the drawings were handed over by the due time.

However, the final result of all this effort was diluted because the factories were not ready to build the aircraft. In fact there was no test aircraft. Only a wooden mock-up was made, the fuselage was assembled 'on the bench', and the dive bomber, designated PB-100 (Pikiruyushchii Bombardirovshcik – dive bomber), had to go into series production at once. Numerous assembly rigs were not ready (they were made at Plant No.156, but the work suffered significant delay). There was no technology for the production of this aircraft, which was quite original in many respects. Moreover, production of the PB-100

was not simple. The most complicated element was its two-spar wing, which had a very thin Duralumin skin 0.6-0.8mm thick, stiffened by a dense assembly of angular cross section stringers and ribs. Later, this wing gave the designers a number of unpleasant surprises.

For the first time in the USSR, the PB-100 made extensive use of electrically-operated controls. Electric motors drove the landing flaps, brake flaps, engine louvres and radiator shutters, control surface tabs and tailplane variable-incidence gear, and served a number of other functions. Series production of the PB-100 required the initiation of the production of several types of electric motor using on-board electrical power. Much time was required to perfect the AP-1 automatic diving system, based on that in the Ju 88, and organise its manufacture.

The shape of a new aircraft was noticeably different from that of the high altitude fighter version. The navigator's and pilot's seats were arranged in a common unpressurised cockpit, and the lower part of the nose was protected by sheets of toughened glass to improve the view for take-off and landing and when searching for targets. The navigator was armed with movable ShKAS machine gun installed on an arc, and was provided with an OPB-1M day sight and an NKPB-3 night sight for bomb aiming. The pilot, who released the bombs in a diving attack, had a PBL-1 sight. Two ShKAS machine guns operated by the pilot and provided with 500 rounds each were fixed in the forward fuselage. The gunner/radio operator, alone in the rear cockpit, operated a hatch gun mounting with the fourth ShKAS, which covered the lower rear zone. An RSB*bis* radio was mounted in the gunner's cockpit. The aircraft's twin-beam antenna worked the RPK-2 Chaika radio compass in addition to the radio. The tailplane tips projecting beyond the fins were removed.

The other differences mainly concerned changes in the powerplant. Removal of the superchargers reduced the cross sectional area of the engine nacelles by 20 to 25%, which combined with the use of ejector exhausts gave a slight increase in speed. The shape of the oil cooler tunnels was changed with the same aim, and their cooling area was increased to improve the operating temperatures of the M-105 engines. The area of the water radiators was increased as well, and louvres replaced bends in the appropriate tunnel exits.

Conversely the new, projecting canopy of the pilot's and navigator's cockpit, the dive-brake flaps and the fairing for the hatch gun mount increased drag. The experimental VISh-42 propellers installed on the '100' had to be replaced by VISh-61Bs.

# Pe-2

Despite their efforts, the factories failed to produce the required number of PB-100s in 1940. They also failed to fulfil another order of the People's Commissariat of the Aircraft Industry, sent after the first and obviously intended to soften the consequences of the failure to fulfil the task set by the Committee of Defence; to roll out the first aircraft by 7th November 1940. Thunder sounded, the directors of Plants Nos.39 and 156 were dismissed, and the director of Plant No.22 was penalised. The flight of at least one production PB-100 before the end of 1940 was the 'last chance' for saving the lives of the leaders of the People's Commissariat of the Aircraft Industry. This flight took place on 15th December 1940, when test pilot N Fedorov of Plant No.39 flew Pe-2 construction number 390101, the lead aircraft of the first series.

The designation Pe-2 replaced PB-100 in accordance with a new rule, introduced in December 1940, of designating the aircraft type by the first two letters of the chief designer's name.

During the following days the aircraft underwent a short, accelerated manufacturer's test programme at the plant. It achieved a maximum speed of 335mph (540km/h) at 16,400ft (5,000m) at a flying weight of 14,991lb (6,800kg), which completely accorded with the specification. But this aircraft and the following four can be considered only token production aircraft. The offensive and defensive armament was in mock-up form, and their combat performance was marred by a long list of defects in the airframe, powerplant and equipment.

Aircraft No.3 was generally left at the disposal of the chief designer for the incorporation of alterations, the first of which was the provision of dual control (from the navigator's seat). Aircraft Nos.1 and 5, which had exceeded the service life of their engines by May, were later handed over to air force technical schools.

The first Pe-2 built at Plant No.22 was received by the military acceptance office on 16th January 1941, and was sent with the first aircraft from Plant No.39 to undergo the state trials at the NII.

The Pe-2's test programme was delayed more than two months owing to the large scale and number of defects discovered. Mass failure of the constant-speed governors for the R-3 propellers was the first unpleasant surprise. Every other flight ended with an emergency landing for NII VVS test pilots Major F Opadchy and Captains A Khripkov, A Siroyegin and L Dudkin because of propeller failure. Another serious flaw was an error made during the design of the shock absorbers of the main undercarriage legs, which, as on the '100', tended to make the aircraft bounce on landing. During the state trials a total of 187 defects in the aircraft produced at Plant No.39 and more than 100 in the aircraft from Plant No.22 were revealed.

Many were quickly resolved, others were listed in the report, and a third group remained 'trademarks' of the Pe-2 throughout its life. Included in this last category were the wing's aerofoil sections, chosen in accordance with the recommendations of the Tsentral'nyi Aerogidrodynamichesky Institut (TsAGI – Central Aerodynamic and Hydrodynamic Institute) specialists for the high altitude fighter and unchanged in the Pe-2, being 'B' at the wing root and 'BS' at rib 13. These profiles had two quite useful properties: a high lift-to-drag ratio at high speeds and a constant position of aerodynamic centre over a wide speed range. The latter was most valuable for the dive bomber, as the speed at the start of a dive was 2 to 2.5 times lower than at the recovery. Without such properties the effort required of the pilot would be much greater, complicating aiming. Such a wing was good in most respects, but the problem was that its stalling angle at low speeds was only 11°. The stall occurred asymmetrically along the span and suddenly when the control column was pulled back hard during landing or in sharp turns. This unpleasant aspect of the Pe-2's handling cost the lives of more than one crew, especially if the pilot was inexperienced.

Nevertheless despite a great many design and manufacturing flaws, the aircraft was successful in general due to its performance.

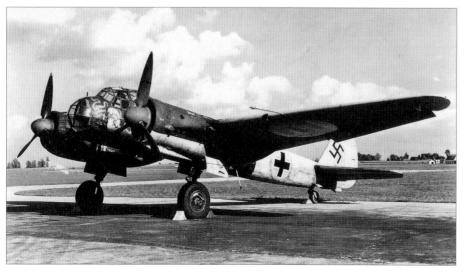

*Photographs on this page:*

**A Pe-2 mock-up under test in a TsAGI wind tunnel.**

**Design of the Pe-2 was greatly influenced by the concept (and hands-on evaluation) of the Junkers Ju 88A.** *Ken Ellis collection*

*Photographs on the opposite page:*

**Early production Pe-2.**

**Close detail of the cockpit and engines of a Pe-2 bomber. Note the crew hatch.**

In addition it was lucky, there being no accidents or serious incidents during the test program at the NII VVS. The Pe-2s of the first few series had a maximum speed of 280mph (452km/h) at sea level and 320mph (516 km/h) at the first altitude limit of 10,000ft (3,000m), and confirmed a maximum speed of 335mph (540km/h) at altitude, achieved for the first time by Fedorov. With a 1,322lb (600kg) internal bomb load the aircraft took 9.2 minutes to reach 16,400ft (5,000m), and its service ceiling was 29,000ft (8,800m). It should be noted that the tests of maximum speed were made with the external bomb suspension points removed and all slots, holes and even small hatches covered. In reality, therefore, the Pe-2 had a slightly inferior performance in 'combat configuration'. But

this did not affect the reconnaissance version, which was built without the air brake grids and with a partly polished skin. This variant was often faster than the pre-production Pe-2.

The internal bomb stowage of the 'Pawn' ('little Pe', a nickname common in both the industry and the air force) was quite original. Besides the internal bomb bay with four suspension points (two on each of two Der-21 cassettes), it had two more in the engine nacelles, using DZ-40 bomb racks. One bomb up to a maximum weight of 220lb (100kg) could be carried on each of the internal suspension points. In addition, four FAB-250 or two FAB-500 bombs could be carried externally on four DZ-40s. The maximum bomb load was 2,204lb (1,000kg) and the normal load was 1,322lb (600kg).

The dive bomber inherited from the '100' high altitude fighter the alternative of having the bomb compartments loaded with K-76 cassettes and K-100 cassettes, schemed some time later. The K-76 cassette contained 76.2 mm tail-less fused projectiles, and the K-100 was loaded with fragmentation bombs of AO-2.5 to AO-10 type. Several test flights showed that the 76.2mm projectiles posed a serious threat to the bomber itself, owing to the weapons tumbling over during release from the cassette, so their use was prohibited almost immediately. The situation with the K-100 cassettes was slightly better, although their design and peculiarities of utilisation did not satisfy the specialists. In this connection the problem of their use on the Pe-2 was unsolved by April 1941.

Left: Snow-camouflaged Pe-2 – note the black (or blue?) outlined red star on the fin/rudder.

Centre: In the autumn of 1941 Pe-2 No.16/32 was equipped with ten RS-82 rockets. This modification was not taken up in service.

Bottom: The Pe-2 became the main Soviet light bomber of the Second World War.

The idea of using the cassette for small bombs was embodied later in the KMB-Pe-2 device, introduced into service in the autumn of 1941.

From the sixth aircraft built at Plant No.39 the Pe-2's movable gun armament was replaced by the production standard installation, consisting of the navigator's upper mounting and an MV-2 hatch mounting with a similar machine gun and ammunition supply. From the very beginning the military saw this as the modern bomber's weak point, so from April and May the series aircraft had the hatched ShKAS replaced by a large calibre BT machine gun with 200 cartridges. The starboard ShKAS in the forward mounting was also replaced by a Berezin machine gun with 150 cartridges, and simultaneously the ammunition for the port ShKAS was reduced to 450 rounds. A special box was provided to collect the very heavy expended links and cartridges of the BT, because they seriously damaged the aircraft's skin and even entered the tunnels of the water radiators. The links discharged by the upper TSS-1 gun were collected in a sack for the same reason. The weight of fire of a Pe-2 armed only with ShKAS guns was 1.152kg/sec, but with the Berezin machine guns it was almost doubled, to 2,208kg/sec.

The Pe-2's 'family roots' had resulted in the first aircraft being fitted with a fighter-type 'joystick'. During the test programme, however, it became clear that it was necessary to replace it with a bomber-type control column so that the pilot could cope with the forces imposed on the control surfaces during manoeuvres. Simultaneously, the Duralumin tubes in the control links were replaced by stronger steel components.

Aircraft Plants Nos.124, 125 and 450 were given the task of Pe-2 production in February 1941. The plan for 1941 provided for the production of 1,100 Pe-2 dive bombers, of which 525 were to be built during the first half of the year. According to information from the factories, however, only 306 were built by the end of May, and Plant No.450 was reorganised to produce another aircraft type. The first production Pe-2s went to two regiments, the 95th High Speed Bomber Air Regiment of the Moscow Military District and the 48th Short Range Bomber Air Regiment of the Kiev Special Military District, in addition to research and test establishments of the People's Commissariat of the Aircraft Industry and the VVS. Aircraft from these regiments participated in traditional May Day military parades in Moscow and Kiev.

The flight and ground staff of VVS service units regarded the new aircraft apprehensively at first. 'The aircraft is too complicated in handling, especially at take-off and landing,' wrote Colonel Pestov, commander of the 95th SBAR. 'Its operation requires pilots with above average qualifications. An ordinary pilot finds it difficult to become familiar with the aircraft'. A number of incidents and accidents took place in service units, though the crew of production plant test pilot Colonel Vorobyov were apparently the first to be killed flying the Pe-2. The peculiarities of the VISh-61B control system caused overspeeding of the propellers on entry into a dive, giving rise to unpleasant experiences for pilots. The slowness of emergency undercarriage extension was also frustrating, but the badly designed air brake flap emergency retraction mechanism turned out to be the most dangerous fault. Although this deficiency might have been quite tolerable in peacetime, it assumed sudden importance with the beginning of war, and was one of the reasons why Pe-2 crews stopped using the aircraft as a dive bomber. If the air brake flaps could not be retracted using the main system after recovery from a dive, the aircraft became easy prey to fighters and flak, being unable to exceed 260-280km/h. By the time the Nazis invaded the USSR, 180 Pe-2s equipped the regiments of five frontier military districts, but only a small number of crews had begun to gain familiarity with the aircraft.

The records of the 16th and 39th Bomber Air Regiments of the Western Front Air Force note that crews of 'Pawns' parried the attacks of enemy fighters most successfully in June and July 1941. On 1st July, for example, six Pe-2s fended off attacks by four Messerschmitt Bf 109s, bringing down two of them. A week later a group of Pe-2s was attacked by four Bf 109s and the bombers again brought down two of their attackers. On both occasions the bombers suffered no losses.

During his interrogation, Major A Mudin of the Luftwaffe's Jagdstaffel 51, brought down in air combat over Bobruisk, affirmed his opinion that the Pe-2 was the best Soviet aircraft: 'It is a high speed aircraft with good armament, and is dangerous to enemy fighters'. This is hardly surprising; he himself was brought down by a Pe-2.

With regard to the first experience of Pe-2 operation by the southern wing of the Black Sea Fleet, a raid on Ploesti in Romania by six aircraft of the 40th Air Regiment was a great success. After spending several days familiarising themselves with their newly received aircraft, the group, led by Captain A Tsurtsulin, set out on its mission. At least a quarter of a million of tons of oil products was burnt in the raid, and the sea was aflame for three days. The Romanian information agency claimed that at least 100 Soviet aircraft had bombed Ploesti. The peculiarity of this singularly successful raid (though losses were suffered), was that that the enemy mistook the Pe-2s for friendly aircraft, and regarded the Soviet fighters and flak as the enemy.

The fate of the 13th SBAR, commanded by V Bogomolov, was typical for the early period of the war. Having begun to convert to the Pe-2 before the war, the regiment was thrown into combat in the region of Yelnya on 16th July. Although the pilots had barely become familiar with circling flight, they quickly gained experience during combat. An attack on a German airfield in the region of Smolensk at the end of July was very successful. The regiment's combat operations were not always successful, and its errors included bad co-operation with escort fighters and the whole group approaching targets at the same altitude. The 13th SBAR lost 20 crews during a month of combat. Among the Pe-2's defects, service pilots listed insufficient defensive armament, a great risk of fire, and insufficient armour, especially for the navigator's and gunner's cockpits.

The first Pe-2 combat operations revealed that a number of the aircraft's assemblies and systems required design changes. The most important concerned armament and survivability. The limited sighting angles of the hatch gun mounting and its poor reliability (the cartridge feed often became jammed after the UBT machine gun's first burst of fire when shooting in extreme positions) were discovered by German pilots, who exploited this weakness effectively. The gun's feed system was urgently modified in the regiments by turning the cartridge box and shortening the hose of the feed. Similar changes were introduced in aircraft built in series in July and August 1941, and it even proved possible to increase the gun's range of movement slightly. An additional, fifth ShKAS machine gun installed on a spherical mounting appeared on aircraft built at Plant No.22 in August. The gun could be moved from one side to the other, was supplied with three cartridge boxes with a total capacity of 225 cartridges, and could fire in the direction normal to the aircraft's centreline and not covered by the hatch and the upper gun mountings.

In some instances when a navigator was killed or severely wounded, physically strong gunners defended the upper hemisphere with this gun, resting its barrel on the edge of the upper hatch. The first attempts to increase the firepower of the navigator's upper gun position were also made at that time. A paired gun mounting with a ShKAS and a large-calibre UBT machine gun on an MV-2 hatch-type turret was tested on aircraft No.9/9 built at Plant No.22. Neither of these mountings were used in series production.

From September 1941 the Pe-2's bombload was increased by fitting cassettes of small KMB-Pe-2 bombs, which allowed the effective destruction of unprotected area targets. During the same period aircraft built at Plants Nos.16 and 32 had rocket projectiles fitted and passed their flight test programme, the installation being recommended for production aircraft. The weight of fire of a salvo of ten RS-132s was equal to a salvo fired by a light cruiser. The negative side of the installation was the significant loss of speed, which fell by 15 to 19mph (25 to 30km/h) without the RS projectiles mounted and 22 to 28mph (35 to 45km/h) with them.

Analysing flight-crew losses of the first production Pe-2s, the military were easily convinced that the navigator and radio operator were the most vulnerable crew members. The navigator was protected to some extent by a small back armour plate, but his head and legs were unprotected against attacks from behind. The gunner/radio operator's armour was really no more than a token gesture. The inadequacies of the armour protection ultimately led to the loss of an entire aircraft and its crew, which at last was understood by designers. They succeeded in slightly increasing the size of the gunner's and navigator's armoured screens, the aft movement of the centre of gravity being partly offset by halving the number of oxygen bottles housed in the rear fuselage. However, the armour provided protection only from rifle-calibre bullets, not from larger-calibre shells or projectiles fired by German Oerlikon guns. On average, ten Pe-2 gunners were wounded for every pilot, and two or three were killed for the loss of one pilot.

One other way of increasing the aircraft's survivability was to modify the fuel tanks. There were two choices: improving the protection and replacing Duralumin tanks with tanks made of fibre, or providing the tanks with a system to fill their voids with inert gas. In the first series Pe-2s, two bottles of nitrogen were installed in the port engine nacelles. However, the system began operating before flight, which resulted in an increased consumption of nitrogen, which was in short supply at the front. Later the fuel tanks were filled by the cooled emissions from the engine exhaust collectors. This system could be turned on and off in flight, as required by the crew.

All the usual difficulties of war, shortages of raw materials, electric power and suitably qualified workers, were aggravated by a major upheaval in October and November 1941, with movement of the main Pe-2 manufacturing plants to the east. Moscow had already suffered air raids, in one of which three newly-completed Pe-2s from Plant No.22 were burnt on Tushino airfield in August.

Plant No.39, which was building mainly the Pe-3, the fighter variant of the 'Pawn', in the autumn of 1941, was evacuated to Irkutsk and soon merged with Plant No.125, and Plant No.22 moved to Kazan and merged with local Plant No.124. Naturally, the move caused a fall in the production rate of the dive bomber.

The four production plants managed to build a total of 1,867 Pe aircraft in 1941, including 196 Pe-3s at Plant No.39. Plant No.22 built 1,120 aircraft, more than a half of the total.

The greatest courage and heroism were demanded of the Soviet Army and the aviation units to counter the German offensive on Moscow, which began in October 1941. The Luftwaffe still had superiority in the air, especially with regard to day bombers. Each Pe-2 was counted, and new aircraft were arranged in new formations and groups to enhance their operation. The Petlyakov bombers flew the most important missions in the battle for Moscow, and new operational methods were devised as experience was gained.

The inexpert navigational skills of the freshly trained flight crews, along with the typically bad autumn weather, resulted in frequent losses of orientation. The well trained pilots and navigators of the 9th Bomber Air Regiment, based in the centre of Moscow, were tasked with leading units and formations of fighters and attack aircraft newly arrived at the front. This was not easy, especially at the final stages, because it was necessary to land on semi-prepared forward airstrips of limited size and with bad approaches.

Operation of the Pe-2 with rocket projectiles became popular in the Moscow region. Sometimes, unusually, they were installed for reverse launch. Having considered the bombers' vulnerability to attacks from behind, technician A Pomazanski suggested installing eight RS-82s so that they could be fired rearwards. The unexpected firing of these projectiles often spoiled attacks by enemy fighters. Later this idea was investigated by the Weapon Research Centre, but it was not widely adopted.

Rocket projectiles were used more often against enemy tanks, the missiles being launched in pairs or fours in a shallow dive. The initiative in developing the methods of using RS-132s against armoured vehicles was provided by Major G Karpenko, the inspector of piloting skills for the Air Force of the Moscow Military District. He also suggested using Pe-2s to illuminate enemy bombers approaching the city at night, thereby allowing fighters to direct their fire at the target thus revealed. Although the number of enemy aircraft brought down in this way was not great, the psychological effect was significant. Enemy bombers caught in the beam of a searchlight would often jettison their bombs before reaching the target, take evasive action and make good their escape.

The speed of production bombers dropped every month. In September 1941 the Pe-2 achieved a maximum speed of 329mph (530km/h) at the second altitude level during a test; in March 1942 the figure was down to 323mph (520km/h), in June it was 314mph

(506km/h) and in September only 306mph (494km/h). During series production the Pe-2 suffered the greatest speed deterioration of all Soviet bombers of the Second World War. This was linked to the increase in flying weight, the fall in production standards (women and very young children were recruited into the factories, and they were physically unable to work resistant Duralumin throughout eleven hour working days), and the change in the aircraft's shape, particularly the navigator's gun mounting.

All the Pe-2s of the 205th series batch were fitted with fairings which gave a speed increase of 3.10 to 4.3mph (5 to 7km/h). At the same time the VISh-61B or VISh-105 propellers of production aircraft were replaced by VISh-61Ps and the antenna mast was moved from the rear of the cockpit canopy to the windshield.

## Pe-2F

Although the quality of Pe-2 production deteriorated slightly at the end of the summer of 1941, it remained satisfactory. Production Pe-2 No.10/35 from Plant No.22, tested at the NII VVS in August and September, achieved a maximum speed of 329mph (530km/h) at 16,400ft (5,000m) and 276mph (445km/h) at sea level. Its time to 16,400ft (5,000m) was slightly better (10 minutes), as was its landing speed (90mph/145km/h). The reduction in flying speed of aircraft built at Plant No.22 was already evident in April 1941, and while this was not unexpected it was necessary to seek ways to eliminate it. As early as March 1941 Petlyakov had submitted a report to the People's Commissariat of the Aircraft Industry regarding a planned radical modernisation of the Pe-2 by replacing its M-105R engines with M-105Fs and M-107s. It was estimated that M-105Fs with TK-2F turbosuperchargers would enable the bomber to reach 372mph (600 km/h) at 22,965ft (7,000m). At the time the new and consequently quite undeveloped M-107 promised a significantly smaller increase in speed, only 360mph (580km/h) at the same altitude, but its potential made it a candidate for the second stage of modification.

It was not only the engines that were changed. The dive bomber Pe-2, converted from the original fighter, had a low wing, and the centre section spars prevented the internal carriage of bombs of 551lb (250kg) or more. To overcome this, the fuselage was lowered in the Pe-2F (as the Pe-2 with M-105F engines and TK-2F turbosuperchargers was designated in the report), and the bomber became a mid-wing aircraft, enabling a pair of FAB-250 bombs or one FAB-500 to be accommodated in the fuselage bomb bay.

*Top:* **A Pe-2 of the 115th production batch during tests at NII VVS, December 1942. This aircraft had a tail section of all-wood construction.**

*Centre:* **A Pe-2 bomber with a dorsal VUB-1 gun mount, enhanced armour and M-105RA engines.**

*Right:* **Often mistakenly called the 'FT', the VUB-1 mount with 12.7mm UBT machine gun.**

Two more large bombs could be carried on external suspension points. Bomb compartments in the engine nacelles were eliminated, but maximum bomb load still rose to 3,306lb (1,500kg), the normal load being 2,204lb (1,000kg). It should be remembered that its small bomb load was one of the main shortcomings of the Pe-2 as a bomber.

The workforce of the experimental department was building the Pe-2F during the late summer and autumn, so it was not until March 1942 that it went for flight testing.

The new year began with a tragic event. Vladimir Petlyakov, the Pe-2's designer, died on 12th January when the aircraft in which he was flying from Kazan to Moscow crashed in the region of Arzamas. Several explanations for the accident were postulated, including fire, engine failure and even sabotage, but the most likely was thought to be that the pilot had flown into a snowstorm, which caused him to lose orientation and collide with a hill.

The bureau was led by Alexander Izakson for some time after the accident, but in March 1943 Alexander Putilov took over. Taking up Petlyakov's proposals for modernising the dive bomber by replacing its M-105RAs with more powerful engines, the new chief designer did not stop work on the Pe-2F, but proposed his own version, powered by air-cooled M-82 radial engines. The flight test programme, completed in April 1942, showed that the Pe-2F powered by M-105Fs was capable of only 347mph (560km/h) at 23,000ft (7,000m) instead of the predicted 372mph (600km/h). The difficulty of controlling the superchargers (the engines did not have the appropriate automatic controls) made the Pe-2F very exhausting to fly, and manageable only by highly skilled pilots. The M-82, being a production engine, was quite a different case. It was some 200 to 400hp (149 to 298kW) more powerful than the M-105RA throughout the whole range of altitudes, and in addition it had a higher altitude margin. This seemed to promise a significant improvement in performance.

Another test aircraft, powered by M-107s, made its maiden flight in September 1942 in the course of the second stage of the Pe-2F programme. The more powerful engines without the tricky superchargers were expected to accelerate the aircraft to 360mph (580km/h) at the second altitude level, but difficulties appeared once again. Almost every flight ended in an emergency landing caused by failure of the powerplant. A month later it was agreed that the test programme could not continue because it might result in an accident. The aircraft was returned to the factory's experimental department to await uprated M-107A engines.

Production of a reconnaissance version of the Pe-2 began at Plant No.22 from August 1941, at a rate of 15 to 20 aircraft a month. In this variant the air brake grids were removed, the fuel tank was suspended inside the fuselage bomb bay and additional tanks were suspended under the centre section. With improved skinning, M-105RA engines and polished wing surfaces (up to one-third chord) this version had a range of about 1,550 miles (2,500km). As well as the Pe-2's standard AFA-B camera, reconnaissance equipment included two AFA-1 cameras and one AFA-27T camera in the radio operator's cockpit. For night operations an NAFA-19 replaced the AFA-B and six to eight FOTAB-50-35 photobombs were carried. These aircraft were supplied to the specially created Long Range Aviation Reconnaissance Regiments of the Supreme Commander-in-Chief.

## Pe-2FT

The inadequacy of the ShKAS machine gun on the TSS-1 upper gun mounting for effectively countering German fighters was discovered at the very beginning of the war, but for some time the factories, preoccupied with launching mass production of the Pe-2, ignored this deficiency. The indignant complaints of a pilot of a fighting unit who had come to Plant No.22 to take delivery of a new aircraft are said to have provided the real impetus for replacing the ShKAS with the more powerful, large calibre UBT machine gun. During a traditional meeting the factory workers and the pilots from the front exchanged slogans on the theme 'the logistics – to the front, the front – to the logistics' (meaning mutual support by those who fight on the fronts and those who work at Soviet factories and farms, supplying the combat units), and mutual gratitude. One of the leaders of the design bureau, L Selyakov, at the back, heard a young pilot say bitterly: 'These meetings are annoying. They bring us down like young chickens at the front, and here …' When discussions began, the need to increase firepower in the upper mounting became clear.

Together with three employees of the bureau, Selyakov designed a new mounting with a 12.7mm UBT machine gun, using components of the production MV-2 hatch mounting. The design was given the official marking 'FT' (Frontovoye Trebovaniye, or 'front requires'. The Pe-2 with the FT or 'Front Task' gun mounting (see the later section on experimental versions of the Pe-2) differed in shape owing to the absence of the navigator's retractable screen, or 'tortoise'. The turret with its large calibre machine gun replaced the TSS-1 mounting, and fuselage station F2 above the fuel tank was covered by a door.

Although the wind blew strongly into the permanently opened navigator's cockpit, especially in winter, this had to be tolerated. But the UBT quickly taught German fighter pilots not to approach the Pe-2 too closely from behind. The FT allowed the same firing angles as the TSS-1: elevation 45°, right to left movement of 45°, and downward to –6°. The ammunition load of 200 rounds was contained in two removable boxes.

The main advantage of the FT mounting was the ease with which it could be installed in aircraft on site, requiring only four to six working hours by two specialists. Aircraft built at Plant No.22 began to come off the assembly line with the FT mounting from the 87th series batch.

Everybody realised that the FT mounting was far from ideal, and could be considered only as a temporary measure. By the spring of 1942, Special Plant No.22 had devised its own version of the upper movable mount for the Pe-2, with the UBT machine gun and a constant belt feed; the so-called 'Torov mounting' (also designated VUB-1 or B-270). The UBK machine gun with pneumatic recharging and electric belt feed was installed on the production VUB-1 instead of the UBT, because the long belt of 200 cartridges often broke during the first shots owing to the increased drag in the feed tube. The mounting rested upon a cast iron gear wheel and was covered with a movable tower-like screen, and theoretically offered significantly greater angles of fire compared with the FT; 110° to the left, 88° to the right and up to 55° upwards. Later it became clear that even physically strong gunners were unable to deflect the machine gun more than 45 to 50° to either side because of the pressure of the airflow on the barrel. Some time later an aerodynamic balance comprising two and, later, one 'petal' positioned above the screen was installed in the turret. The prototype turret was installed for the first time in a Pe-2F, and a similar firing position was then fitted to a Pe-3bis from Plant No.39. During the test programme of the Pe-3bis it became evident that the VUB-1 mounting reduced the 'Pawn's' maximum speed by 4.9 to 7.4mph (8 to 12km/h) compared with the TSS-1 mounting installed in earlier production aircraft.

## Experimental Pe-2s

In the summer and autumn of 1942 the design bureau of Vladimir Klimov, designer of the M-105 engine, conducted trials in connection with augmenting the M-105P and M-105R engines by increased blowing. The 'P' series engines differed from the 'R' series in the design of the reduction gear, which allowed a gun to be installed between the cylinder blocks.

*Top:* **Pe-2 with a new FZ mount and canopy, tested at the NII VVS in June 1943.**

*Above left:* **Modified FZ gun mount. This was not placed into production.**

*Above right:* **Wind tunnel testing of a Pe-2 with redesigned navigator's compartment.**

The augmented engines were designated M-105PF and M-105RF respectively; the first was immediately put into series production, but the second was less successful. Despite a slight improvement in the performance of the Pe-2 powered by M-105RFs – the maximum speed increased by 9.9 to 13mph (16 to 21 km/h), the time to climb to 16,400ft (5,000m) was reduced by 1.5 minutes and the take-off run by 131 to 164ft (40 to 50m) – the M-105PF was not put into production because it was not sufficiently reliable. Instead, it was decid-

ed in the autumn of 1942 to replace the M-105RAs in the Pe-2 with typical fighter-type M-105PFs rated at 1,210hp (902kW). This had both positive and negative consequences. While the aircraft's speed increased at altitudes from ground level to 9,900ft (3,000m), it fell from there upwards because of the engines' inferior high altitude capabilities.

NII VVS objected to this engine substitution. In a letter to Repin, the principal engineer, Major General Fyodorov, deputy chief of the NII VVS, affirmed: 'The installation of M-105PF engines in the Pe-2 gives no advantages. The aircraft's speed will be [24.8 to 43.4mph] 40 to 70km/h lower than that of the Bf 109 throughout the whole range of altitudes ...'.

Nevertheless, replacement of the M-105RA with the M-105PF went ahead. Initially the VISh-61B propellers optimised for the 'RA' version were retained on production Pe-2s, though they were not at all suitable for the

'PF' and it was necessary to impose a strict limit on engine revolutions, thereby reducing power.

The main reason for the engine replacement was obviously to reduce the number of different engines produced and thereby increase production.

In the autumn of 1942 the general deterioration of the situation at the front, and the German occupation of the wide territories up to Volga, caused a sharp drop in the amount and types of Duralumin sheet and metal parts produced by the industry. In a number of cases the thickness of aircraft skins had to be increased from 0.8mm to 1mm, or from 1.2mm to 1.5mm, with a consequent increase in aircraft weight. Deliveries of sheets of smaller sizes and containing flaws such as waves and cracks made unintended joints, often overlapping. Wingtips began to be made of several pieces.

This had a negative effect on the performance of production Pe-2s, and because of the deterioration in the material supplied, Plant No.22, the sole manufacturer of Pe-2 dive bombers from late 1942, and the design bureau headed by A Putilov, sought to replace the aircraft's all-metal components. A wooden rear fuselage (F3), with wooden frames and plywood skinning, was fitted to aircraft number 20/115. Its tailplane had the same structure, though metal fins were retained. The gunner/radio operator's entrance hatch was changed, being made to open outwards to facilitate egress in an emergency. The aircraft had an RPK-10 radio compass (the RPK-2 was installed in one aircraft of every three produced from autumn 1941, and later only in reconnaissance aircraft).

Major Ashitkov flew the complete test programme of the wooden-tailed Pe-2, including dives at angles of 60 to 65° with and without the air brake grids extended, pulling loadings of up to 3 to 3.5g in the recovery. There were no deformations or failures, but eyewitnesses recall that the military representative of the plant doubted the strength of the junction of the tailplane and rear fuselage. The aircraft was passed to the TsAGI, where a number of improvements recommended by local specialists were made, in addition to strength investigations. L Selyakov, the leading engineer of Plant No.22's design bureau, demanded that he be allowed to fly in the aircraft during the test programme, while it made steep dives and 70 to 80° turns. He got into the tail section of the aircraft without a parachute, so that once the tests were completed the military would be left in no doubt about the machine's safety. Selyakov recalled that he emerged from the aircraft neither alive nor dead after the flight, but that he convinced the military representative of its strength. Later the wooden F3 fuselage section and tailplane were installed on some Pe-2s in different series, but as Plant No.22 was unable to undertake large scale production of these units (it was working exclusively with metal), mixed-structure Pe-2 production was relatively small-scale. Only the wooden tail tip was fitted, and this was later the subject of adverse reports from service units because its plywood skin tended to warp and swell.

The first two Pe-2 trainers, with an instructor's cockpit in place of the fuselage fuel tank, were built during November-December 1942. Later this variant was built in series at a production rate of 10 to 15 aircraft a month.

Another interesting version of the Pe-2, with a movable cannon and an AKAB machine gun battery mounted under fuselage, was under test at the end of 1942. The AKAB installation was worked out at Plant No.32 under the leadership of Georgy Mozharovsky and Ivan Venevidov. Two paired gun carriages for a ShVAK gun and a UBK machine gun with a special device to allow for altitude, speed and the angle of the gun, allowed sustained firing against small targets while the aircraft was in horizontal flight, which significantly increased the density of destructive fire. The dropping of bombs on selected targets was accomplished automatically and simultaneously with the firing of the machine

**Two views of Pe-2 prototype No.19/31 fitted with M-82 engines during the winter of 1942.**

A production Pe-2 with M-82FN engines. Of the 100 ordered, only 22 were delivered.

gun and cannon. A number of faults in the design of the battery were revealed during the test programme, but they were not major shortcomings. Later, in 1944, such batteries were installed in a modified version of the Lend-Lease Douglas A-20G attack aircraft, and were successfully used in combat.

Nevertheless, the most important task for Putilov was the creation of high altitude versions of the Pe-2. Two were schemed: the high-altitude fighter or VI (vysotny istrebitel), and the high altitude reconnaissance aircraft or VR (vysotny razvedchik). The mock-up commission for the VI took place at the end of January 1943. The aircraft looked like the Pe-2 but was slightly changed, being powered by two M-105PDs with Dollezhal superchargers. The new forward part of the fuselage (F1) had a single-seat pressurised and ventilated cockpit, and the attack armament included one ShVAK gun with 250 rounds. The rear fuselage (F3) was also revised; the radio operator/gunner's cockpit was removed and an electrically operated remote mounting with a UBK machine gun was installed in the tail. The wing area was increased by 26.9ft$^2$ (2.5m$^2$), using new frames made of wood. This was the next stage in the replacement of Duralumin in the aircraft's structure by readily available wood. The project was ruined by lack of co-ordination in the production of some new elements of the structure. As a result, when the M-105PD engines were delivered to the factory the cockpit and the new wing components had not arrived. Putilov therefore decided to install the engines in an ordinary production Pe-2 so that trials of the powerplant could be started. When the pressurised cockpit and fuselage section were ready it became clear that there were no more M-105PDs available, and the delivery schedule was in doubt. Putilov decided to install ordinary production M-105PFs and metal wings in the VI to enable testing of the pressurised cockpit to begin. Plant No.23 had to produce the outer panels of the wooden wing, which greatly delayed completion of the order. Moreover, work on the remote controlled gun installation was proceeding slowly. It was mounted in the third aircraft to be completed. And the main task was to extend the experimental works; the mock-up commission concerning the VR was to take place in May, and this aircraft was supposed to be powered by M-82NV engines with TK-3 superchargers. The building of a VI second prototype with the same powerplant began.

Meanwhile, the situation became complicated for Plant No.22's chief designer. Despite the numerous requirements laid down by the People's Commissariat of the Aircraft Industry and the SCD, performance of Pe-2 dive bombers built at the plant continued to deteriorate. In March 1943 production aircraft achieved a maximum speed of only 295 to 299mph (475 to 482km/h) without external stores at 10,500 to 11,000ft (3,200-3,400m). A number of new defects became apparent, one of the most serious being the impossibility of the pilot and navigator abandoning the aircraft after the middle portion of the cockpit canopy had been jettisoned. On Pe-2s built before the 110th series the navigator lowered the TSS-1 fairing to its lowest position and the pilot jettisoned the middle part of the canopy, after which they had only to jump from the aircraft, pass beneath the tailplane and open their parachutes. The pilots did not like jumping from the lower hatch. It was quite difficult for them to force their way through to it in a tumbling aeroplane, and it often failed to jettison in an emergency.

The installation of the VUB-1 turret in the Pe-2 made a significant difference. In April 1943 Colonel Nevinny, chief engineer of the First Air Army, reported to General Repin, the head engineer of the VVS: 'Pe-2, factory No.8/137, with a VUB-1 gun mounting, belonging to the 2nd BAR, was damaged by an Fw 190 fighter in air combat on 19th March 1943. Subsequent investigation revealed that the navigator refused to jump from the lower hatch and moved to the cockpit. The roof of the canopy failed to jettison by use of the emergency handle. The aircraft was not under control at the time, and was diving at an angle of 60-70°. By their combined efforts the pilot and navigator succeeded in jettisoning the canopy, but at that moment the pilot was thrown against the glazing of the VUB-1. His legs remained in the cockpit, and he was pressed so strongly against the turret that he could not jump out, so he released his parachute and was pulled away. The navigator failed to get out of the cockpit and died... a pilot and navigator of the 261st BAR perished the same day in similar circumstances.'

VUB-1 gun mount with single-blade compensator, on test at TsAGI.

Again, as in the case of the FT, the designers at the aircraft factory proved to be faster than their colleagues at Plant No.32. A test Pe-2, factory No.7/187, with a new cockpit canopy and a new firing position for the navigator, the so-called FT or 'Front Task' mounting, had already begun its test programme in June 1943. The cockpit canopy was 4¾ to 6in (120 to 150mm) higher, and the crash pylon was reintroduced (aircraft with the VUB-1 had it, and it was major omission on the Pe-2, which had a tendency to nose over in a rough landing). The F3 fuselage section was faired into the contours of the canopy and, most importantly, significantly better working conditions were provided for the navigator. This was achieved by rearranging the cockpit, reducing the instrument panels, improving the navigator's workplace and greatly improving his view. The middle section of the canopy comprised two parts which separated when jettisoned. Although a number of defects were revealed during the first stage of the test programme, and though the new gun installation provided slightly fewer firing angles than the VUB-1, the modification was a great step forward. Unfortunately, despite the NII VVS's insistence that the F3 assembly be adopted for production aircraft, it was not built in series owing to the position taken by the People's Commissariat of the Aircraft Industry.

## Pe-2 with M-82s

The design bureau of Plant No.22 worked in several directions, seeking a means of increasing the maximum speed of the production aircraft.

The prototype M-82 powered Pe-2 first flew in June 1942. The aircraft, No.19/31, was allocated for experimental work, and its powerplant was underdeveloped and caused the designers many problems. The engine control system did not give reliable operation at idle, and it was therefore necessary when landing to switch off and make a gliding approach and touchdown. This was extremely dangerous, because an overshoot and go-around for a second landing attempt was out of the question. Sometimes the engines caught fire on starting up, and this prolonged completion of the aircraft by three long months. Test pilot Major Khripkov made several successful flights in the M-82-powered Pe-2, and the maximum speed of 338mph (545km/h) at 19,400ft (5,900m) attained during one of these flights was the most important reason for continuing the tests, because it was 31 to 34mph (50 to 55km/h) faster than production aircraft built during the autumn and the beginning of winter 1942-43.

In the summer of 1943 Vladimir Myasishchev, having finished work on the '102' long range high altitude bomber, took over as head of the design bureau of Plant No.22. The new chief designer had his own point of view regarding Pe-2 development. He immediately dropped the VR project and the VI was transferred to another plant for completion, where it 'died successfully'. But work on the Pe-2 with M-82 and M-107A engines continued. The M-82 engined Pe-2 went into series production during the 'Myasishchev period'. Some of these aircraft were built in the series from 227 to 250, and differed from their contemporaries with M-105PF engines in having AV-5L-118 propellers and reduced armament of only one large calibre machine gun for each crew member. In addition, auxiliary fuel tanks with a capacity of 43.9 gallons (200 litres) were arranged in the wings in place of the radiators. The production aircraft achieved a maximum speed of 338mph (545km/h) at 20,300ft (6,200m) with a normal bomb load of 1,322lb (600kg) at a flying weight of 19,235lb (8,725kg).

Two circumstances had a profound influence on the fate of this advanced version; the shortage of M-82FN engines, which were also installed in Lavochkin La-5 fighters being built in numerous factories, and a large numbers of defective oil radiators destined specially for the Pe-2 with the M-82FN. The radiator honeycombs were blocked because of poor quality soldering, and the oil went round the cooling system via the bypass valve. This caused the engines to overheat rapidly and fail, making normal operation of the aircraft impossible. Plant No.22 built a total of 32 Pe-2s with M-82 engines (100 were ordered initially), and these were completed to combat capable state in the autumn and winter of 1943-1944, after which they were delivered to various regiments. The 48th Guard Bomber Regiment and the 11th and 99th Special Reconnaissance Air Regiments were among the first to receive several such aircraft. In accordance with an air force decision, the M-82-engined aircraft were to be named Pe-4 from 21st June 1943, but this designation was not widely adopted because of the small number produced. The designation Pe-6 was reserved for the variant with M-107As, but this was also seldom used.

## Pe-2A

Myasishchev gained the assistance of the TsAGI and the People's Commissariat of the Aircraft Industry to improve the production Pe-2. A number of modifications were made to aircraft No.19/205 to reduce drag and increase maximum speed. In addition, the reasons for the deterioration in performance of production aircraft were investigated using the Pe-2A modification of the aircraft (the so-called 'first stage of improvement'), and a programme for large-scale improvement of the Pe-2's structure was worked out. It included the following principal measures:

- changing of the empennage – the rudders became cut through, and the teeth of the tailplane were enlarged, which reduced the drag of the tail surfaces in level flight;
- a new cockpit canopy was installed, similar to that fitted on aircraft No.7/187;
- the water radiators were enlarged and the shape of their intake tunnels improved;
- the exhaust collectors were positioned closer to the cowlings, and the intakes of emission were retracted inside of the wing and cowls of the engines;
- the RDK-10 frame was installed in the wood forward of the fuselage F1, and the antenna became a single wire (only to the starboard fin);
- the external bomb racks were relocated inside the wing.

Some of the innovations tested on the Pe-2A were introduced on production aircraft. The most important characteristic of the aircraft – the maximum speed, began to improve steadily at the end of the summer and in the autumn of 1943. Aircraft No.18/209, which had been modified to have a second internal area filled with neutral gas, achieved a speed of 315mph (507km/h) at the second altitude margin during its test programme in November 1943.

The idea behind the second area containing neutral gas was that, in addition to the fuel tanks, the compartments in which they were housed were also filled with cooled exhaust emissions, reducing the possibility of fire if the wing and tank were shot through.

Another aircraft, No.18/206, was equipped with an experimental exhaust system, the quality of its wing surfaces was improved and VISh-61P propellers were installed. These changes enabled the aircraft to attain a maximum speed of 321mph (518km/h).

## Pe-2B

The next step forward was the Pe-2B, the 1944 version with 1,260hp (939kW) VK-105PF engines. In addition to further aerodynamic improvements and the installation of the combined pilot and navigator's cockpit in the F3 fuselage section at Plant No.19/223, the wooden wing which had by then been ordered by Putilov for the VI high altitude fighter was used. This wing had a NACA 230 section and its area was increased by $26.9\text{ft}^2$ ($2.5\text{m}^2$), which reduced wing loading, improved take-off and landing performance and lessened the tendency of the Pe-2 to fall into a corkscrew at low speeds. The outer wing panels were replaced by the traditional metal units at a later stage of the test programme, but with a changed leading edge of NACA 230 profile up to the front spar. The maximum speed attained by the Pe-2B during the test programme, at a weight of 18,915lb (8,580kg), was 331mph (534km/h) at 12,800ft (3,900m); the time to 16,400ft (5,000m) was 10.5 minutes and its range was 745 miles (1,200km).

## Pe-2RD

Tests with an RU-1 rocket powerplant mounted in the rear fuselage of Pe-2 No.15/185 began in the summer of 1943. The leading engineer for the test programme was Sergei Korolev, later to create the world-famous Soviet space vehicles. The aircraft was powered by an RD-1 rocket with a thrust of 661lb (300kg) at sea level, initially with electric ignition and later with chemical ignition. Two tanks containing kerosene and nitric acid were mounted ahead the engine, and the test engineer was seated in the gunner's position. Compressed air containers were also arranged in the fuselage for 'sub-pressurising' the respective fuel constituents in their tanks. The pumps were gear-driven from the aircraft's M-105PF piston engines.

Test flights showed that the Pe-2 with the RU-1 gained an increase in speed of about 37.2 to 40.3mph (60 to 65km/h) at medium altitudes. However, the motor's deficiencies and brief endurance, the aircraft's reduced fuel load, the aft displacement of the cg, the

Two views of Pe-2 No.19/223 – the Pe-2B – undergoing development tests as the 'Standard for 1944'.

The Pe-2B's redesigned cockpit and gun mount.

Pe-2B prototype used to test a dorsal ShKAS gun mount.

Modified dorsal FZ gun mount during flight test. It was not adopted.

low reliability of RD-1 (Korolev had a narrow escape when the engine exploded on one flight), and also the prolonged period of testing (it continued until mid-1945) determined the fate of the aircraft. Unlike the Lavochkin and Yakovlev fighters fitted with the auxiliary RU-1, the rocket powered 'Pawn' was not built in series.

## Pe-2D, Pe-2M-1, Pe-2I, Pe-2M and Pe-2K

Myasishchev continued the work begun by Putilov on the Pe-2F with M-107A engines and a 'lowered' fuselage (in particular the Pe-2D fitted with the F3 canopy and cockpit), modification of the production Pe-2 with M-107A engines, and a new development of the Pe-2 powered by the M-1. This engine, created by specialists of Plant No.16 of the People's Commissariat of the Aircraft Industry, was a direct development of the M-105, and retained the shape and principal dimensions of the latter (although the cylinder diameter was increased). According to the calculations, the M-1 would give a maximum power of 1,350hp (1,007kW) at ground level and 1,300hp (969 kW) at the second altitude limit of 20,400ft (6,200m). The Pe-2 powered by these engines could reach a speed of 357mph (575km/h) at that altitude without significant changes in the powerplant, but unfortunately the M-1 was not put into production.

Myasishchev then devised a radical modernisation, the Pe-2I, which promised great advances in performance and combat characteristics, in addition to subtle improvement of the production Pe-2 by a considerable number of minor modifications. There was no connection between this version and the Pe-2I (Istrebitel – fighter, or literally 'destroyer') designed in August 1941. Myasishchev's Pe-2I was clearly a further development of the Pe-2F, and repeated the latter concept in its general features: more powerful engines (VK-107As in 1944) and a bigger bomb load (bombs of up to 220lb/100kg in the internal bays), owing to the adoption of the mid-wing configuration. But other components and systems of the Pe-2I were also changed. The aircraft became a two-seater, a mounting for a remote-controlled UBK machine gun (from the VI) was installed in the tail, and the wing structure was changed to that of the last version of the Pe-2B, giving a significantly higher angle of attack.

The Pe-2I's performance was impressive. It had a maximum speed of 407mph (656km/h) at altitude and 343mph (552km/h) at sea level, climbed to 16,400ft (5,000m) in 7.1 minutes and a range of 1,317 miles (2,120km). It was often described as the 'Soviet Mosquito' or the 'Pe-2I Mosquito', likening its operational versatility to that of the celebrated high speed British fighter/bomber/reconnaissance aircraft. Its poor take-off and landing performance was a drawback, as was the non-completion of the remote-control gun mount, series production of which was achieved only with great difficulty.

Being preoccupied with this significant aircraft, Myasishchev and the leadership of People's Commissariat of the Aircraft Industry missed the opportunity to introduce the new F3 cockpit canopy into series production. This was a big mistake. More than a year was lost hoping for a quick introduction of the Pe-2I into production. Throughout 1944 and even at the beginning of 1945 the military specialists of the NII VVS insisted on the necessity of the F1 conversion, as well as adoption of the cockpit as fitted to aircraft No.7/187, but the People's Commissariat of the Aircraft Industry and the leadership of Plant No.22, as though hypnotised by anticipation of the Pe-2I entering large scale production, deferred this requirement and did not take the necessary measures. But production of the Pe-2I never became a flood; there was only a trickle of five aircraft in a small series completed during February-May 1945. These aircraft did not reach the Front and were never used in combat.

The next intended production version became the simplified Pe-2M, which had significantly more powerful defensive armament (in response to the requirements of the military) comprising one fixed UB-20 cannon and two of the same weapons in the navigator's

turret and in the newly introduced gunner/radio operator's position. This variant was short-lived; an edict requiring that work on combat versions of the Pe-2 should cease sealed its fate in June 1945. The four aircraft already built were not received by the VVS. The Pe-2K was slightly more successful. This version of the standard production 'Pawn', fitted with rocket assisted take-off gear, was built in small numbers in February 1945.

A government decree ordered work to be stopped on the last version of the Pe-2, the all-metal PB-2VK-108 with still more powerful engines, and on the VK-109 powered version, which did not progress beyond the drawing board. Plant No.22 was turned completely to the production of training aircraft for combat units and VVS pilots' schools, beginning from

the 492nd series, but the production of this modification also ended in late 1945. During 1940-45 the VVS received a total of 10,574 Pe-2s, including the five Pe-2Is. The overwhelming majority of this total, 9,563 dive bombers, were built at Plant No.22, while Plant No.39 built 895 and Plant Nos.124 and 125 built 104 and 144 respectively.

*For technical data, see Table E, page 169.*

*Top:* **Pe-2A exhaust stubs, the so-called 'TsAGI Mushrooms'.**

*Bottom:* **Retro-fitted Pe-2 No.19/205, becoming the Pe-2A.**

*Top:* **Myasishchev's Pe-2M-1 prototype.**

*Above:* **The Pe-2I featured much cleaner lines than its predecessor. It featured VK-107A engines and a remotely-controlled aft-firing gun.**

*Left:* **De Havilland's Mosquito (high-flying PR.34 illustrated) inspired the Pe-2I and indeed the latter type was referred to as 'the Soviet Mosquito'.** *Ken Ellis collection*

*Below:* **UPe-2 (or sometimes Pe-2UT or Pe-2S) bomber trainer, built and tested after the end of the war.**

The emblem on the nose of this Pe-2 denotes its use with a Guards regiment.

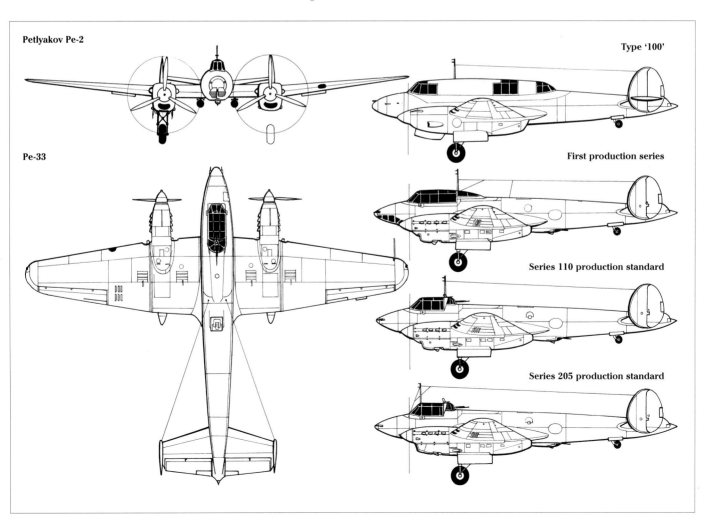

Petlyakov Pe-2

Type '100'

Pe-33

First production series

Series 110 production standard

Series 205 production standard

# TB-7 (Pe-8)

The TB-7 bomber is perhaps one of the few Soviet warplanes built before the war whose history clearly reflects all the distinctive features of aircraft development under the onerous totalitarian Soviet regime of the 1930s and 1940s. The fact that even its designation changed twice (from ANT-42 to TB-7 and then Pe-8) gives food for thought, not to mention that it was twice withdrawn from production.

Preliminary work on a four-engined heavy bomber, initiated at the Konstruktorski Otdel Opytnovo Samolyotostroeniya (KOSOS – Experimental Aircraft Design Section) of TsAGI in July 1934 and headed by Andrei Tupolev, was motivated by the need to continue the TB-1 (ANT-4) – TB-3 (ANT-6) heavy bomber line. As in the case of the TB-3, the design team was led by Vladimir Petlyakov. Its creators thought that the new bomber should be invulnerable to anti-aircraft fire and contemporary fighters and able to hit strategic targets, mainly by virtue of its high altitude capabilities, powerful defensive armament and significant bomb load.

The project, later given the KOSOS designation ANT-42, was based upon the AM-34 engine designed by A Mikulin's team. Series production of this powerful engine, which provided 800hp (596kW) for take-off, had been initiated at the end of 1933. However, it was not a high altitude engine, and it therefore provided a challenging technical problem which was successfully solved by fitting the aircraft with a supplementary engine to drive a compressor for the main engines. KOSOS designers elected to use a liquid-cooled M-100 to drive the compressor. This engine, rated at 860hp (641kW), entered series production in 1935 and was derived from the Hispano-Suiza 12Y by Klimov.

At the beginning of the 1930s Andrei Tupolev had designed the TB-3 heavy bomber, which entered service but did not meet the long term requirements of the VVS. In July 1934 the team led by Petlyakov, which was an organic part of the Tupolev OKB staff, began to design the ANT-42 (TB-7).

In 1931 the NII VVS had raised questions about the development of a modern bomber, and the specifications and requirements were passed to the TsAGI. The aircraft's primary missions were seen as strikes against targets of national importance and strategic significance, the bombing of fleet bases and mass paratroop operations. Its structure was to allow the bomber's alternative use as a heavy escort cruiser with additional gun mountings instead of bombs.

On 27th July 1934 Andrei Tupolev directed the department responsible for the construction of prototype landplanes to begin designing the four-engined TB-7. The aircraft was given the in-house code '42', and during the process of development it was designated '42' or ANT-42, corresponding to the initials of the general designer. The preliminary design was submitted to the VVS in December 1935, and at that time the mock-up was reviewed.

The modern heavy bomber was to be a high altitude aircraft, and a variety of ways of increasing the engine's altitude capabilities were examined, and also the supplementary equipment. It took a long time to find the answer, but at last the idea of the isolated auxiliary engine was conceived. This consisted of an engine coupled to a special supercharger, feeding the bomber's main engines with compressed air in flight. The unit, known as the ATsN (Agregat Tsentralnovo Nadduva) was mounted in the upper part of the fuselage directly above the wing centre section, a location that offered the most convenient layout for the 6ft 6in (2m) diameter air ducts linking the compressor unit with the main engines, which were to be Mikulin AM-34FRNs rated at 1,120hp (835kW) each. Use of a similar engine to drive the supercharger would have facilitated maintenance, but it was too large and was replaced by the compact Klimov M-100, which fitted comfortably.

The Soviet central aero engine institute, the Tsentral'nyi Institut Aviatsionnogo Motorostoeniya (TsIAM – Central Institute of Aviation Motors), was charged with developing a special supercharger and also with integrating it with the M-100. This group worked under the leadership of B Stechkin, A Mikulin and K Minkner. The routing of the air ducts through the airframe, from the supercharger to the main engines, posed many problems.

At the same time means of increasing the speed were found. The angular shape of the first TB-1 and TB-3 heavy bombers, which had caused high drag, was streamlined by the use of wing root fairings, and the corrugated metal skin was replaced by a smooth one. The new bomber's undercarriage design remained the same, with a castoring tailwheel, but the main wheels were made retractable to reduce drag. Variable-pitch propellers were fitted. Due to these alterations, it did not even bear a superficial resemblance to its precursor, the TB-3. It marked a qualitative leap from low to high speed bomber design.

Externally, the aircraft was notable for its different fuselage shape. Because the upper fuselage directly over the wing centre section was the most convenient location for the ATsN, both for installation and maintenance, and its engine nacelle protruded considerably above the fuselage outline, it was possible to fair the canopy into the ATsN housing. For this purpose the pilots' seats were positioned in tandem, installed on a special pilots' floor on the tubular front spar structure of the wing centre section.

The lower fuselage under the wing centre section, where the bomb bay was located, remained wider and corresponded to the fuselage mid-section. This enabled the required bomb load to be stowed there. In the end the mid-fuselage cross-section became pear-shaped. The fairing for the auxiliary engine ended in a powered dorsal turret. Up to the tail the fuselage was of oval section, and ended in a tail gun turret.

The radio operator was positioned on the port side of the fuselage, and the air mechanic was on the starboard side in the pilots' compartment, under the pilots' floor. The reserve navigator's seat was behind him.

The forward fuselage section was oval. A spherical gun turret, rotating on a vertical axis, was mounted in the nose. Behind the turret was the navigator's seat, in a separate glazed nacelle projecting well below the fuselage outline. This gave the navigator-bombardier an excellent field of view for rapid target location and good bomb aiming.

The bomb bay and external brackets mounted under the wing centre section between the fuselage and the inner engines were provided with special carriers which allowed up to 8,818lb (4,000kg) of bombs to be carried, comprising bombs weighing from 220lb (100kg) to 4,409lb (2,000kg) each.

The bomber's defensive armament was very powerful and ensured good cover in all directions. The rear hemisphere, the area most frequently subjected to enemy fighter attacks, was particularly well defended. In the tail there was a rotating turret with a ShVAK gun which covered the entire rear area. In addition, the upper rear hemisphere was covered by a dorsal turret immediately aft of the ATsN, which also covered all of the upper front hemisphere. The underside was very effectively defended by two Berezin large calibre machine guns mounted in the tail ends of the undercarriage housings. Twin 7.62mm ShKAS machine guns were mounted in the nose turret. With such heavy armament the aircraft was a veritable 'flying fortress', and its defensive power and efficiency were borne out in combat during the war.

The latest electrical, radio and navigation equipment was installed, an electrical system being used to power some of the engine control drives, in particular the radiator shutters. The '42' bettered the American Boeing B-17 in bomb load and defensive armament.

ANT-42 undergoing assembly at the Tupolev experimental plant.

The ANT-42 prior to first flight.

State trials of the ANT-42 were carried out side-by-side with the manufacturer's tests, during the winter of 1938-1939.

It could carry 40 x 220lb (100kg) bombs, compared with 16 in a B-17, or two 4,409lb (2,000kg) bombs. The gun armament included two turrets with 20mm guns, whereas the B-17's turrets had only two machine guns.

On 9th November 1936 the completed ANT-42 first prototype was transported to the airfield minus engines. Four AM-34FRNs and one M-100 for the ATsN were received on 23rd December, and the bomber's maiden flight occurred on the 27th. The crew of the massive aircraft included TsAGI test pilot Mikhail Gromov, well known for his long distance flights to the USA, and airman M Zhilin. Manufacturer's development tests began that day, but the aircraft flew for a long time without using the ATsN. Finally, on 11th August 1937, the first day of the state acceptance trials, the ATsN engine was used for the first time. During the tests the aircraft attained a maximum speed of 250mph (403km/h) at 26,250ft (8,000m), a service ceiling of 35,500ft (10,800m). Range was 1,864 miles (3,000km).

The commission noted a number of shortcomings, such as the powerplant's low level of development, difficult controllability and excessive weight. At that time the AM-34FRN engine had not yet undergone state tests, and it did not enter production. Moscow aircraft production Plant No.156, where the design bureau was located and the prototype was constructed, had to eliminate all of the faults by 10th December 1937.

Design of the second prototype ANT-42 had begun in April 1936, and a number of the shortcomings of the first prototype had already been taken into account during the preliminary studies. The fuselage was widened by 4in (100mm), and the rear end was modified to incorporate a new empennage. In accordance with an NII VVS requirement a 20mm gun was installed in the rear turret instead of a machine gun. The wing centre section was widened, the wing structure was improved slightly, and the tailplane's external bracing struts were eliminated. Cables in the flap control system were replaced by tubular linkages near the wing centre section. The undercarriage and the structures of other systems were changed.

Development of the second prototype was finished by 1st January 1938, and it was completed in May of the same year. In the meantime the first prototype ANT-42 underwent joint manufacturer's and state acceptance tests with AM-34FRNV main engines and the M-100 supercharger engine from 6th March to 30th April.

Performance was determined at three gross take-off weights; 52,910lb (24,000kg), 57,319lb (26,000kg) and 61,728lb (28,000kg). Maximum speed at 28,200ft (8,600m) was 267, 260 and 252mph (430, 420 and 406 km/h) respectively, and the time to climb to 16,400ft

(5,000m) was 16.3, 18.8 and 23.3 minutes.

According to a resolution of the State Committee the bomber had the required ceiling and speed, exceeding the performance of many contemporary fighters, and the NII VVS insisted that it be put into production. During the state tests the aircraft was generally referred to as the TB-7 (Tyazhyoly Bombardirovshchik – heavy bomber).

The second prototype's joint VVS and state tests began on 11th August 1938. Its powerplant consisted of four AM-34FRNV engines plus one M-100A engine for the ATsN. Its defensive armament differed from that of the first prototype. Twin 7.62mm ShKAS machine guns were placed in the nose turret instead of the 20mm ShVAK gun, and a similar change was made in the rear turret. The ShVAK guns in the wing positions were also replaced by ShKAS machine guns. Some firing positions, including that of the pilot, were eliminated.

The NII VVS test results for the second prototype were similar to those for the first machine. This aircraft was to set the standard for the initial TB-7 production run at Plant No.124.

Preparation for series production had begun as early as 1937, but was not completed until 1939. It was a long time before a plant was found to build the supercharger units, and this caused great anxiety. When series production started, Plant No.124 obtained ATsNs for the first four aircraft only, and the TsIAM refused to manufacture any more. This was a sad blow, as without the ATsN the bomber's service ceiling was greatly reduced, along with other performance parameters. The advisability of TB-7 production became questionable.

Delivery problems with the AM-34FRNV main engines arose in the second half of 1939, and TB-7 production was halted. The plant had managed to complete only the first two production bombers, and several more were in various stages of construction. Only two of these featured the ATsN superchargers.

At the beginning of 1940 the People's Commissariat of the Aircraft Industry (Aviaprom) gave aircraft Plant No.124 directions and construction of the TB-7 was finally halted, but the Aviaprom authorities realised the need to supply the VVS with the new bombers. At the same time a number of aero-engine design bureaux proposed alternative powerplants for the TB-7.

The newly-appointed director of aircraft Plant No.124, Mikhail Kaganovich, brother of Lazar Kaganovich, one of Stalin's high-ranking officials, also paid great attention to the bomber, and obtained enough of the new 1,200hp (895kW) AM-35A engines to equip the six aircraft then under construction. At the same time a powerplant using Aleksei Dmitriyevich Charomskii's M-30 and M-40 diesel engines was designed.

In the spring of 1941 the first TB-7 powered by M-40s, with a nominal power of 1,000hp (746kW) and a take-off power of 1,500hp (1,119kW) was rolled out. Kaganovich invited Georgy Baydukov, well-known throughout the USSR as a crew member on Valery Chkalov's record-breaking long range flights, to act as its test pilot.

Simultaneously another aircraft powered by M-30s, subsequently redesignated ACh-30B after Charomskii, was constructed. The M-30 and M-40 were essentially the same, but differed in turbo-supercharger dimensions and number. However, in the process of running the diesels it was found that they were unreliable. They were liable to cut out at high altitude because the manually-controlled fuel feed depended on a certain rate of revolutions per minute being maintained, and they could only be restarted at about 1,500m. The M-30 was more reliable in this respect because it had a centrifugal supercharger.

By the end of 1940 Plant No.124 had completed 18 aircraft and delivered them to the VVS, despite constant production stoppages. After the outbreak of war the plant began production of Pe-2s, which drew heavily on the factory's resources, but TB-7 production continued. Complicated and skilful work was undertaken to ensure the aircraft's efficiency. In August 1941 TB-7 formations were organised, one of them led by the well-known Arctic flyer M Vodopyanov. On 9th August the first air raid by these bombers was made on Berlin.

Most of the TB-7s built in 1942 had AM-35As, which were considered more reliable, but engine deliveries suffered frequent hold-ups. It was therefore proposed that Shvetsov-designed 1,850hp (1,380kW) air-cooled M-82s be fitted, though their installation posed problems because wing and engine nacelles needed to be reconstructed and complicated exhaust collectors had to be fitted. Nevertheless, these more powerful engines were installed, and were provided with two-speed superchargers to increase their altitude capability. At first the M-82s ran irregularly because of the turbosuperchargers, but this problem was later eliminated. Adoption of the M-82 meant that Plant No.124 was not short of engines in 1943, and steady production began. In the middle of the war the bomber was redesignated Pe-8 in acknowledgement of Vladimir Petlyakov, who led the team that designed it. He later became leader of the design collective. The bomber's development was controlled by the chief designer at Plant No.124, Joseph Nezval, one of A Tupolev's best assistants, who had taken a most active part in its design.

Production of the M-82-powered Pe-8 continued in 1944. It was believed at the plant that the versions with M-30s and M-40s would no longer be built, but another four aircraft were

*Top left:* **One of the four M-34FRNB engines powering the ANT-42.**

*Top right:* **Each of the inner undercarriage/engine nacelles carried a rearward facing turret.**

*Right:* **ANT-42 nose turret.**

*Below and bottom:* **Two views of an M-40 diesel-engined Pe-8.**

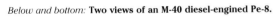

constructed with modified M-30s. However, the performance was not greatly improved.

With a 4,409lb (2,000kg) bomb load and full fuel tanks the Pe-8 powered by AM-35As had a maximum range of 2,236 miles (3,600km). With M-30 or M-40s its range increased to 3,392 miles (5,460km), and with M-82s it was 3,604 miles (5,800km). Most production TB-7s (Pe-8s) had AM-35As, which were the most reliable. Unlike the first prototypes, aircraft powered by M-30s, M-40s, AM-35As and M-82s had no ATsN to enhance their altitude capabilities. In total, 93 aircraft were built (96 according to some sources).

Practically all of the available TB-7 heavy bombers were delivered to the 14th Heavy Bomber Air Regiment, which was non-operational at the beginning of the war. Most of its four-engined giants were awaiting planned modernisation of their engines and replacement of their defensive armament.

A week after the outbreak of war, Stalin took an interest in the status of this unique VVS unit. He summoned to the Kremlin the regiment's commander, Colonel Novodranov, and Colonel Lebedev of the NII VVS, who was responsible for refining the TB-7. The leader, who had repeatedly raised objections against production of the aircraft, regarded the four-engined bomber as a retribution weapon, even if only symbolically, but it was ideal for striking blows against targets deep in the enemy's rear. On Stalin's initiative it was decided to strengthen the regiment immediately by drawing air and ground crews from civil aviation and the NII VVS.

The re-formed regiment was named the 412th, and later the 432nd, and Lebedev became its new commander. Nine of the dozen aircraft built had diesel engines, while the rest had AM-35As. After initial preparations eight M-40-powered aircraft were detached for an attack on the Reich capital. Computations showed that the desired radius of operation could be guaranteed by using the advance airfield at Pushkin, in the environs of Leningrad. Of eight TB-7s that took off on 10th August 1941, only five dropped their bombs on Berlin. The serious losses were due to the low reliability of the diesel engines, which failed to come up to expectations. Seven TB-7s were lost during August 1941, one in a crash, rendering the regiment practically useless. Command quickly took corrective action, re-engining the remaining aircraft with AM-35As. This increased their altitude to 16,400ft (5,000m), clear of anti-aircraft fire.

In October 1941, after replenishment with new aircraft from Plant No.124, the regiment launched raids on Berlin, Königsberg, Danzig and other objectives. In the winter of 1941-42 it was given the unusual tasks of bombing a railway bridge across the Volga in the Kalinin region and delivering a special agent to the Zhitomir area, in the enemy's rear. In April 1942 a crew captained by Major Asyanov accomplished a non-stop flight to Great Britain, carrying embassy officials and diplomatic mail. This flight presaged another, to the USA and back via England, on 19th May 1942. On board for this trip were the Soviet Minister of Foreign Affairs, Vyacheslav Molotov, and his staff. In spite of great difficulties the flight was successful, and the aircraft's commanding officer and navigators Major Romanov and Major Shtepenko were made Heroes of the Soviet Union.

In brief, the results of TB-7 operations at the beginning of the war were as follows. From August 1941 to May 1942 the regiment flew 226 operational missions and dropped 606 tonnes of bombs. The total attrition was 14 aircraft (nine were non-combat losses) and 61 crew members. Seventeen new and modernised TB-7s replaced the casualties.

In May 1942 the government decided to increase TB-7 production in Kazan. As a result the 746th Long Range Regiment (as the unit was named in 1942) was expanded into a two-regiment division. As Colonel Lebedev took command of division, Major N Egorov was placed in command of the 746th Regiment and Major A Lebedev led the newly-created 890th Regiment.

After a short training period the division returned to combat. Its TB-7s bombed enemy positions in the Orel, Bryansk, Kursk and Poltava regions in the summer of 1942, and in August 1942 alone they made as many flights as they had during the preceding ten months.

In the autumn, and especially in the winter of 1942-43, the activities of the TB-7 (redesignated Pe-8 at that time) diminished somewhat. This was partly due to the increased difficulty of operating in winter conditions, and partly to the discovery of serious manufacturing deficiencies which meant that barely half of the available aircraft were usable.

In 1943 Kratovo was the 45th Air Division's main base. Operating from there it bombed enemy airfields, railway lines and stations, and echelons of troops. One of the regular targets was Gomel, in Belorussia, and from February to September 1943 753 tonnes of bombs were delivered on the railway station and other targets, resulting in 139 large conflagrations and 79 explosions.

Operations against troops and material in occupied towns and enemy territory were no less important. The use of 'superheavy' FAB-500 bombs dates from this period, the first being dropped on Königsberg in April 1943.

In July 1943 the Germans strengthened their defences against Soviet heavy night bombers, and their Messerschmitt Bf110 night fighters shot down four aircraft. This was due firstly to the increase in night fighter activity in the Kurskaya Duga area, and sec-

ondly to the fact that the new Pe-8s with M-82 radials were more visible in the night sky because they lacked flame-damping exhausts.

Crews noted both the advantages and disadvantages of the M-82-engined Pe-8. Among the new variant's obvious merits, its increased range was especially appreciated. With a 4,409lb (2,000kg) bomb load it covered almost 3,106 miles (5,000km), some 932 miles (1,500km) further than the AM-35A-powered aircraft. First among the shortcomings was the complex throttle control of the M-82s. Uneven increase of power during take-off could cause the aircraft to veer off, with the attendant danger of damaging its undercarriage. In 1943 alone, six Pe-8s were lost to such accidents. Shortly after the arrival of the M-82-powered aircraft, Pe-8s with ACh-30B diesel engines entered service with the 45th Air Division. Although this engine was considerably more mature than the M-30 and M-40 it was not flawless, suffering frequent failures of its compressor bearings and piston rings. In 1943-1944 the heavy bomber pilots fondly remembered the less powerful and economical but far more reliable AM-35A, the production of which was curtailed.

By the spring of 1944 it was clear that the 45th Division could not be equipped solely with the Pe-8. The production rate was too low, and in the whole of 1944 only five were built. Consequently the VVS Command decided to equip the newly formed 362nd Air Regiment and, partially, the 890th Air Regiment, with US-built North American B-25 Mitchells. From June the flight hours accumulated by the division's Mitchells increased all the time, but even in 1944 the Pe-8s completed 276 operational sorties, including attacks on Helsinki, Nazi-occupied Tallinn and Pskov. However, the number of Pe-8s available decreased steadily, and on the night of 1st/2nd August 1944 the type flew its last operation.

It was clearly necessary to bring Pe-8 operations to an end. In 1942 the loss rate was one aircraft for every 103 flights, but by 1944 on it was up to one for every 46 flights. The aircraft had evidently become obsolescent, and it was impossible to continue using it as a long range heavy bomber. Its high-altitude capability, speed, defensive firepower and reliability were now inadequate. The Pe-8 served in the transport role beyond the war's end.

*For technical data, see Table F, page 172.*

**Production TB-7 (Pe-8) with four AM-37As.**

**A production Pe-8 with M-82s undergoing state flight tests and operational trials at NII VVS.**

*Right:* **A Pe-8 undergoing maintenance under camouflage netting. Note the cased FAB-250 bombs in the foreground.**

A formation of Pe-8s en route to a target.

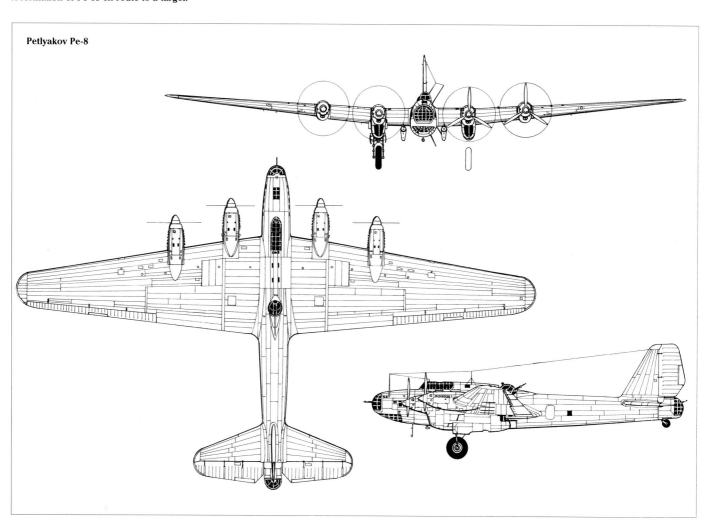

Petlyakov Pe-8

# Polikarpov

## NB('T')

Manufactured in the autumn of 1943, the NB (Nochnoi Bombardirovshchik – night bomber) prototype had been designed at the Polikarpov Design Bureau and was given the factory designation 'T'. It had refined aerodynamics, a twin-fin empennage and high capacity bomb bay, and its overall dimensions were practically the same as those of the production Ilyushin Il-4, though its flying weight and bomb load were significantly greater. The bomber's structure incorporated several innovations, and it had a crew of five. A 4,409lb (2,000kg) bomb load was attached to special carriers in the bomb bay, and externally mounted bombs brought the total bomb load to 1,102lb (5,000kg).

The NB's powerplant consisted of two 1,850hp (1,380kW) ASh-82FNV air cooled engines. Variants were projected powered by 2,000hp (1,492kW) ASh-71s and water cooled AM-39s. Its armament consisted of a fixed 12.7mm UB machine gun mounted in the nose, one UB in an upper turret, and another machine gun in a lower hatch mount.

The maiden flight of the NB(T) took place on 23rd May 1944, and manufacturer's tests began in August. The bomber attained a speed of 316mph (510km/h) at 16,400ft (5,000m), which was rather good at that time. Consequent upon Nikolay Polikarpov's death the tests were not completed and development work ceased.

*For technical data, see Table F, page 172.*

**The five-seat NB was built in the autumn of 1943 and featured wide cockpits and a capacious bomb bay.**

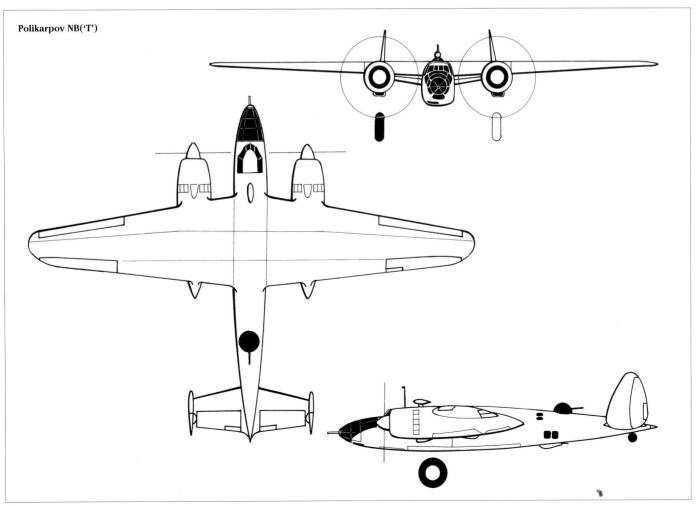

Polikarpov NB('T')

# Tupolev and Arkhangelsky

The name of Tupolev appears rarely in the numerous publications about aircraft of the Second World War. It occurs in connection with the ill-fated SB tactical strike bomber, and with one of the best aeroplanes of the war, the Tu-2, which appeared in late 1942 but was used effectively only at the war's end, when Soviet victory over the Nazis was beyond doubt. Warplanes such as the TB-1, TB-3 and R-6 of the 1930s, the period when Soviet heavy aviation was created, are very seldom mentioned. These aircraft were mainly used in the logistical units of civil aviation, but they were also employed in other activities. During those years a great many munitions factories were functioning without problems, because raw materials and spare parts were delivered on time by air.

The idea of creating the first Soviet heavy bomber arose in the mid-1920s. In late November 1925, test pilot A Tomashevsky first flew the ANT-4, the prototype TB-1 (Tyazhyoly Bombardirovshchik – heavy bomber). After some finishing off and completion of the flight tests, the TB-1 was put into series production. That same year the specialised technical bureau for military inventions, the Ostekhbyuro, offered the Andrei Tupolev Design Bureau the opportunity to develop and build a new heavy aircraft exceeding the TB-1 in payload capability, range, speed and reliability, using all available experience. The Air Force Department of the Soviet Army was also interested in this project. The specified performance of the new aeroplane was as follows: maximum cruising speed, 93mph (150km/h); range, 186 to 217 miles (300 to 350km); and payload capability 3,747lb (1,700kg), including 2,204lb (1,000kg of bombs).

The design task was far from easy, as the methods of prediction and of design itself differed dramatically from those used hitherto. In addition, it was necessary to overcome the conservatism of many foreign aviation companies, which until the 1930s continued to adopt the biplane layout for large aircraft, placing the engines between the wings. Another problem was the lack of an indigenous engine of sufficient power for such a heavy aeroplane. At the same time it was felt of great importance to overcome the Soviet dependence on foreign aviation industries. When the draughting of the design was almost finished and most of the calculations had been done, the powerplant was still undetermined. The new aircraft was to be an all-metal cantilever monoplane with a monoplane tailplane and four engines mounted along the wing.

The designers had to overcome the many differences which constantly arose between them on the one side and the Ostekhbyuro and Air Force Administration on the other. In March 1927 the VVS approved an additional role, according to which the heavy bomber was also to have night capability. It was to be powered by four engines rated at 2,400hp (1,790kW).

Andrei Tupolev, who was working on several other state orders at the time, realised that it would be impossible to build the new aeroplane in time. The reasons for this included the enormous amount of work, the lack of production capacity, and impossibility of complying with constantly changing customer demands. Only by using his authority and diplomacy was Tupolev able to persuade the Aviatrest (the Ministry of the Aircraft Industry) to defer the new experimental heavy bomber's maiden flight until 1930. At an airfield in the suburbs of Moscow on 22nd December 1930 test pilot Mikhail Gromov lifted the experimental ANT-6, powered by four American-built Curtiss Conqueror engines, into the air for the first time. Once the factory and state flight tests were completed in February 1931, the new bomber was adopted by the Soviet Army Air Force under the designation TB-3.

## TB-3

At the very beginning of serial production the American engine was replaced by a German-built BMW-VI and then by the M-17F, the Soviet copy of the German engine. In late 1931 a new engine, designated M-34 and rated at 750 to 830hp (559 to 619kW), passed all of its tests and went into serial production. In January 1933 the drawings for replacement of the M-17Fs with the M-34 were ready, and on 8th March the ANT-6 made its first flight with the new powerplant. Unfortunately it suffered an accident and was heavily damaged. It was not until the autumn that the second prototype was moved to the Air Force Scientific Research Institute for flight testing. This aircraft passed all the tests without any trouble, and showed its superiority over the earlier M-17F-engined version in speed, payload capacity, stability and controllability, as well as in its take-off and landing performance. When the modified M-34 with an increased compression ratio, designated M-34R, and the M-34RN with an even greater compression ratio and supercharging (the power increased to 840 to 970hp – 626 to 723kW) were put into production, all of the TB-3's flying characteristics were significantly improved.

The flypast of the first nine new production bombers over Red Square during the May Day celebration caused a sensation and puzzled Western air force attachés.

Changing the powerplant was not the only way to improve the aircraft. In 1933 the spring shock absorbers of the undercarriage were replaced by oleo-pneumatic shock examples, enhancing safety during take-off and landing. In 1935 the corrugated surface was replaced by a smooth skin, and tests of this modification showed much better flying characteristics. The first serial production bombers had a maximum speed of about 112mph (180km/h) and a service ceiling of 12,500ft (3,800m). Installation of the new powerplant increased maximum speed to 179mph (288km/h) and service ceiling to more than 12,500ft (3,800m). With its new engines the bomber could carry four tonnes of bombs, and the maximum range with a two-tonne bomb load increased to 1,553 miles (2,500km). Defensive armament comprised a single or twin TUR-6 gun turret with 7.62mm-calibre DA machine guns, movable TUR-5 turrets installed immediately aft of the wing and housing one or two DA machine guns, and a dorsal turret with one DA machine gun.

The bombers with M-34R and M-34RN engines differed from the first production TB-3s in the design of their engine cowlings, and the M-34FRN also had a fully glazed cockpit canopy. The two inboard engines of aircraft powered by M-34RNs were installed closer to the fuselage and had four-blade propellers, while the two outboard engines had two-blade propellers. Three-blade propellers were installed on M-34FRN engines.

A large number of heavy bombers were needed to equip the Soviet Army Air Force's newly-created long range bomber force. Only one factory was producing the TB-3, and it could not meet demands. Peotr Baranov, head of Aaviaprom, issued an order for TB-3 production to begin at a second plant which was then busy producing smaller aircraft. Andrei Tupolev appointed Joseph Nezval, a very experienced designer, consultant and director for the introduction of new technologies at the chosen plant.

*Photographs on the opposite page:*

**By the start of the Second World War, the M-17F-powered TB-3 was obsolete, but it still had a useful role to play.**

**Formation of TB-3s.**

**The upper gunner was not protected from the air flow.**

**The rear gunner was situated below the rudder.**

External bomb carriers on the TB-3 were
actuated by a cable drive.

TB-3s also earned their keep as paratroop
platforms.

Paratroops departed the TB-3 via the trailing edge
of the wing.

*Photographs on the opposite page:*

A Polikarpov I-16 suspended under the wing of a
TB-3. This SPB composite was used to good effect
during the war.

An I-16 armed with a pair of FAB-250 bombs slung
under the wing of a TB-3.

Large numbers of TB-3s served with the air
force. A bomber with big bomb load and
strong defensive armament was a significant
force in mid-1930s and the very existence of
the TB-3 served to restrain Japanese mili-
tarism on the USSR's eastern borders.

The TB-3 was used in real combat conditions for the first time in the late 1930s. In the
summer of 1938, 60 TB-3s, flying in large formations, attacked Japanese ground forces in
the region of Hasan Lake. The same tactic
was used in the spring of 1939, during the
Japanese invasion in Khalkhin-Gol. In January 1940 the TB-3s bombed Finnish troops on
the Karelia peninsula.

Under direction of the Headquarters of the
Supreme Commander-in-Chief, during six
days in August 1941 TB-3s repeatedly attacked the German tank columns in the Star-
odub, Trubachevsk and Unech regions.

In the late 1930s the speed of fighters grew
considerably, so the demands placed upon
bombers also had to change. At the very beginning of the Second World War it became
obvious that Soviet long range aviation force
must be equipped with new types of aeroplanes. The TB-3 was used as a heavy
bomber only in the first year of war. As the
fighter units had suffered heavy losses, the
bombers flew their missions without escorts,
and mainly at night.

It was still not really safe to use the aircraft
for bombing, so in an attempt to avoid heavy
losses the command decided to use it only as
a transport to drop cargo by parachute. The
TB-3 had been evaluated in this role before
the war. In the Kiev Military District in September 1935, large scale manoeuvres by different
Soviet Army arms took place. During these
manoeuvres, for the first time in Soviet military history, a mass airborne invasion force including 1,188 paratroopers was used. In an
operation lasting only 110 minutes, heavy aircraft delivered 1,975 soldiers, one T-37 tank,
six trucks and ten artillery pieces on to a 'captured enemy airfield'. To transport bulky

Many difficulties were encountered, and as
a result the products suffered from a mass of
production defects. Nevertheless, work continued and progress was made in spite of the
problems. The first aircraft rolled out of this
factory was flown by Yulian Piontkovsky, and
most of the production bombers were tested
by Valery Chkalov.

From 1932 to 1939 the factories manufactured 818 TB-3s of different variants for a
number of roles. In addition, under the designation G-1 and G-2 the type was also used in
civil aviation as a long range heavy cargo carrier to transport bulky loads to Siberia and the
Far East. Using specially modified aircraft,
personnel and equipment were delivered
right to the North Pole, and on some flights
landings were made on drifting ice. Some of
the most skilled Russian pilots; Mikhail
Vodopyanov, Vasily Molokov, Anatoly Alex-
eev, Ilya Mazuruk and Mikhail Babushkin,
took part in these historic flights.

loads the TB-3 was fitted with a special suspended frame, and it could also accommodate 35 soldiers with ammunition or 30 equipped paratroopers.

In the autumn of 1941, having an advantage over the Soviet Army in combat capable troops and weapons, the Germans opened an offensive in the direction of Moscow. There was a threat that German troops attacking from the south would take Moscow and also capture the Soviet 3rd and 13th Armies, and ground forces in the Orel area required urgent reinforcement.

The Soviet command decided to transport the 5th Air Assault Corps to the region, and 6,000 personnel along with ammunition, armament, trucks and guns were delivered there by air in three days. Two-thirds of the 60 aeroplanes which participated in this operation were TB-3s, and all of the flights were made in daytime without fighter escort. No losses were reported during the operation.

From 18th to 22nd January 1942 TB-3s participated in an operation in which two battalions of the 201st Airborne Brigade and the 250th Airborne Regiment were delivered to the region south of Vyazma. In late September 1942 an airborne force of many thousands was landed at the Bukrinsk foreland by order of Georgy Zhukov, to support units that had crossed the Dnepr. The 53rd Air Division, commanded by Col I Georgiev and equipped with TB-3s, took part.

## SPB Zveno

One of the most persistent problems for long range heavy bombers was that of defence against attack by enemy fighters. The TB-3 had a powerful machine gun defensive armament, and thanks to good design there were no blind spots. Moreover, each zone was covered by two or more gun positions simultaneously. Even this, though, was not a 100% guarantee of protection.

In 1930 engineer Vladimir Vakhmistrov suggested to Andrei Tupolev the idea of a flying aircraft carrier, consisting of a large aeroplane serving as a carrier for several fighters. By this means the combat range of the fighters was considerably increased, for they could be released from the parent aircraft in flight, fulfil their mission and return to either the nearest airfield or their home base. This idea was approved by the Air Force Department, and in late 1931 the first airborne aircraft carrier based on the TB-1 bomber was tested.

Later a TB-3 was converted for the same purpose. In this form it was able to carry five fighters at a time, two I-5s, two I-16s and one I-Z, the last of which hooked on to the undercarriage in flight. The state tests in September 1933, flown by test pilots Peotr Stephanovsky, Stepan Suprun, Vasily Stepanchonok and others, showed the high reliability of this system, which was named Zveno (link). During the next ten years the system was improved, and

more TB-3s were converted into flying aircraft carriers. In one variation of the Zveno system two Polikarpov I-16 fighters, attached beneath the wings of the carrier, were able to take two 551lb (250kg) bombs each and act as high speed dive bombers once released. This new variation of the system was named Skorostnoy Pikiruyuschy Bombardirovschik (SPB – high speed dive bomber). The SPB was successfully used in the Black Sea Fleet in the defence of Sevastopol.

On 1st August 1941 two TB-3s carried four I-16s armed with eight FAB-250 bombs to the Romanian city of Konstanza. During their mission they totally destroyed a floating dock, the oil refining plant in Ploesti and several military ships. One of the most difficult tasks was the destruction of the Chernovodsk bridge over the Danube, on the region's main supply line, along which enemy fuel and technical equipment was transported to the front line. On several occasions Pe-2s and Il-4s had tried to carry out the mission, but without success. In August 1941 the SPBs made two attacks. During the first flight four I-16s launched from a pair of TB-3s blew up the central 459ft (140m) pier, together with the oil pipeline and the coastal oil pumping station. During the second raid six I-16s released from three TB-3s completely destroyed the railway.

*For TB-3 technical data, see Table F, page 172.*

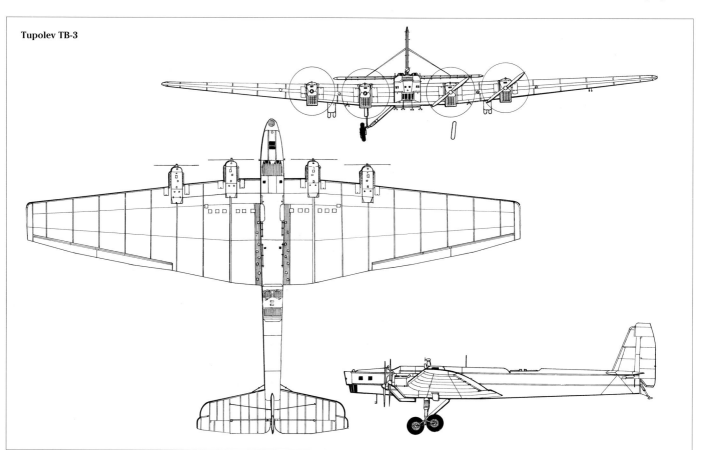

**Tupolev TB-3**

First prototype SB, with Wright Cyclone engines.

## SB (ANT-40)

The SB bomber was one of the aircraft designed in the mid-1930s which took part in the Second World War. In the early 1930s the average speed of bombers was 155 to 167mph (250 to 270km/h), and they could operate only with a fighter escort, so a design requirement was issued for a bomber able to fly missions unescorted.

Andrei Tupolev and his associate Aleksandr Arkhangelsky received the VVS's new request for proposals enthusiastically. On 21st February 1934 the chief of the TsAGI chaired a meeting at which a plan for the design of the ANT-40 twin-engined high speed bomber was adopted. In March the VVS sent the TsAGI a technical specification outlining the required performance of the ANT-40 bomber. It had to have a maximum speed of 205mph (330km/h) at 13,200ft (4,000m), a service ceiling of 26,250ft (8,000m), a range of 434 miles (700km) and the ability to carry a 1,102lb (500kg) bomb load. Its defensive armament was to include a nose gun mounting with two 7.62mm ShKAS machine guns, and an upper turret and lower hatch mountings with the same weapons.

Following detailed discussion with the VVS representatives, the designers decided to develop a completely new aircraft embodying the latest aerodynamics, technology and metallurgy. The corrugated Duralumin skinning used hitherto had caused high aerodynamic drag, and simply covering the corrugated skin

with fabric or plywood resulted in a structure that was too heavy and lacked strength, apart from the technological difficulties.

On 1st January 1934 a new team headed by Arkhangelsky was organised at the TsAGI to design the new aircraft. A month later, when the plans had yet to be adopted, the designers began the major design task.

Three months later, on 8th March 1934, after intensive work, the preliminary design for the new bomber was presented to the VVS for adoption. The airframe and primary structural members were designed to a new concept. The layout was based on that idea that the overall dimensions should be the smallest possible to carry the specified 1,102lb (500kg) bomb load and powerful armament, and the whole bomb load was to be housed internally in the fuselage. Tupolev had decided to use Duralumin skinning, and the aerodynamic lines were perfect, without any protrusions. On 10th March the mock-up was approved, and at the same time it was decided to build the first ANT-40 prototype, powered by American-built 730hp (544kW) Wright Cyclone air cooled radial engines, by 15th July 1934, and the second, powered by French Hispano-Suiza engines, by 15th August.

Construction of the first aircraft began on 25th April, and on 7th October 1934 it made its first flight, piloted by K Popov. The bomber's Cyclone engines drove three-bladed variable pitch propellers. During production tests from 7th to 31st October nine flights were made. During its last test flight the aircraft crashed on landing, and was delivered to the TsAGI for repair. This took three months, and the second phase of testing did not begin until 5th

February 1935, by which time the aircraft was slightly modified. Although the wing had the same span (62ft 4in – 19m), its area was reduced from 512.3 to 498.3ft$^2$ (47.6 to 46.3m$^2$). At a flying weight of 10,399lb (4,717kg) the aircraft had a maximum speed of 201mph (325km/h) at 13,100ft (4,000m), a service ceiling of 22,300ft (6,800m) and a landing speed of 62 to 68mph (100 to 110km/h).

By 31st July 1935 the tests had been completed, and the prototype was converted into an experimental aircraft and turned over to the TsAGI's Experimental Flight Test Department as a flying test-bed. Retractable skis and Hamilton variable pitch propellers were tested from 21st February to 11th March 1936.

Construction of the second ANT-40 prototype began on 15th May 1934. Its two 780hp (581kW) Hispano-Suiza 12Ybrs water-cooled engines drove two-bladed propellers of 11ft 2in (3.4m) diameter, produced at Plant No.28. Because of the greater weight of the engines, the wingspan was increased to 66ft 7in (20.3m), the area being correspondingly greater at 559ft$^2$ (51.95m$^2$). On 30th December this aircraft was ready, and immediately began preliminary production testing. On that same day pilot I Zhukov took it on its maiden flight, and the tests continued until 21st January 1935. The greatest speed attained at 13,100ft (4,000m) was 267mph (430km/h), considerably higher than the specified speed. A test commission noted in the conclusions of its report that the aircraft had a high performance and could be used as a high speed bomber. However, it was necessary to conduct a second series of tests to obtain a more objective performance estimation.

The first stage of the state trials of the second ANT-40 prototype were conducted at the NII VVS and TsAGI from 8th February to 3rd March 1935. The aircraft was equipped with a ski undercarriage, and its flying weight was 11,022lb (5,000kg). Although the aircraft's maximum speed fell to 218mph (351km/h) at 13,200ft (4,000m), its absolute service ceiling increased to 30,800ft (9,400m).

On 3rd March the aircraft crashed when the wing skin failed owing to vibration, and the tests were interrupted while the cause was investigated. At the TsAGI the nature of the failure was investigated by future academician Mstislav Keldysh. The cause was determined to be wing-aileron flutter, and this was eliminated a few days later by fitting aileron mass balances. From then onwards it became standard practice to fit mass balance weights to the control surfaces of high speed aircraft.

Repair work continued until April. During that time the engines were moved forward 4in (100mm) and the leading edge sweep back of the outer wing panels was increased from 4.5° to 9°. From 9th April to 16th June 1935 the TsAGI conducted development tests to improve the bomber's structure and performance according to the NII VVS requirements.

On 16th June the aircraft was handed over to the military representative for its state trials. After modification the aircraft's empty weight had increased by 1,435lb (651kg) to 8,527lb (3,868kg), having been 7,092lb (3,217kg) at the time of the preliminary production tests. The second stage of the state trials lasted from 16th June to 17th July.

For this stage of the tests, which it passed, the bomber was equipped with a conventional wheeled undercarriage. Flying weight was reduced to 10,709lb (4,858kg), its maximum speed at 16,400ft (5,000m) was 251mph (404km/h) and its service ceiling was unchanged.

The State Commission noted a number of shortcomings and defects, and demanded that additional tests be conducted after these had been eliminated. These tests were conducted from October 1935 to April 1936, after which the aircraft was passed to Moscow Plant No.22 to serve as a standard for series production.

On 2nd March 1936 pilot M Alexeyev submitted to the TsAGI a report concerning the possibility of establishing new world payload-to-height records using the ANT-40 which he saw as an ideal aircraft for such prestigious ventures. His estimates were proved completely correct. On 1st November 1936 the Hispano-Suiza powered ANT-40 reached an altitude of 41,650ft (12,695m) with a 2,204lb (1,000kg) payload, but this achievement was recorded only as a national record.

## SB-2M100 and SB-2M100A

The problem of introducing the new bomber into series production had been solved much earlier, in March 1934. The Soviet Air Force urgently needed such a bomber, and for that reason the delivery of technical documentation to Plant No.22 had begun as early as March 1935, before the state trials were completed. In mid-1936, at the decision of the government, the 5th TsAGI brigade of the Experimental Flight Test Department, headed by Arkhangelsky, was sent to the plant as a separate design bureau to update the ANT-40 and prepare it for production. The aircraft was redesignated SB (Skorostnoy Bombardirovschik – high speed bomber).

The pre-production SB, manufactured in the spring of 1936, was powered by 750hp (559kW) M-100 engines, licence-built Hispano-Suizas. Like the second prototype this aircraft had 11ft 2in (3.4m) diameter two-blade propellers, but it had greater wing and tailplane areas, which increased its weight. Its armament consisted of three gun mountings. Two movable 7.62mm ShKAS machine guns provided with 1,000 rounds were installed in the fuselage nose, a turret with a ShKAS machine gun and 1,000 rounds was mounted in the upper rear fuselage, and there was a hatch mounting with a ShKAS machine gun and 500 rounds. The bomb bay was in the middle of the wing centre section. The bombs, one of 1,102lb (500kg) or up to six to a total of 1,322lb (600kg), were carried on racks.

To assess the bomber's performance, service trials were conducted from 25th March to 31st July 1936. Six aircraft of the initial batch (constructor's Nos.221, 222, 226, 227, 228 and 229) participated in these tests. The average flying weight was 12,407lb (5,628kg), and empty weight 8,950lb (4,060kg). The maximum speed at 17,000ft (5,200m) was 244mph (393km/h), and service ceiling was reduced to 29,500ft (9,000m). Although performance was inferior to that of the second machine, the aircraft nevertheless met the VVS requirements. In the final report on the service tests it was recommended that the SB-2M100 be introduced into the inventory.

Full scale production of the SB was an important milestone for the Soviet aircraft industry. As early as 7th November 1936 production aircraft flew over Red Square, and earlier, in September, the crews of the SBs had engaged in aerial combat over Spain, on the side of the Republican Army.

Mass production of the SB had some negative aspects. Simplification of the technology and the elimination of lightened structural members made the aircraft overweight and increased its aerodynamic drag, thereby reducing maximum speed. To improve performance, more powerful engines were installed. In December 1936 SB bomber production No.22200 was built with new 860hp (641kW) M-100As. Flying weight increased to 12,636lb (5,732kg), maximum speed at 13,200ft (4,000m) increased up to 268mph (432km/h), and the service ceiling was 31,300ft (9,560m). Production of the M-100A powered version was started.

Combat experience in the Spanish Civil War also resulted in changes to the bomber's structure, armament and equipment. In 1937 several structural changes were made. A new MV-3 machine gun mounting and a lower hatch mount with an OP-2 optical sight were installed; the pilot's and navigator's cockpits were joined by means of three shields, and the bulkhead behind the pilot's seat was removed; the instrument panels were re-equipped; and an additional faired rear view mirror was positioned over the windshield.

Test of the updated bomber were conducted in May-June 1937, attention being concentrated on revised armament, equipment and armour. Take-off weight had increased to 12,808lb (5,810kg), and maximum speed at 13,200ft (4,000m) was slightly reduced to 256mph (412km/h). The aircraft passed its state trials and was put into production.

## SB-*bis*-2M103 and SB-*bis*-2 2M103

In the middle of 1937 there arose the possibility of fitting the SB with new, more powerful M-103s rated at 960hp (716kW). A prototype was built at two Moscow Plants, Nos.22 and 156, and differed significantly from the production aircraft. The M-100As were replaced by M-103s, and new radiators had to be installed. The engine cowlings were also changed, and three-bladed variable pitch propellers replaced the two-bladed VISh-2s. The undercarriage, flaps and lower engine cowling control systems were redesigned, a new castoring tailwheel with a lock, controlled from the cockpit, was installed, and the navigator's cockpit was enlarged to accommodate dual controls. The aircraft's equipment was also changed. As a result the flying weight rose considerably to 14,166lb (6,426kg).

During the state trials the Commission noted a series of shortcomings, including a decreased margin of safety and the increased complexity of the navigator's task in his new cockpit. Moreover, it was noted that the redesigning of the powerplant gave no benefits because the bomber's aerodynamics had suffered. A series of recommended modifications was worked out, to be tested on the prototype in 1938. Plant No.22 was ordered to build several SB prototypes incorporating all of the alterations adopted during the testing of the SB-2M100A, but powered by the new M-103.

In September 1937 pilot M Alexeyev set a new world payload-to-height record flying the SB-bis-2M103, reaching 40,178ft (12,246.5m) with a 2,204lb (1,000kg) payload. In March 1938 an SB powered by M-103s driving VISh-2 propellers, and with a polished wing surface and a ski undercarriage, underwent state trials at the NII VVS. Thanks to the increased power the take-off run was reduced to 820 to 918ft (250 to 280m).

## SB-bis-3 2M103 and SB-2M103

On 1st November 1937 the M-103 powered SB-bis-3 prototype with modifications to the powerplant installation went for its state trials. Duct-type coolers were used instead of nose radiators, and the water cooled oil radiators replaced by air cooled units. These changes improved the aircraft's aerodynamics, and hence its performance. At a flying weight of 13,256lb (6,013kg) its maximum speed was 233mph (375km/h) at sea level, 276mph (445km/h) at 14,750ft (4,500m) and 253mph (408km/h) at 23,000ft (7,000m). On 17th January 1938 the state trials were completed. In spite of the unreliability of the powerplant, the Commission recommended that the Air Force Administration introduce the SB-bis-3 with updated engines into series production. Plant No.22 was ordered to retrofit the powerplant and to submit the aircraft for testing once again. Development of the bomber continued throughout 1938, and during that time a number of production SBs were built with the SB-bis-3-type powerplant. These aircraft were designated SB-2M103.

The state trials of SB-2M103 No.1/83 were carried out at the NII VVS from 27th July to 19th September. This aircraft, which was intended to set the production standard for the second half of 1938, had the following significant features:

• Der-19 underwing bomb racks to carry 551 and 1,102lb (250 and 500kg) bombs were installed – the bomb load was increased to 3,306lb (1,500kg);
• an AFA-13 camera was fitted;
• the undercarriage operating system was replaced by one using electro-hydraulics;
• an additional mechanical bomb dropping system controlled from the pilot's cockpit was introduced;
• a ¼in (6mm) thick armoured pilot's seat was fitted in the cockpit.

In overload the bomber could carry three 1,102lb (500kg) bombs. It was tested at the normal flying weight of 13,613lb (6,175kg) and at a maximum weight of 17,085lb (7,750kg).

At normal weight it reached a speed of 160mph (258km/h) at sea level and 260mph (419km/h) at 13,200ft (4,000m), while the corresponding figures at maximum weight were 205 and 234mph (330 and 378km/h). The rate of climb was considerably reduced, as was service ceiling at 24,600ft (7,500m). The M-103 powered aircraft with the additional bomb load and full tanks had a performance equal to that of a production SB-2M100A, and it was recommended as a standard for series production. During 27th-28th September the same version underwent additional testing with overload. It was determined that an automatic propeller was necessary to increase the maximum speed of the aircraft in this condition.

In order to increase range, an SB-2M103 from the 96th series built at Plant No.22 was equipped with two 83.5 gallon (380 litre) external fuel tanks. The state trials of this aircraft, conducted at the NII VVS from 20th September to 8th October 1938 at a flying weight of 13,613lb (6,175kg), yielded maximum speeds of 211mph (340km/h) at sea level (224mph/362km/h without external tanks) and 243mph (392km/h) at 4,000m (257mph/415km/h). Time to climb to 16,400ft (5,000m) was 9.1 minutes (8.1 without external tanks). Although this performance with increased range met VVS requirements, the method of dropping the fuel tanks was underdeveloped, and it was necessary to conduct additional tests to ensure safe release in different modes of flight.

Aircraft No.13/221, which Plant No.22 handed over for testing in November 1939 as a standard for series production, had undergone the following changes:

• new ducted water coolers with constant inlets were installed;
• the gap between the propeller spinner and engine cowling was closed;
• fairings were fitted at the inlet pipe and where the control surfaces were hinged to the flying surfaces;
• a separate adjustable water cooler cap control was rigged up;
• the aircraft was given two coats of paint and the wing and empennage leading edges were polished.

In addition, several other changes were introduced. This version proved successful, being recommended as the standard for the 201st production series. At a flying weight of 14,065lb (6,380kg) its maximum speed at 13,500ft (4,100m) was 279mph (450km/h).

The SB was in large scale production at two factories, and in the late 1930s output reached eleven aircraft per day. From 1936 to 1940 a total of 6,656 SBs of all versions were produced.

When its opponents encountered the new Soviet bomber in operation with the Spanish

Republican Air Force they had a great surprise. The SB's high speed (almost matching that of the fighters), powerful armament and ability to fly both day and night missions allowed heavy strikes to be delivered against hostile troops.

In 1937 the bomber successfully participated in Chinese Army operations during the war with Japan, and the SB squadrons played a significant role in the conflict near Lake Hasan. In the summer of 1939 they took part in the bombing of the Japanese front line near the Khalkhin-Ghol River. During 1939-1940 SBs were in action in the war with Finland. A few were captured, and after repair were operated by the Finnish Air Force.

The SB high speed bomber was operated by the Soviet Air Force until the end of 1942. By that time, however, the aircraft's speed and bomb capacity were insufficient to meet VVS requirements, and those remaining were gradually turned over to the Civil Air Fleet.

## USB

The appearance of a considerable number of high speed bombers in VVS units led to the need for a trainer version. Such an aircraft, based on the SB-2M100A production bomber and equipped with a special trainer cockpit, was developed at Plant No.22. An additional cockpit for the instructor replaced the navigator's cockpit in the nose, and was provided with dual control and all the necessary equipment and instrumentation. The cockpit was designed in such a way that it could be installed in place of the navigator's position by VVS units in the field.

Although the trainer version successfully passed its state trials during 11th-16th March 1938, only the new cockpit was recommended for production. This could be retro-fitted to production SBs if necessary. The Commission, which made some suggestions concerning the trainer's cockpit, proposed that Plant No.22 should modify it further and then re-submit it for further tests. Nevertheless, only a small series of USB (Uchebnyi - trainer, SB) were produced.

## MMN-2M105

After the designers of the Tupolev Design Bureau had been modifying the SB for five years, the requirements for that class of bomber changed. To attain the speed of 310mph (500km/h) now desired, it was necessary not only to improve the aerodynamics but also to use more powerful engines.

In September 1939 the MMN (modified

smaller lifting surface) high speed bomber prototype powered by with two 1,050hp (783kW) M-105 engines was sent to the NII VVS for its state trials. A further development of the SB bomber, it featured an 86ft$^2$ (8m$^2$) reduction in wing area. The structure of the outer wing panels was simplified, the spars being replaced by shielded walls and the truss ribs being pressed parts. The fuselage nose was more streamlined and housed only one 7.62 ShKAS machine gun instead of two, dual control was installed in the navigator's position, the lower gun mounting was closed by a hatch, and an MV-3 turret was installed in the dorsal position. Two additional fuel tanks each of 45 gallon (205 litre) capacity were fitted in the outer wing panels, the areas of the ailerons and tail surfaces were changed and the flap area was considerably increased, and an emergency undercarriage extension system was installed in the cockpit.

In spite of its considerable structural alterations, simplified production technology and new powerplant, the bomber did not yield the desired improvement in performance. With the same flying weight during its flight tests the MMN had a maximum speed of 284mph (458km/h) at 13,800ft (4,200m) and 251mph (405km/h) at sea level, while it took 9.3 minutes to reach 16,400ft (5,000m). Early in 1949 such performance was completely unsatisfactory, and development of the MMN was halted. Nevertheless, the State Commission recommended that several of the MMN's new structural features be introduced in the structure of the production SB bomber. The fuselage nose was changed to take a new gun mount and a dual control, the upper turret of TUR-9 type was replaced by an MV-3, the LU hatch mounting was replaced by an MV-2 turret, and the emergency undercarriage extension system was fitted in the cockpit.

## SB in service

The final episode in the Tupolev SB's history began with the invasion of the Soviet Union by Hitler's Wehrmacht. By the middle of June 1941, 71 of the 82 Bomber Air Regiments operated different and already outdated versions of the SB. Of these, 45 were located in the Leningrad, Baltic, West Kiev and Odessa air force military districts on the eve of the invasion. German reconnaissance estimated the total number of SBs near the border at 1,200 to 1,500, but in fact at the beginning of the war there were 1,428, of which 1,262 were airworthy.

A number of problems prevented the use of this force. Firstly, combat aircraft were distributed unevenly among the Air Regiments. At the beginning of February 1941, for exam-

ple, the 134th Short Range Bomber Air Regiment of the Moscow military district received an additional 19 Arkhangelsky Ar-2s, and although its 19 SBs appeared to be surplus to requirements they remained in the regiment until the middle of May. At the same time the regiments of the 23rd Air Division had only half of their required quota of aircraft.

Secondly, bombing accuracy was too low. Although special Dive Bomber Air Regiments equipped with SBs and Ar-2s had been established before the war, their crews had not undergone any intensive training and the regiments differed only slightly from ordinary units.

Thirdly, many combat regiments were located ineffectively near the borders. The 22 Ar-2s and 22 SBs of the 13th Mixed Bomber Air Regiment of the 9th Mixed Bomber Air Division, based at Borisovshchina airfield, only 43 miles (70km) from the border, suffered significant damage at the beginning of the invasion. Even more unfortunate was the 16th Mixed Bomber Air Regiment of the 11th Mixed Bomber Air Division, which lost 23 SBs and all of its new high speed Pe-2s in one blow.

In summing up the events of the first day of the war, it can be said that, on the whole, bombers suffered less than fighters, but their activities were hampered by the breakdown in control and communication, as well as by the inadequate combat training of the pilots. Especially heavily burdened were the crews of the 12th and 13th Bomber Air Division, who accomplished a difficult task, namely destroying a Nazi tank force which had penetrated the Soviet front in the region of the Suvalkin salient. There were no escort fighters at all, because the air force of the Western Military District had lost 528 fighters during the first day. On the following day, 22nd June 1941, nine of the SBs were attacked by eleven Bf109s, and in the ensuing combat three Messerschmitts and four bombers were destroyed. A real air battle raged in the Western Military District on 30th June, when German troops were crossing the Beresina river. Several aviation units opposed them, in particular the SBs of the 128th, 6th, 121st, 125th, 130th and 24th Bomber Air Regiments. Led by G Beletsky, the pilots of the last unit, who had some combat experience, particularly distinguished themselves.

But the regiments suffered incredible losses. In some air combats more than nine SBs were shot down. According to German records their fighters shot down 110 Soviet aircraft that day, and these figures are almost certainly correct. The SB formations manoeuvred badly, and their gunners could not provide effective defensive fire. In appreciation of the SB, German General Schwabedissen, referring to German experts, wrote, on page

143 of *The Russian Air Force in the Eyes of German Commanders*:

'The SBs carried a crew of three and were armed with three swivel-mounted machine guns. Their firepower was inadequate against fighters, in spite of the fact that their bottom gondola, a feature unknown to the Luftwaffe before the war, made it possible for them to fire downwards to the rear and sideways to the rear. They could carry a bomb load of 2,200lb [997kg]. The main weakness of these aircraft was their high inflammability. Their fuel tanks were unprotected, and the gravity-feed tanks over the engines were easily ignited by gunfire, thus causing the engines to burn.'

The SBs on the South Western Front fought more successfully. They too suffered heavy losses during the first days of fighting, but they did not lose their fighting efficiency. The 94th Mixed Bomber Air Regiment, commanded by Colonel Nikolaev, delivered particularly effective blows against tank clusters. Their SBs, in contrast with those of neighbouring units, fought in small groups, and were based close to the front line so that they could carry higher bomb loads, but their losses were also heavy, totalling 14 aircraft.

At the beginning of the war the greatest operation on the Northern Front, under Commander-in-Chief General A Novikov, was a blow delivered against enemy airfields located on Finnish territory. A total of 236 bombers, most of them SBs, were escorted by 224 fighters, and up to 30 aircraft were destroyed on the airfields and another eleven enemy fighters fell in the air battles. The Soviet Air Force lost 23 SBs, almost all over the hostile airfields, which they attacked without fighter escort. This pre-emptive strike gave the Soviets air superiority for a time, and the Luftwaffe was forced to withdraw its aircraft into the deep rear. On this occasion the Tupolev bomber units were well organised.

It was on the Northern Front that the first Soviet Second World War pilots to become Heroes of the Soviet Union appeared. Among them were SB formation commanders Captain A Michailov of the 10th Mixed Bomber Air Regiment and First Lieutenant P Markutsa, who were so honoured on 22nd July 1941. Markutsa's SB was shot down during a reconnaissance flight. He escaped from the aircraft in the enemy's rear, met soldiers of the 749th Rifle Regiment in a forest, trying to make their way home, and led them out of encirclement. Like many of his comrades this bold pilot died in battle, in December 1941.

Aware of the mistakes made by Soviet bomber units on other fronts, the SB crews of the 1st and 2nd Mixed Air Division of the Northern Front tried to keep close formation when attacked by enemy fighters, thereby achieving the greatest possible concentration

*Top left:* **Detail view of the rear upper turret.**

*Top right:* **SB nose turret.**

*Centre and above:* **Early production series SB with M-103 engines and honeycomb radiators.**

of defensive fire. Due to their successful co-ordination the gunners frequently managed to keep the enemy at a distance.

Attempts to use the SB's high speed to break away from attacking Messerschmitts proved unsuccessful. This tactic, which pilots had used in Spain and Mongolia, was useless against Luftwaffe pilots. The bomber was at least 62mph (100km/h) slower than Bf 109E and 46mph (75km/h) slower than the Bf 110C, so the break-away manoeuvre would fail, the combat formation was opened out, co-ordinated defensive fire became impossible and the bombers suffered losses.

Under these conditions from 5th to 10th July 1941 a total of 60 SBs were lost on the Northern Front. Fortunately, because there was no firm front line, two-thirds of the crews shot down managed to return to their regiments. In one month the huge armada of SBs on the Western Front practically ceased to exist. By 24th July there were only 875, representing 57% of all tactical bombers. The SBs soon began to operate with fighter escort and to fly at night.

Tupolev SBs were used in the same manner during the battle for Moscow. Existing combat units were considerably battered, so General Headquarters decided to transfer the 1st, 34th and 459th Bomber Air Regiments, with 60 SBs, from the rear areas and place them at the disposal of the Commander-in-Chief of the Western Front VVS. In October, during the first air battles for Moscow, the crews of the 173rd and 321st Bomber Air Regiment, partly equipped with SBs, distinguished themselves. According to German documents and prisoners' statements the effectiveness of the night bombers was relatively high, and the enemy suffered considerable losses to their attacks.

During the battle for Moscow the SB (ANT-40) was used as well as the PS-41 (ANT-41) transport aircraft to carry equipment, food

and ammunition to combat units which, for a variety of reasons, had become separated from their main formations.

The aircraft also supported Moscow Air Defence units. A specially formed night air group led by Major Karpenko was used to distract German bombers from their intended targets and to illuminate hostile aircraft at night, using powerful lights installed on the wings of the SBs for that purpose. Although the group operated in the region of Medyn for only a short time, it played an important part.

On the whole, however, the SB's role in the air war was not great. It was difficult to replace losses owing to the shortage of aircraft, and only 97 SBs remained in the combat units by the time of the winter counter-offensive by Soviet troops. Of these, only 60 could be considered as airworthy.

Late in 1941 the SB's operational service was assessed. The Luftwaffe had destroyed more than 1,700 front line aircraft; two-thirds of the total losses. The SB was also used by Soviet naval aviation. It can be confidently stated that no other combat aircraft suffered losses as high as the SB bomber.

In 1942 SBs were not used so intensively. The crews of the combat regiments had learned how to avoid interception, putting an end to daytime flights. Because of this it should come as no surprise that losses in the SB fleet for the whole of 1942 were ten times lower than those in the second half of 1941.

The 33rd Mixed Bomber Air Regiment, led at first by Colonel F Pushkaryov and later by Major K Rasskazov, was one of the most successful SB regiments in 1942 and the beginning of 1943.

Above: Night operations with ski undercarriage.

Left: The lack of ski conversion kits forced most SBs to operate on snow using their wheeled undercarriage.

# SB-RK (Ar-2)

A most interesting version of the SB bomber originated from the Arkhangelsky OKB during 1938-1939. This was powered by two new 1,050hp (783kW) M-105s with two-stage superchargers, driving 9ft 10in (3m) diameter VISh-22E propellers, the pitch angles of which were automatically adjusted in flight from 21° to 41° by means of an engine speed governor. Instead of having the radiators under the nacelles, the designers mounted them for the first time in the wing leading edges, greatly reducing drag. The whole powerplant was lowered to merge smoothly into the wing, and this also improved the view from the cockpit. The wingspan was reduced to 59ft (18.0m), and the wing area to 518ft² (48.2m²). Designated SB-RK, the aircraft was built in 1940.

While it was still in design and development the SB-RK became obsolete, and it was decided to convert it into a dive bomber. The nose was made more streamlined, the navigator's cockpit redesigned and provided with a movable seat, and dual controls were fitted to increase survivability. Total fuel capacity was increased to 490 gallons (2,230 litres) by the addition of two 81 gallon (370 litre) external fuel tanks. One 7.62mm ShKAS machine gun was installed in the forward fuselage, instead of the SB-RK's two, and the maximum bomb load was 3,306lb (1,500kg).

The elevator trim tab setting made the aircraft enter a dive easily, and recovery was made automatically after the bombs had been dropped. The aircraft's maximum level speed was 313mph (505km/h), and its service ceiling increased to 31,200 to 32,800ft (9,500 to 10,000m). Maximum range with a 1,102lb (500kg) bomb load was over 1,304 miles (2,100km) and with a 2,204lb (1,000kg) bomb load it was 621 miles (1,000km). The modified bomber successfully completed its state trials, and the government decreed it was to replace all other SBs from August 1940. Production did not begin until October 1940.

In December the production SB-RK was given the designation Ar-2, incorporating the name of the chief designer of Plant No.22 in Moscow. By March 1941 198 Ar-2s had been produced at the plant, when concentrated on the more advanced Pe-2. Ar-2s served during the early years of the Second World War.

**These very rare illustrations of Ar-2s are of captured examples on former Soviet airfields.**

**Arkhangelsky Ar-2**

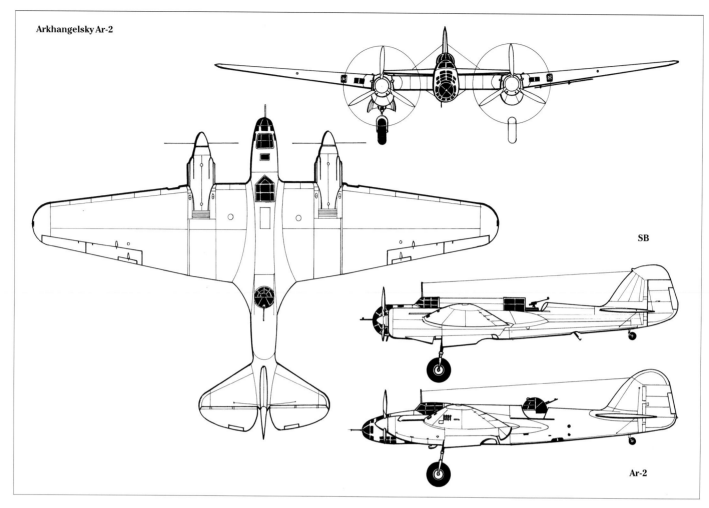

SB

Ar-2

## SBB-1 ('B')

The designer of the SB, Arkhangelsky, tried to increase its speed and bomb load to convert it into a dive bomber even after it had gone into full-scale production. Late in 1939, with experience gained in SB and SB-RK production, he began designing a new dive bomber with two M-105s, designated 'B', at Plant No.22. This was a three-seat mid-wing monoplane with twin fins and rudders, carrying a crew consisting of a pilot, navigator and radio operator/gunner. It had an all-metal structure and a streamlined fuselage. The increased area of glazing provided a good view compared with that from the MMN.

The two-spar wing had a metal stressed skin. The water radiators were mounted between the spars in the wing centre section. The main undercarriage and tailwheel were retractable. Armament comprised two 7.62 ShKAS machine guns. The navigator's gun protected the aircraft from frontal attacks, while the gunner's turret-mounted machine gun defended the upper rear hemisphere. The SBB-1's normal bomb load was 1,322lb (600kg), while in overload it could carry up to 2,204lb (1,000kg) of bombs, 1,763lb (800kg) being accommodated in the bomb bay.

The 'B' prototype bomber made its maiden

flight early in 1941, and it underwent tests as the SBB-1 (Skorostnoy Blizhniy Bombardirovschik – high speed, short range bomber). Flying weight was 13,227lb (6,000kg). During the tests it attained a maximum speed of 282mph (454km/h) at sea level, and 335mph (540 km/h) at 16,000ft (4,900m). Time to 16,400ft (5,000m) was 6.35 minutes. Its performance was therefore similar to that of a production Bf109E fighter. Careful fitting of the undercarriage fairings, the installation of ejector exhaust pipes and some other modifications increased its top speed by 12 to 16mph (20 to 25km/h). Noting the aircraft's high performance, the test pilots recommended that it be introduced into the inventory after troubleshooting. Final completion of the SBB-1 under wartime conditions was deemed unnecessary owing to the start of full scale production of the Pe-2, with better performance and having more powerful armament.

## Type '103' (ANT-58) and '103U' (ANT-59)

An order to design a new front line bomber designated Tu-2, to replace the obsolete SB high speed bomber, was issued to Andrei Tupolev before the war. A group of designers

*Opposite page from top to bottom:*

**Prototype of the '103', powered by AM-37s.**

**The '103U' prototype.**

**Rear view of the '103U' showing the gun position in the rear cockpit and the dorsal gun glazing.**

led by Tupolev began to design the aircraft in the NKVD prison, as Tupolev, like many other designers including Petlyakov, Myasishchev and Tomashevich, had been arrested and falsely accused of spying for Germany. The project was originally called ANT-58. Preliminary design of the prototype was complete by February 1940. According to calculations the aircraft, powered by Klimov M-120s, would have a flying weight of 17,195lb (7,800kg), a top speed of 434 to 459mph (700 to 740km/h), a range of 1,553 miles (2,500km). Its defensive armament was to consist of eight machine guns, and it would carry a bomb load of up to 2,204 to 4,409lb (1,000 to 2,000kg).

The ANT-58 mock-up was examined and approved on 21st April 1940, after which the prototype was designated '103'. In accordance with a State Committee of Defence (GKO) resolution dated 1st August 1940, Plant No.156 was to build three '103' prototypes, the first powered by AM-37s and the second

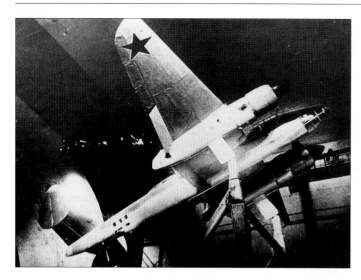

and third by M-120s with TK-2 turbosuperchargers. Construction of the first aircraft began in May 1940 and was completed on 8th January 1941. On 29th January M Nyukhtikov took it on its maiden flight, and manufacturer's tests lasted from January to May 1941. The '103' then underwent state trials from June to July of that year.

In May 1940 Soviet Air Force officials issued revised requirements. These included increasing the crew of the '103' to four, with the navigator located near the pilot as in Junkers aircraft, and installing an additional gun mounting. The second prototype '103' was designated '103U' (ANT-59). As M-120 development had suffered delays, AM-37s were also installed in this machine, and because of an increase in maximum cross section and flying weight the '103U's performance turned out to be worse than that of the first prototype.

The '103U' was completed by 9th April 1941 and Nyukhtikov made the first flight on 18th May. During June and July the '103U' underwent state trials together with the '103'. According to the test results, at normal take-off weight 23,004lb (10,435kg) the '103U' had a top speed of 291mph (469km/h) at sea level and 379mph (610km/h) at 25,600ft (7,800m), it reached 16,400ft (5,000m) in 9.5 minutes, its service ceiling was 34,500ft (10,500m) and it had a range of 1,180 miles (1,900km). In the final stage of the tests a new fin and rudder were installed.

The performance met requirements, and the GKO decided that production of the '103U' should start on 27th June 1941. However, the AM-37 engine was underdeveloped owing to the wartime conditions then prevailing, and it became necessary to find an alternative powerplant.

Tu-2 in the wind tunnel at TsAGI.

Static tests underway on a Tu-2 at TsAGI.

Production ASh-82-powered Tu-2 with three-bladed propellers.

## Type '103V' (ANT-60)

A new '103U' prototype powered by Shvetsov M-82 air-cooled engines and redesignated '103V' (ANT-60) represented the production Tu-2 prototype. The '103V' was completed following evacuation to Plant No.166 in Omsk in November 1941, and its maiden flight was performed by pilot Vasianin on 15th December 1941. Joint manufacturer's and state trials were conducted from 15th December 1941 to 22nd August 1942. On 28th March 1942 the aircraft was given the production designation Tu-2. Owing to the unsatisfactory behaviour of its engines, the first '103V' prototype was taken off the tests and replaced by a production '103V' initially designated '103VS' (Tu-2 No.308).

At a normal flying weight of 23,231lb (10,538kg) the maximum speed at 10,500ft (3,200m) was 323mph (521km/h), the time to 16,400ft (5,000m) was 10.2 minutes, the service ceiling was 29,500ft (9,000m) and the range was 1,255 miles (2,020km). Armament consisted of three 7.62mm ShKAS machine guns, two 12.7mm UB machine guns, two 20mm ShVAK guns and ten 132mm PS-132 rocket projectiles. The normal bomb load was 2,204lb (1,000kg), and the maximum was 6,613lb (3,000kg). After the '103V' was replaced by the '103VS', the former was returned to the factory and re-engined with new M-82FNVs (the initial designation of the M-82FN). In June 1943 the '103V' underwent manufacturer's tests in this form, when it had a maximum speed of 328mph (528km/h) at sea level and 352mph (568km/h) at 18,000ft (5,500m), while the M-82 powered '103V' was capable of 308 and 338mph (496 and 545km/h) respectively.

On the basis of the test results, the decision to put the M-82FN-powered Tu-2 into production was adopted on 20th July 1943.

# Tu-2

Preparations for '103V' production began just after the evacuation of Tupolev and his design team from Moscow to Omsk. The work, in which Plants Nos.166 and 156 in Omsk were involved, became particularly intensive at the end of 1941. The first three bombers were completed in February, 1942, and in the summer of 1942 three Tu-2s (the production designation of the '103V') were prepared for service trials, but were delayed by defects in their M-82 engines. It was not until September 1942 that the bombers arrived at the 3rd Air Army combat units. During their service tests the aircraft, based at Migalovo airfield, flew 25 combat missions without loss. Each aircraft flew once a day, and average flight range was about 310 miles (500km), the bomb load being from 2,204 to 4,409lb (1,000 to 2,000kg).

The flights were performed by combat pilots and crews from the NII VVS. Most of the flights were made by Captain Chernichenko from the NII VVS (eight) and First Lieutenant Sviridov (seven). On the whole the Tu-2 received a more favourable assessment from the pilots than the Pe-2. It was noted that the aircraft had a powerful armament, was faster by almost 62mph (100km/h) at low and medium altitudes, and could carry up to 6,613lb (3,000kg) of bombs. Several shortcomings were also pointed out.

The 132nd Bomber Air Regiment commanded by Major A Khlebnikov soon arrived at the front. By the beginning of the Soviet counter-offensive at Stalingrad 17 Tu-2s were operational, of which 15 were combat ready. All were in the 3rd Air Army at the Kalinin Front. Marshal Novikov, Commander-in-Chief of the Soviet Air Force, wrote in a report to Stalin that these aircraft were essential to the front line regiments. After stating that the Pe-2s had insufficient range, and that it was difficult to organise the co-operation of the bombers on different fronts, he concluded that the Tu-2 was necessary.

Novikov's report and the report on the results of the Tu-2's service trials were late. An order stopping the bomber's production in Omsk and replacing it with Yak-9 fighter production was adopted on 7th October 1942. Having lost his production base, Tupolev tried to have the decision cancelled, and went to Moscow to argue his case.

Nevertheless, the 80th and last production Tu-2 was assembled in January 1943. When Tu-2 production was interrupted, the documents concerning the results of its service tests, with the pilots' and commanders' assessments, reached the Central Committee Secretariat and Stalin in person. The aircraft was praised, and Aircraft Industry People's Commissar A Shakhurin, who was summoned to the Kremlin by Stalin regarding the matter, remembered how the decision to restore Tu-2 production was reached:

Stalin suddenly said: 'We were wrong when we stopped the aircraft's production. I am very displeased with you. You have done wrong.' 'What is wrong?', I asked. 'You should have complained of me to the Central Committee', said Stalin, as he walked along the hall, smoking. Apparently nobody in the Central Committee complained about Stalin. After a pause I said: 'Production of the bombers is being restored at the evacuated plant. The production rate will not be as great as in Siberia, but it is possible to put the Tu-2 back into production.' Stalin answered: 'Well, prepare a proposal'.

The decision was taken on 17th June 1943. It was specified that the bomber's speed should not be lower than 310mph (500km/h) at sea level and 341mph (550km/h) at 18,000ft (5,500m), that its service ceiling should be 29,500ft (9,000m), and that its range with a 2,204lb (1,000kg) bomb load should be not less than 1,242 miles (2,000km). The plant to which Shakhurin had referred was Moscow Plant No.23, which had just started production of the Il-4 and was now going to build the modern Tupolev bomber.

In spite of the interruption in production, the Tupolev OKB continued Tu-2 development work. Three production bombers built in Omsk in October 1942 were chosen to undergo structural improvement. The most comprehensive changes were made to Tu-2 No.100716. Among other alterations, the air brake grids and automatic dive recovery control system were removed, the nose machine gun was removed, the tailplane was made non-adjustable, the control system was made simpler and the fuel system was considerably simplified.

Believing in the ultimate success of their work, the Tupolev team continued to improve the bomber's structure and production technology. Slight structural changes enabled the aircraft to perform different roles. Its survivability was improved by halving the weight of wiring, simplifying the hydraulic system, reducing the number of controls and instruments from 93 to 38, and making a four-fold reduction in the total length of hydraulic pipelines. Structural weight of production Tu-2s decreased by 881lb (400kg).

In August 1943 Tupolev and his team returned to Moscow from Omsk. At that time the Tu-2's unreliable M-82 engines were replaced by M-82FNs from aircraft No.716. The latter engine also powered Lavochkin's fighters. On 26th August 1943 the first fully modified Tu-2, No.716, flew for the first time, and its manufacturer's and state trials began soon after.

These suffered protracted delay, which was the fault of leading engineer A Sokolov, but the report on the tests concluded that the Tu-2 had a better performance than other bombers of the same type, such as the Pe-2 and Douglas Boston serving with the Soviet Air Force. The service ceiling and range were even better than specified, and the changes had improved survivability and controllability, but directional stability was still inadequate and much worse than that of the Boston and Yer-2.

The pilot's and navigator's views were poor. Although the augmented M-82FN engines considerably enhanced the aircraft's performance they had proved unreliable during the tests, and there were many troubles with the AV-5-167A propellers owing to the danger of overspeeding.

By the end of the Tu-2's state trials in December 1943, deliveries from Plant No.83 had begun. Sixteen aircraft were ready at the end of the year, and the first unit to have the new Tu-2s was the 47th Reconnaissance Regiment. On one occasion pilots of the 28th Guard Fighter Air Regiment, flying Bell P-39 Airacobras, were delayed at take-off and failed to rendezvous with the Tu-2s they were to escort. Fortunately the bombers returned safely.

By the beginning of June 1944 the Tu-2 was in service in large numbers, and the 334th Bomber Air Division, commanded by Colonel I Skok, was fully equipped with the type. It was introduced into service under the personal control of Stalin, who ordered: 'Take care of the division as if it were the pupil of an eye', and repeatedly questioned Marshal A Novikov about Tu-2 operations. The bomber justified expectations, a particularly strong blow being delivered against Vyborg railway terminal on 17th June 1944 by 59 Tu-2s. After this operation the division was awarded the title Leningradskaya (Leningrad) by General Headquarters.

When, at the beginning of June 1944, it was decided to conduct service trials of the Tu-2, the 334th Red Banner Bomber Air Division had 87 of them, of which 74 were airworthy. The Tupolevs were used only for level bombing in daytime. They were loaded with FAB-500 and FAB-1000 bombs and RAB-3 bomb cassettes which the Pe-2s could not carry, in addition to the usual load in the bomb bay and on the external hardpoints. Because the supply of bombs was irregular, the average bomb load during the first two months was 2,645lb (1,200kg). Not until September 1944 did it increase to 2,976lb (1,350kg).

Soviet Air Force Command used the whole division to deliver blows, the Tu-2s operating at ranges of 186 to 310 miles (300 to 500km) from their airfields. All missions were flown with Yak-9 and Airacobra fighters providing escort, but in spite of this the Luftwaffe fighters engaged the Tu-2s energetically, and in three months shot down ten and damaged another 14. Seven were shot down by German anti-aircraft artillery. The average loss rate of the Tupolev bomber was one aircraft for every 46.5 sorties.

Assessing the Tu-2 from the results of the service trials, Lt Colonel Bugay, commanding the 132nd Bomber Air Regiment, wrote that it was an excellent and modern twin-engined bomber. He praised its easy handling, its ability to fly on one engine, and its high speed, adequate range and capability to carry large bombs. Bugay wrote: 'The pilots of the regiment appreciated the Tu-2 and successfully flew combat missions'.

Intensive efforts were made to increase Tu-2 production, but the capacity of Plant No.23 was modest compared with the massive Nos.1 and 22 plants. Consequently in 1944 little more than 30 aircraft per day were being built. By the beginning of 1945, in addition to the 334th Bomber Air Division of the 3rd Air Army of the Baltic Front, which was equipped with 111 Tu-2s, the 326th Bomber Air Division of the 4th Air Army of the Belorussian Front had 94 aircraft. These units and the 47th Long Range Reconnaissance Air Regiment were the main units operating the Tu-2. The total of

278 Tupolev bombers, 264 of them airworthy, comprised about 9% of the whole bomber fleet of the Soviet Army Air Force. This low percentage was due to the fact that the Tu-2 could not replace the Pe-2 in the dive bomber role, and pilots had become accustomed to the Pe-2. For this reason the Tu-2 was used for level bombing missions in the final stages of the war.

Up to the end of the war 1,013 Tu-2s were built of a final production total of 2,527 aircraft. Using the production Tu-2S as a basis, the Tupolev OKB and Plant No.156 combined their efforts to develop a range of prototypes, some of which appeared after the war.

## Tu-2Sh

A few Tu-2Sh (Shturmovik – armoured attacker) prototypes, based on the Tu-2S but powered by ASh-82FN engines, were built. They also had different armament. As proposed by A Nadashkevitch, chief of the armament brigade, production Tu-2S No.13/14 had 48 PPSh sub-machine guns installed in its fuselage, with which to attack hostile infantry. Although a fierce fusillade of fire was possible for a short period of time, it was impossible to reload the numerous guns quickly, so work on this project was abandoned.

Another production Tu-2S was fitted with a 75mm gun reloaded by the navigator, for use against enemy trains, in addition to its standard armament. This aircraft was tested but did not go into production.

In 1946 a production Tu-2S was armed with two 45mm NS-45 guns and two 37mm NS-37 guns under the fuselage nose, and two 20mm ShVAK guns near the fuselage sides. The upper rear hemisphere of the aircraft, which had a crew of two, was protected by a turret mounted 12.7mm UBT machine gun. This version, too, remained only a prototype.

On production Tu-2 No.26146, instead of the four guns of the aforementioned prototype, a single 57mm RShR anti-tank gun was installed in the bomb bay. The barrel, fitted with a recoil compensator, protruded approximately 0.5m from the aircraft's nose. This two-seat attack aircraft prototype had completed its state trials by 28th February 1947.

## ASh-83 powered Tu-2

On 18th May 1945 test pilot A Perelyot took Tu-2S No.100716 into the air for the first time as a modified production aircraft with a new powerplant. This aircraft had passed its combined manufacturer's and state tests in the

second half of 1943, but its original M-82FNV engines had now been replaced by more powerful, high altitude Shvetsov ASh-83s. Trials showed that there was an increase in maximum speed but a slight reduction in range. The variant progressed no further because the ASh-83 did not go into production.

## Tu-2R (Tu-6)

Work on the installation of the photographic reconnaissance equipment in the Tu-2 began in 1942, and the first photo-reconnaissance prototype was built in 1943. After the war, in 1946, testing began of the Tu-6 with more refined equipment. The cameras tested included AFA-33s with focal lengths of 20cm, 33cm, 50cm, 75cm and 100cm, and the NAFA-3S/50 and AFA-3S/50. When the AFA-33/100 with a focal length of 100cm was installed, the lens projected beyond the fuselage and had to be faired. An additional fuel tank was installed in the bomb bay.

State trials of the Tu-6 were conducted until 9th April 1947, and a standard for the photo-reconnaissance aircraft for 1947 to 1948 was established. Tu-2S production had ended by that time, and only a few aircraft of this type were built.

## Tu-2T

In the second half of 1944 the Tu-2T was designed for naval use, based on the production Tu-2S bomber. One or two 45-36-AN torpedoes with TsAGI-type stabilisers were mounted under the wing centre section on special TD-44 carriers with Der-4-44U locks. In February-March 1945 the Tu-2T prototype passed its joint manufacturer's and state tests. Its maximum speed was 313mph (505km/h) with one torpedo and 306mph (493km/h) with two. The aircraft did not go into production because a project for a long range torpedo-carrier based on the '62' (Tu-2D) bomber had been developed.

*For technical data, see Table G, page 174.*

*Photographs on the opposite page:*

**Tu-2 No.7/58 under test, equipped with a new four-bladed propeller and anti-icing system.**

**View of a Tu-2's capacious internal bomb bay.**

**Tu-2 formation.**

**Later production standard Tu-2S.**

## Type '62' (Tu-2D) and '62T'

In 1941, after the Tupolev Design Bureau had designed the '103' (ANT-58), a long range version was formulated, having greater span and wing area. However, at that time there was no possibility of building such an aircraft because the bureau was engaged on the '103V'. It returned to the idea of a long range development of the bomber at the end of 1943.

The standard Tu-2S, designed in 1943, could quickly be converted into a long range bomber by enlarging the outer wing panels and tail surfaces and increasing fuel capacity. This enabled the bureau to prepare the drawings for the new variant with the minimum of effort. Two Tu-2s manufactured at Plant No. 166 in October 1942, Nos.714 and 718, were used for flight tests. Modified at Plant No.156 in Moscow in 1944, they were given the manufacturer's code '62' and designated Tu-2D. Aircraft 718 was completed in June 1944, and first flew on the 17th of that month. Manufacturer's tests under test pilot A Perelyot continued until 23rd September 1944, and the state trials were conducted from 20th November 1944 to 23rd April 1945. This prototype differed from the production Tu-2 in having greater wing and empennage areas, increased fuel capacity, new canopies for the pilot's and navigator's cockpits to improve their view, and new propellers. The consequent increase in weight reduced the speed and altitude performance, but its range increased to 1,758 miles (2,830km).

Aircraft No.714 was rebuilt at Plant No.154, being completed in September 1944. It differed from No.718 in having its crew complement increased to five and a lengthened nose housing the navigator's position. The co-pilot, who could also double as a gunner, occupied the former navigator's cockpit. The special equipment was changed, and the maximum bomb load was increased from 6,613 to 8,818lb (3,000 to 4,000kg). Manufacturer's tests were conducted from 20th October 1944 to 1st March 1945, again with test pilot A Perelyot in charge. State trials began on 18th June 1945 and were completed on 31st October. The maximum range remained approximately the same at 1,733 miles (2,790km), but speed and ceiling were inferior even to those attained by Tu-2D 718. After its state trials, 714 was delivered to Plant No.156 for conversion into a long range torpedo-carrier. This work was completed in June 1946, and on 2nd August the first flight was performed by F Opadchy and V Morgunov. Designated '62T', it had an additional fuel tank in the bomb bay and could carrying one or two torpedoes. Because the end of the war halted Tu-2D production, the '62T' bomber and torpedo carrier progressed no further, though they did form the basis for other post-war versions.

## SDB ('63')

In May 1944 the Tupolev Design Bureau and Plant No.156 produced a new type of front line bomber, the SDB (Skorostnoy Dnevnoy Bombardirovschik – high speed day bomber), which by virtue of its speed and high altitude capabilities would be almost invulnerable to enemy fighters and could bomb hostile targets in daytime. In accordance with a GKO decision of 22nd May 1944, Plant No.156 was required to build two SDBs and prepare them for tests by 1st June 1944 and 15th October 1944 respectively. Both aircraft were given the factory code '63'. The first SDB prototype was a version of the '103' aircraft fitted with more-powerful 1,870hp (1,395kW) AM-39 engines instead of AM-37s. Its dive brake grids were removed because the aircraft was not intended for dive bombing, the armament was changed, initially to two 20mm ShVAK guns and a single 12.7mm UB machine gun, and the crew was reduced to two.

The first flight was made by leading test pilot A Perelyot on 21st May 1944, and the ensuing manufacturer's tests lasted ten days, being completed on 31st May. State trials began on 5th June and were completed on 6th July. At a normal flying weight of 22,266lb (10,100kg), top speed increased to 327mph (527km/h) at sea level and 400mph (645 km/h) at 21,800ft (6,650m). The bomber's rate of climb also improved, the time 16,400ft (5,000m) being 7.45 minutes. The range remained approximately the same at 1,137 miles (1,830km), and the ceiling was slightly lower at 32,800ft (10,000m).

The second SDB prototype was finished in October 1944, in accordance with the VVS request issued during the tests of the first prototype. Many structural components of the production Tu-2S were incorporated in the second SDB prototype, which differed from the first in the following ways:

- single-strut main undercarriage legs;
- augmented AM-39Fs instead of AM-39s;
- improved view for pilot and gunner;
- maximum bomb load increased from 6,613 to 8,818lb (3,000 to 4,000kg);
- slightly changed wing centre section;
- vertical tail surfaces of increased area;
- cockpit armour for the crew of three;
- an additional 12.7mm UB machine gun;
- fuel capacity increased from 472.9 to 519.1 gallons (2,150 to 2,360 litres).

The aircraft underwent development testing from 29th November 1944 to 4th April 1945, in concert with the NII VVS. The state trials of the second prototype were conducted from 5th April to 16th May 1945. The normal flying weight increased to 24,085lb (10,925kg) and maximum speed at 22,500ft (6,850m) was slightly lower at 397mph (640km/h), and even increased at sea level to 339mph (547

km/h). Compared with the first SDB prototype the service ceiling increased by 328ft (100m), owing to the augmented engines, but the rate of climb decreased.

A serious shortcoming noted during the SDB's tests was the poor view provided for the navigator. Moreover, the Tupolev design team were pinning their hopes on the new Tu-10 ('68'), which they hoped would replace the Tu-2S in production, and work on the SDB was therefore discontinued.

## Tu-10 ('68')

In accordance with VVS demands, the Tupolev Design Bureau constantly improved the production Tu-2S bomber. By the end of the war a new version of the aircraft had been prepared, powered by 1,850hp (1,380kW) AM-39FNV water cooled direct injection engines. In addition, the following changes were introduced:

- the canopy was widened;
- one large window replaced the three side windows;
- radiators were installed in the wing centre section;
- the rear sections of the wing were redesigned because fuel tanks Nos.6 and 7 were replaced by one common tank;
- the area of the vertical tail surfaces was increased;
- the tailplane was made hydraulically controllable;
- a new tailwheel was installed and the main landing gear struts were slightly modified.

In addition, the bomber's armament was improved. The navigator's VUSh gun mounting was replaced by a VUS-1, and the radio operator/gunner's VUB-2M gun mounting was replaced by a VUB-65. The hatch machine gun and the bomb-lifting system were modernised, and the maximum bomb load was increased from 6,613 to 8,818lb (3,000 to 4,000kg).

The prototype, designated Tu-10 (manufacturer's code '68') and employing the airframe of production Tu-2S No.16120, was completed by 1st May 1945, and on 19th May test pilot A Perelyot undertook the maiden flight. Manufacturer's tests began on 6th June, and the aircraft then went for its state trials, which lasted from 28th June to 30th July.

**First prototype of the '63' (or SDB) powered by AM-39s.**

**Second prototype of the '63' (SDB) with AM-39F engines, under test during the winter of 1944-1945.**

**The Tu-10 ('68'), a modified Tu-2 with AM-42s.**

Compared with a production Tu-2S, maximum speed increased to 323mph (520km/h) at sea level and 394mph (635km/h) at 23,300ft (7,100m). On 30th June 1945 the aircraft was damaged in a wheels-up landing, and from then until 16th November it was under repair, the opportunity also being taken to eliminate some defects.

On 17th November the aircraft was handed over for its second series of state trials, which continued until 8th March 1946. The NII VVS concluded that the Tu-10 ('68') could be recommended for introduction into the inventory if all of the noted faults were eliminated, and the aircraft was therefore transferred back to the factory, where new AM-39FN2 engines and AV-9K-22A four-bladed propellers were installed, the vertical tail area was increased, a larger tailwheel was fitted and the dihedral was reduced by 1°30'.

On 24th May 1946 Plant No.156 completed the modifications and the bomber was delivered for flight testing. On 28th May Perelyot lifted the improved aircraft into the air and began the manufacturer's tests, which lasted until 10th August 1946. On 16th September the Tu-10 went for its state trials, which finished on 20th November. Its rate of climb, ceiling and range were all improved, attaining a maximum speed at 24,750ft (7,550m) of 393mph (634km/h).

According to the conclusions of the NII VVS, the Tu-10 ('68') was satisfactory and could be introduced into the inventory on condition that its range was increased to 2,100km. By order of the People's Commissariat of the Aircraft Industry, production of the aircraft with AM-39FN2s driving three-blade AV-5LV-22A propellers was initiated, but only ten were built. By the beginning of 1947 piston-engined front line bombers had no future, and the Tupolev design bureau began to develop projects for jet aircraft based on the Tu-2.

## Type '65' (Tu-2DB)

One more prototype of the Tu-2D long range bomber was built, powered by AM-44TK water cooled engines with TK-1B (TK-300B) turbo-superchargers, driving 12ft 5in (3.8m) diameter three-bladed AV-5LV-166B propellers. On 1st July 1946 test pilot F Opadchy took the '65' on its maiden flight, but the new engines proved unreliable and development was abandoned.

## 'Type 67' (Tu-2D)

A '62' prototype powered by ACh-30BF diesel engines received the plant designation '67'. It made its first flight on 12th February 1946 with A Perelyot at the controls, but in 1947 further development was cancelled owing to frequent engine failures.

## Type '69' (Tu-8)

The prototype designated '69' was built in an attempt to increase the range of the Tu-2. Although its wingspan was the same as that of its predecessor, the Tu-2D ('62'), its wing area was enlarged by increasing the chord of the outer wing panels and ailerons, and the undercarriage was given larger wheels and reinforced. The powerplant was the same as that of the production Tu-2S. The crew of five was accommodated in larger and wider cockpits, the pilots sat side-by-side and the nose glazing was increased.

Armament consisted of a 20mm B-20 gun in the nose, and a B-20 gun in an electrically operated turret for the second pilot and for each of the two gunners. Bomb load was increased to 9,920lb (4,500kg), which brought the flying weight to 31,415lb (14,250kg), or 36,926lb (16,750kg) in overload. All of the performance parameters worsened with the exception of the range, which was estimated to be 2,547 miles (4,100km).

The aircraft was completed in May 1947 and passed its state trials, but its performance was disappointing for the period and it was not sufficiently strong and stable in flight. By that time the first Soviet jet bombers had been designed, and there was no reason to continue to develop the Tu-8.

## Tu-2 'Paravan'

By September 1944 two production Tu-2Ss, Nos.21/57 and 21/59, had been converted into special 'Paravan' aircraft, intended for overcoming enemy balloon barrages. Each aircraft had a 19ft 8in (6m) long Duralumin cone mounted on its nose, and cables with sharp cutting edges were stretched from the tip of the cone to the wingtips. To maintain the correct cg, 330lb (150kg) of ballast was installed in the aircraft's tail. The 'Paravan' did not go into production.

*For technical data, see Table G, page 174.*

*Photographs on the opposite page:*

**Production Tu-2 No.12/57 reworked into a 'Paravan' for the destruction of balloon barrages.**

**The '65' (or Tu-2DB) long range bomber. Powered by two AM-44s with turbo-superchargers.**

**The fate of the '67' was similar to the '65', both were troubled by powerplant choice.**

*This page, below:*

**The Tu-2 prototype fitted with a 57mm RShR anti-tank cannon.**

*Above:* **One of the last versions of the Tu-2, the Tu-8 was tested after the war.**

*Left:* **Naval Tu-2T torpedo bomber prototype. Note the stowage of the torpedoes on the fuselage sides.**

**Tupolev Tu-2S**

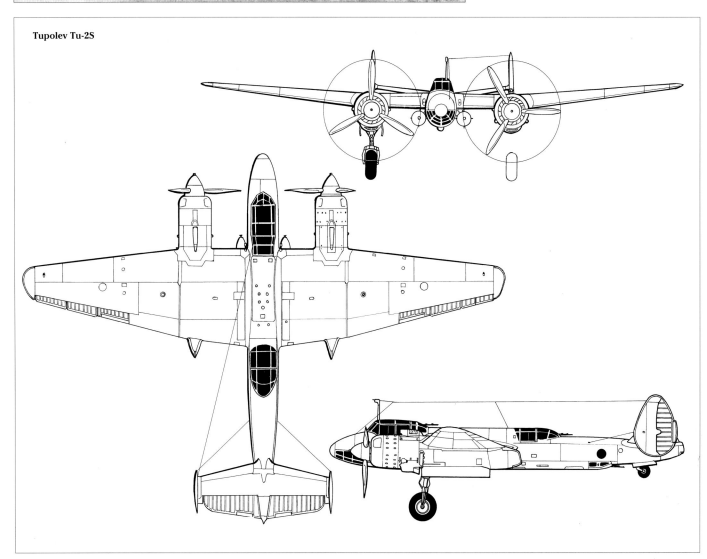

# Data Tables

Table A

## Twin-engined Fighters

| | OKO-6 | Ta-3 | Ta-3bis | SAM-13 | TIS (A) | TIS (MA) | MiG-5 (DIS) | MiG-5 (DIS) | '100' | Pe-3 | Pe-3 | Pe-3bis | Pe-2I | Tu-1 (63P) |
|---|---|---|---|---|---|---|---|---|---|---|---|---|---|---|
| Year of Production | 1940 | 1941 | 1943 | 1940 | 1941 | 1943 | 1941 | 1942 | 1940 | 1941 | 1944 | 1942 | 1941 | 1946 |
| Crew | 1 | 1 | 1 | 1 | 2 | 2 | 1 | 1 | 3 | 2 | 2 | 2 | 2 | 3 |
| Powerplant | 2 x M-88 | 2 x M-89 | 2 x M-89 | 2 x MV-6 | 2 x AM-37 | 2 x AM-39 | 2 x AM-37 | 2 x M-82F | 2 x M-105 | 2 x M-105RA | 2 x VK-105PF | 2 x M-105RA | 2 x M-105RA | 2 x AM-43V |
| Power at altitude – (hp) | 1,000 | 1,250 | 1,250 | 220 | 1,400 | 1,700 | 1,400 | 1,330 | 1,050 | 1,100 | 1,260 | 1,100 | 1,100 | 1,950 |
| – (kW) | 746 | 932 | 932 | 164 | 1,044 | 1,268 | 1,044 | 992 | 783 | 820 | 939 | 820 | 820 | 1,454 |
| Length – (m) | 9.81 | 9.83 | 9.83 | 7.68 | 11.7 | 11.7 | 10.875 | 12.14 | 12.69 | 12.66 | 12.45 | 12.66 | – | 13.6 |
| – (ft-in) | 32-2 | 32-4 | 32-4 | 25-2 | 14-0 | 14-0 | 35-8 | 39-9¾ | 41-7½ | 41-6 | 40-9½ | 41-6 | – | 44-7½ |
| Wingspan – (m) | 12.65 | 12.65 | 13.38 | 7.3 | 15.5 | 15.5 | 15.1 | 15.1 | 17.15 | 17.13 | 17.13 | 17.13 | 17.13 | 18.86 |
| – (ft-in) | 41-6 | 41-6 | 43-10½ | 23-11 | 50-10 | 50-10 | 49-6 | 49-6 | 56-3 | 56-2 | 56-2 | 56-2 | 56-2 | 61-10 |
| Wing area – (m²) | 25.4 | 25.4 | 28.1 | 9.0 | 34.8 | 34.8 | 38.9 | 38.9 | 40.8 | 40.8 | 40.5 | 40.5 | 40.8 | 48.8 |
| – (ft²) | 273.4 | 273.4 | 302.4 | 96.8 | 374.5 | 374.5 | 418.7 | 418.7 | 439.1 | 439.1 | 435.9 | 435.9 | 439.1 | 525.2 |
| Empty weight – (kg) | – | 4,738 | 4,934 | 754 | 5,800 | – | 6,730 | – | 5,887 | 5,730 | 5,795 | 5,858 | – | 9,460 |
| – (lb) | – | 10,445 | 10,877 | 1,662 | 12,786 | – | 14,836 | – | 12,978 | 12,632 | 12,775 | 12,914 | – | 20,855 |
| Gross weight – (kg) | – | 5,998 | 6,626 | 1,183 | 7,840 | – | 8,000 | 8,000 | 7,200 | 7,860 | 8,270 | 8,000 | 7,735 | 12,755 |
| – (lb) | – | 13,223 | 14,607 | 2,608 | 17,283 | – | 17,636 | 17,636 | 15,873 | 17,328 | 18,231 | 17,636 | 17,052 | 28,119 |
| Speed at sea level - (km/h) | 488.0 | 477.0 | – | – | 490.0 | – | – | – | 455.0 | 444.0 | 465.0 | 438.0 | 454.0 | 479.0 |
| – (mph) | 303.2 | 296.4 | – | – | 304.4 | – | – | – | 282.7 | 275.8 | 288.8 | 272.1 | 282.1 | 297.6 |
| Speed at altitude- (km/h) | 567.0 | 595.0 | 600.0 | 560.0 | 535.0 | 570.0 | 610.0 | 604.0 | 538.0 | 535.0 | 527.0 | 530.0 | 540.0 | 641.0 |
| – (m) | 7,550 | 7,000 | 7,000 | 5,800 | 7,000 | 7,000 | 6,800 | 5,000 | 6,600 | 5,000 | 3,850 | 5,050 | 5,000 | 8,600 |
| – (mph) | 352.3 | 369.7 | 372.8 | 347.9 | 332.4 | 354.1 | 379.0 | 375.3 | 334.3 | 332.4 | 327.4 | 329.3 | 335.5 | 398.3 |
| – (ft) | 24,750 | 22,950 | 22,950 | 19,000 | 22,950 | 22,950 | 22,300 | 16,400 | 21,650 | 16,400 | 12,650 | 16,550 | 16,400 | 28,200 |
| Climb to 5,000m – (min) | 5.5 | 6.3 | – | – | 7.3 | – | 5.5 | 6.3 | – | 9.0 | – | 6.65 | 8.5 | 11.6 |
| – (to 16,400ft - min) | 5.5 | 6.3 | – | – | 7.3 | – | 5.5 | 6.3 | – | 9.0 | – | 6.65 | 8.5 | 11.6 |
| Service ceiling – (m) | – | 10,400 | – | 10,000 | 10,250 | – | 10,800 | 9,800 | – | – | 8,800 | 9,100 | 9,500 | 11,000 |
| – (ft) | – | 34,100 | – | 32,800 | 33,600 | – | 35,400 | 32,200 | – | – | 28,900 | 29,900 | 31,200 | 36,100 |
| Take-off run – (m) | – | 1,060 | 2,065 | 850 | 1,720 | – | 2,280 | 2,500 | 1,400 | 2,150 | 1,650 | 1,500 | 1,780 | 2,250 |
| – (ft) | – | 3,477 | 6,774 | 2,788 | 5,643 | – | 7,480 | 8,202 | 4,593 | 7,053 | 5,413 | 4,921 | 5,839 | 7,381 |
| Landing roll – (m) | – | – | – | – | 1,000 | 1,000 | 1,000 | 1,000 | 1,000 | 700 | 500 | 700 | 700 | 1,000 |
| – (ft) | – | – | – | – | 3,280 | 3,280 | 3,280 | 3,280 | 3,280 | 2,296 | 1,640 | 2,296 | 2,296 | 3,280 |
| Armament – (mm) | 4 x 20 | 4 x 20 | 4 x 20 | 4 x 7.62 | 2 x 20 | 2 x 37 | 2 x 23 | 2 x 23 | 2 x 20 | 2 x 12.7 | 1 x 20 | 1 x 20 | 2 x 20 | 2 x 45 |
| | 2 x 7.62 | 2 x 7.62 | 2 x 7.62 | | 6 x 7.62 | 2 x 12.7 | 2 x 12.7 | 2 x 12.7 | 3 x 7.62 | 2 x 7.62 | 2 x 12.7 | 3 x 12.7 | 2 x 12.7 | 2 x 23 |
| | | | | | | 1 x 7.62 | 4 x 7.62 | 4 x 7.62 | | | | 1 x 7.62 | | 2 x 12.7 |
| Page in main text | 37 | 37 | 37 | 20 | 34 | 34 | 17 | 17 | 22 | 25 | 25 | 27 | 33 | 41 |

See the Glossary and Notes, pages 14 and 15, for details of measurement units etc.

*Right:* **The updated Pe-2bis prototype bomber was accomplished by the Petlyakov Design Bureau in September 1941 and was tested at the NII VVS in September and October of that year.**

*Below:* **Polikarpov's TIS(A) twin-engined fighter followed the established format of its day.**

Table B

## Ilyushin Attack Aircraft

| | TsKB-55 | TsKB-57 | Il-2 | Il-2 | Il-2 | Il-2 | Il-2 | Il-2U | Il-10 | Il-8 No.1 | Il-8 No.2 |
|---|---|---|---|---|---|---|---|---|---|---|---|
| Year of Production | 1939 | 1940 | 1940 | 1942 | 1941 | 1942 | 1943 | 1943 | 1944 | 1943 | 1944 |
| Crew | 2 | 1 | 1 | 1 | 2 | 2 | 2 | 2 | 2 | 2 | 2 |
| Powerplant | 1 x AM-35 | 1 x AM-38 | 1 x AM-38 | 1 x AM-38 | 1 x M-82 | 1 x AM-38 | 1 x AM-38F | 1 x AM-38F | 1 x AM-42 | 1 x AM-42 | 1 x AM-42 |
| Take-off power – (hp) | 1,350 | 1,660 | 1,660 | 1,660 | 1,700 | 1,660 | 1,750 | 1,750 | 2,000 | 2,000 | 2,000 |
| – (kW) | 1,007 | 1,238 | 1,238 | 1,238 | 1,268 | 1,238 | 1,305 | 1,305 | 1,492 | 1,492 | 1,492 |
| Length – (m) | 11.6 | – | 11.653 | 11.653 | 11.653 | 11.653 | 11.653 | 11.653 | 11.12 | 12.931 | 12.932 |
| – (ft-in) | 38-0 | – | 38-2¾ | 38-2¾ | 38-2¾ | 38-2¾ | 38-2¾ | 38-2¾ | 36-5¾ | 42-3½ | 42-3½ |
| Wingspan – (m) | 14.6 | 14.6 | 14.6 | 14.6 | 14.6 | 14.6 | 14.6 | 14.6 | 13.4 | 14.6 | 14.6 |
| – (ft-in) | 47-10¾ | 47-10¾ | 47-10¾ | 47-10¾ | 47-10¾ | 47-10¾ | 47-10¾ | 47-10¾ | 47-10¾ | 47-10¾ | 47-10¾ |
| Wing area – ($m^2$) | 38.5 | 38.5 | 38.5 | 38.5 | 38.5 | 38.5 | 38.5 | 38.5 | 30.0 | 39.0 | 39.0 |
| – ($ft^2$) | 414.4 | 414.4 | 414.4 | 414.4 | 414.4 | 414.4 | 414.4 | 414.4 | 322.9 | 419.8 | 419.8 |
| Empty weight – (kg) | 3,615 | 3,792 | 3,990 | 4,261 | 3,935 | 4,525 | 4,625 | 4,300 | 4,650 | 5,245 | 5,110 |
| – (lb) | 7,969 | 8,359 | 8,796 | 9,393 | 8,675 | 9,975 | 10,196 | 9,479 | 10,251 | 11,563 | 11,265 |
| Gross weight – (kg) | 4,725 | 4,988 | 5,310 | 5,788 | 5,655 | 6,060 | 6,160 | 5,091 | 6,300 | 7,250 | 7,610 |
| – (lb) | 10,416 | 10,996 | 11,706 | 12,760 | 12,466 | 13,359 | 13,580 | 11,223 | 13,888 | 15,983 | 16,776 |
| Max take-off weight – (kg) | – | – | 5,510 | 5,988 | 5,855 | 6,260 | 6,360 | 5,355 | 6,500 | 7,650 | 7,830 |
| – (lb) | – | – | 12,147 | 13,201 | 12,907 | 13,800 | 14,021 | 11,805 | 14,329 | 16,865 | 17,261 |
| Speed at sea level - (km/h) | 362.0 | 423.0 | 433.0 | 380.0 | 365.0 | 370.0 | 375.0 | 396.0 | 507.0 | 435.0 | 461.0 |
| – (mph) | 224,9 | 262.8 | 269.0 | 236.1 | 226.8 | 229.9 | 233.0 | 246.0 | 315.0 | 270.3 | 286.4 |
| Speed at altitude – (km/h) | 422.0 | 437.0 | 450.0 | 414.0 | 396.0 | 411.0 | 390.0 | 414.0 | 551.0 | 470.0 | 509.0 |
| – (m) | 5,000 | 2,800 | 2,460 | 2,500 | 2,500 | 1,200 | 1,200 | 1,500 | 2,300 | 2,240 | 2,800 |
| – (mph) | 262.2 | 271.5 | 279.6 | 257.2 | 246.0 | 255.3 | 242.3 | 257.2 | 342.3 | 292.0 | 316.2 |
| – (ft) | 16,400 | 9,200 | 8,100 | 8,200 | 8,200 | 4,000 | 4,000 | 4,900 | 7,500 | 7,350 | 9,200 |
| Climb to 1,000m – (min) | 2.3 | 1.7 | 1.6 | 2.2 | 1.8 | 2.4 | 2.2 | 2.0 | 1.6 | 1.97 | 2.6 |
| – (3,300ft – min) | 2.3 | 1.7 | 1.6 | 2.2 | 1.8 | 2.4 | 2.2 | 2.0 | 1.6 | 1.97 | 2.6 |
| Service ceiling – (m) | 9,000 | 8,500 | – | 6,200 | – | 6,000 | 6,000 | – | 7,250 | 6,800 | 6,900 |
| – (ft) | 29,500 | 28,000 | – | 2,000 | – | 19,700 | 19,700 | – | 23,800 | 22,300 | 22,600 |
| Operational range – (km) | 618 | 850 | 638 | 740 | 700 | 685 | 685 | – | 800 | 1,180 | 1,140 |
| – (miles) | 384 | 528 | 396 | 459 | 434 | 425 | 425 | – | 497 | 733 | 708 |
| Take-off run – (m) | 340 | 250 | 450 | 420 | 524 | 400 | 370 | 385 | 475 | 318 | 520 |
| – (ft) | 1,115 | 820 | 1,476 | 1,377 | 1,719 | 1,312 | 1,213 | 1,263 | 1,558 | 1,043 | 1,706 |
| Bomb load, normal – (kg) | 400 | 400 | 400 | 400 | 400 | 400 | 400 | 200 | 400 | 600 | – |
| – (lb) | 881 | 881 | 881 | 881 | 881 | 881 | 881 | 440 | 881 | 1,322 | – |
| Bomb load, max – (kg) | 600 | 600 | 600 | 600 | 600 | 600 | 600 | – | 600 | 1,000 | 1,000 |
| – (lb) | 1,322 | 1,322 | 1,322 | 1,322 | 1,322 | 1,322 | 1,322 | – | 1,322 | 2,204 | 2,204 |
| Armament – (mm) | – | – | 2 x 20 | 2 x 20 | 2 x 20 | 2 x 20 * | 2 x 20 * | – | 2 x 23 | 2 x 23 | 2 x 23 |
| | | | | or 2 x 23 | | or 2 x 37 | or 2 x 37 | | or 4 x 23 | | 1 x 20 |
| | 5 x 7.62 | 4 x 7.62 | 2 x 7.62 | 2 x 7.62 | 1 x 12.7 | 2 x 7.62 | 2 x 7.62 | 2 x 7.62 | 2 x 7.62 | 2 x 7.62 | 2 x 7.62 |
| | | | 8 x RS-82 † | 8 x RS-82 † | 2 x 7.62 | 1 x 12.7 | 1 x 12.7 | 2 x RS-82 | 1 x 12.7 | 1 x 12.7 | |
| | | | | | 8 x RS-82 † | | | | 4 x RS-132 | | |
| Page in main text | 43 | 43 | 47 | 47 | 47 | 47 | 47 | 52 | 55 | 61 | 62 |

* or 2 x 23 † or 8 x RS-132 See the Glossary and Notes, pages 14 and 15, for details of measurement units etc.

*Left:* **Two-seat version of the Il-2, with an experimental gun turret, undergoing tests at NII VVS.**

*Below:* **The Il-2 achieved the highest production figures of any aircraft to date. This is a record unlikely to be beaten!**

Table C · **Sukhoi Light Bombers and Attack Aircraft**

| | 'Ivanov' SZ-2 | 'Ivanov' SZ-3 | 'Ivanov' SZ-3 | BB-1 production | Su-2 production | Su-2 prototype | Su-2 production | Su-2 prototype | Su-4 production | ShB | Su-6 (SA) | Su-6 (SA) | Su-6 (SA) | Su-8 (DDBSh) |
|---|---|---|---|---|---|---|---|---|---|---|---|---|---|---|
| Year of Production | 1937 | 1939 | 1939 | 1939 | 1940 | 1941 | 1941 | 1941 | 1941 | 1940 | 1941 | 1942 | 1944 | 1943 |
| Crew | 2 | 2 | 2 | 2 | 2 | 2 | 2 | 2 | 2 | 2 | 1 | 2 | 2 | 2 |
| Powerplant | 1 x M-62 | 1 x M-87A | 1 x M-87B | 1 x M-88 | 1 x M-88 | 1 x M-88B | 1 x M-88B | 1 x M-82 | 1 x M-82 | 1 x M-88 | 1 x M-71 | 1 x M-71F | 1 x AM-42 | 2 x M-71F |
| Take-off power – (hp) | 820 | 950 | 950 | 950 | 1,100 | 1,100 | 1,100 | 1,700 | 1,700 | 1,100 | 1,900 | 2,200 | 2,000 | 2,200 |
| – (kW) | 611 | 708 | 708 | 708 | 820 | 820 | 820 | 1,268 | 1,268 | 820 | 1,417 | 1,641 | 1,492 | 1,641 |
| Length – (m) | 9.92 | 10.25 | 10.25 | 10.25 | 10.25 | 10.25 | 10.25 | 10.46 | 10.79 | 10.25 | 9.24 | 9.24 | 9.5 | 13.5 |
| – (ft-in) | 32-6½ | 33-7½ | 33-7½ | 33-7½ | 33-7½ | 33-7½ | 33-7½ | 34-3¾ | 35-4¾ | 33-7½ | 30-4 | 30-4 | 31-2 | 44-3½ |
| Wingspan – (m) | 14.3 | 14.3 | 14.3 | 14.3 | 14.3 | 14.3 | 14.3 | 14.3 | 14.3 | 14.3 | 13.58 | 13.58 | 13.58 | 20.5 |
| – (ft in) | 46-10¾ | 46-10¾ | 46-10¾ | 46-10¾ | 46-10¾ | 46-10¾ | 46-10¾ | 46-10¾ | 46-10¾ | 46-10¾ | 44-6½ | 44-6½ | 44-6½ | 67-3 |
| Wing area – (m²) | 29.0 | 29.0 | 29.0 | 29.0 | 29.0 | 29.0 | 29.0 | 29.0 | 29.0 | 29.0 | 26.0 | 26.0 | 28.0 | 60.0 |
| – (ft²) | 312 | 312 | 312 | 312 | 312 | 312 | 312 | 312 | 312 | 312 | 279 | 279 | 301 | 645 |
| Empty weight – (kg) | 2,604 | 2,816 | 2,800 | 2,918 | 2,930 | 2,970 | 2,970 | 3,220 | – | 3,100 | 3,727 | 4,110 | 4,370 | 9,208 |
| – (lb) | 5,740 | 6,208 | 6,172 | 6,432 | 6,459 | 6,547 | 6,547 | 7,098 | – | 6,834 | 8,216 | 9,060 | 9,634 | 20,299 |
| Gross weight – (kg) | 3,937 | 4,030 | 4,080 | 4,345 | 4,360 | 4,150 | 4,345 | 4,700 | 4,620 | 4,500 | 5,250 | 5,534 | 6,200 | 12,736 |
| – (lb) | 8,679 | 8,884 | 8,994 | 9,578 | 9,611 | 9,149 | 9,578 | 10,361 | 10,185 | 9,920 | 11,574 | 12,200 | 13,668 | 28,077 |
| Speed at sea level – (km/h) | 360.0 | 375.0 | 375.0 | 375.0 | 375.0 | 410.0 | 375.0 | 459.0 | 450.0 | – | 510.0 | 480.0 | 492.0 | 485.0 |
| – (mph) | 223.6 | 233.0 | 233.0 | 233.0 | 233.0 | 254.7 | 233.0 | 285.2 | 279.6 | – | 316.9 | 298.2 | 305.7 | 301.3 |
| Speed at altitude – (km/h) | 403.0 | 468.0 | 468.0 | 467.0 | 460.0 | 512.0 | 468.0 | 486.0 | 486.0 | – | 527.0 | 514.0 | 521.0 | 550.0 |
| – (mph) | 250.4 | 290.8 | 290.8 | 290.1 | 285.8 | 318.1 | 290.8 | 301.9 | 301.9 | – | 327.4 | 319.3 | 323.7 | 341.7 |
| Climb to 5,000m – (min) | 16.6 | 11.5 | 12.0 | 12.0 | 12.0 | 11.3 | 12.0 | 9.8 | 10.5 | – | 9.5 | 10.6 | 11.0 | 9.0 |
| – (to 16,400ft – min) | 16.6 | 11.5 | 12.0 | 12.0 | 12.0 | 11.3 | 12.0 | 9.8 | 10.5 | – | 9.5 | 10.6 | 11.0 | 9.0 |
| Service ceiling – (m) | 7,440 | 8,800 | 8,800 | 8,900 | 8,800 | 9,120 | 9,000 | 8,400 | 9,500 | – | 7,600 | 8,100 | 8,000 | 9,000 |
| – (ft) | 2,450 | 28,900 | 28,900 | 29,200 | 28,900 | 29,900 | 29,500 | 27,550 | 31,200 | – | 24,900 | 26,600 | 26,250 | 29,500 |
| Operational range – (km) | 1,200 | 1,160 | – | 1,200 | 1,200 | 1,000 | 1,190 | 1,100 | 1,000 | – | 576 | 972 | 790 | 600 |
| – (miles) | 745 | 720 | – | 745 | 745 | 621 | 739 | 683 | 621 | – | 357 | 603 | 490 | 372 |
| Take-off run – (m) | 380 | – | 280 | – | 380 | – | – | 345 | 350 | – | 520 | 410 | 540 | 350 |
| – (ft) | 1,246 | – | 918 | – | 1,246 | – | – | 1,131 | 1,148 | – | 1,706 | 1,345 | 1,771 | 1,148 |
| Landing roll – (m) | 240 | – | – | – | 425 | – | – | – | – | – | – | – | – | – |
| – (ft) | 787 | – | – | – | 1,394 | – | – | – | – | – | – | – | – | – |
| Bomb load – (kg) | 400 | 400 | 400 | 400 | 400 | 400 | 400 | 400 | 400 | 600 | 400 | 200 | 200 | 600 |
| – (lb) | 881 | 881 | 881 | 881 | 881 | 881 | 881 | 881 | 881 | 1,322 | 881 | 440 | 440 | 1,322 |
| Armament – (mm) | 5 x 7.62 | 5 x 7.62 | 5 x 7.62 | 6 x 7.62 | 6 x 7.62 | 6 x 7.62 | 6 x 7.62 | 2 x 12.7 2 x 7.62 | 2 x 12.7 2 x 7.62 | 6 x 7.62 | 2 x 23 4 x 7.62 | 2 x 37 1 x 12.7 2 x 7.62 | 2 x 37 1 x 12.7 2 x 7.62 | 4 x 45 1 x 12.7 5 x 7.62 |
| Page in main text | 72 | 72 | 72 | 73 | 73 | 73 | 73 | 77 | 77 | 78 | 80 | 80 | 80 | 82 |

See the Glossary and Notes, pages 14 and 15, for details of measurement units etc.

*Above:* **The greatest part of the Sukhoi BB-1 (Su-2) fleet was fitted with the M-88B engine. This illustration is of the prototype under test.**

*Right:*
**Su-6 with an AM-42 water-cooled engine.**

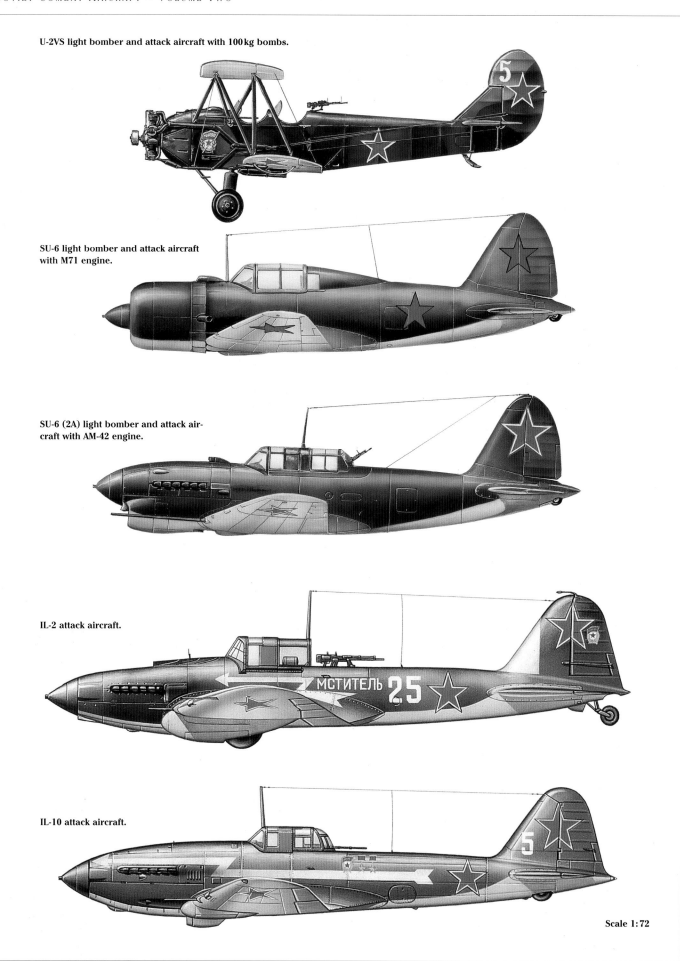

U-2VS light bomber and attack aircraft with 100 kg bombs.

SU-6 light bomber and attack aircraft with M71 engine.

SU-6 (2A) light bomber and attack aircraft with AM-42 engine.

IL-2 attack aircraft.

IL-10 attack aircraft.

Scale 1:72

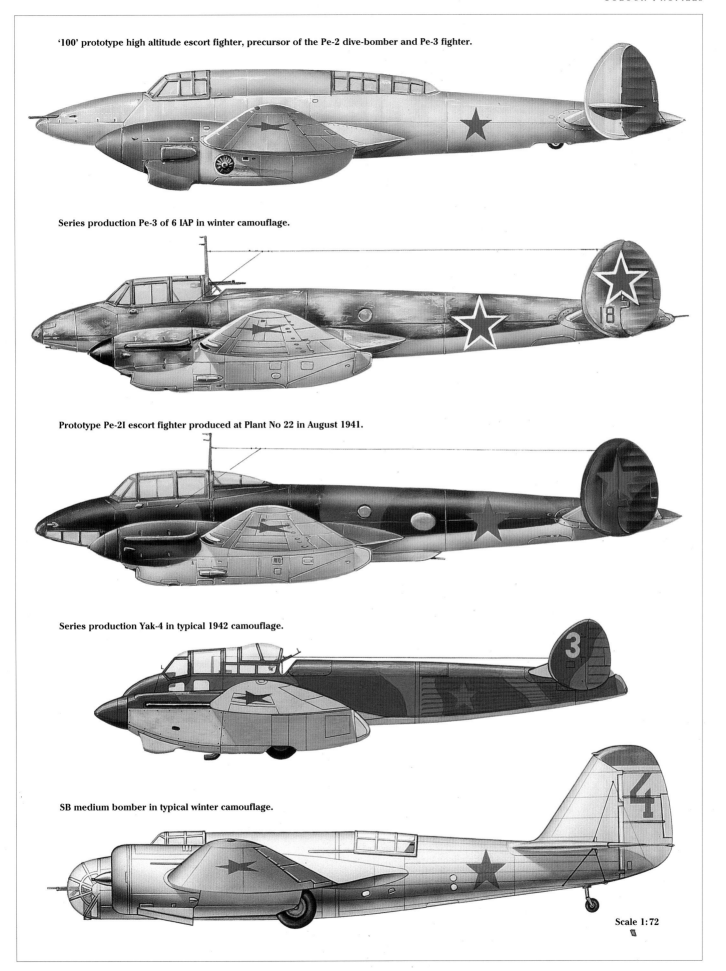

'100' prototype high altitude escort fighter, precursor of the Pe-2 dive-bomber and Pe-3 fighter.

Series production Pe-3 of 6 IAP in winter camouflage.

Prototype Pe-2I escort fighter produced at Plant No 22 in August 1941.

Series production Yak-4 in typical 1942 camouflage.

SB medium bomber in typical winter camouflage.

Scale 1:72

Table D

## Miscellaneous Light Bombers, Attack and Reconnaissance Aircraft

| | R-5 | U-2VS | VIT-1 | VIT-2 | SPB (D) | S-2M103 | OPB-5 | 'Pegasus' | KhAI-5 | R-10 | R-10 standard | KhAI-52 | KhAI-52 | No.22 (BB-22 No.1) | BB-22 No.2 | Yak-2 | Yak-4 |
|---|---|---|---|---|---|---|---|---|---|---|---|---|---|---|---|---|---|
| Year of Production | 1934 | 1933 | 1937 | 1938 | 1939 | 1940 | 1941 | 1943 | 1936 | 1938 | 1939 | 1939 | 1939 | 1939 | 1940 | 1940 | 1940 |
| Powerplant | 1 x<br>M-17F | 1 x<br>M-11F | 2 x<br>M-103 | 2 x<br>M-105 | 2 x<br>M-105 | 2 x<br>M-103 | 1 x<br>M-90 | 2 x<br>M-11F | 1 x<br>Cyclone | 1 x<br>M-25V | 1 x<br>M-25V | 1 x<br>M-62 | 1 x<br>M-63 | 2 x<br>M-103 | 2 x<br>M-103 | 2 x<br>M-103 | 2 x<br>M-105 |
| Power at altitude – (hp) | 730 | 140 | 960 | 1,050 | 1,050 | 960 | 1,425 | 140 | 712 | 750 | 750 | 820 | 1,100 | 960 | 960 | 960 | 1,050 |
| – (kW) | 544 | 104 | 716 | 783 | 783 | 716 | 1,063 | 104 | 531 | 559 | 559 | 611 | 820 | 716 | 716 | 716 | 783 |
| Length – (m) | 10.56 | 8.17 | 12.7 | 12.25 | 11.2 | 13.2 | 8.28 | 8.35 * | 9.3 | 9.4 | 9.4 | 9.6 | 9.6 | 9.34 | 9.34 | 9.34 | 10.18 |
| – (ft-in) | 34-7½ | 26-9½ | 41-8 | 40-2 | 36-9 | 43-4 | 27-2 | 27-4½ * | 30-6 | 30-10 | 30-10 | 31-6 | 31-6 | 30-7½ | 30-7½ | 30-7½ | 33-4½ |
| Wingspan – (m) | 15.5 | 11.4 | 16.5 | 16.5 | 17.0 | 11.4 | 10.4 | 11.5 | 12.2 | 12.2 | 12.2 | 12.2 | 13.42 | 14.0 | 14.0 | 14.0 | 14.0 |
| – (ft-in) | 50-10 | 37-4¾ | 54-1½ | 54-1½ | 55-9¼ | 37-4¾ | 34-1½ | 37-9 | 40-0 | 40-0 | 40-0 | 40-0 | 44-0 | 45-11 | 45-11 | 45-11 | 45-11 |
| Wing area – ($m^2$) | 50.2 | 33.15 | 40.4 | 40.76 | 42.93 | 22.9 | 18.0 | 26.6 | 26.8 | 26.8 | 26.8 | 26.8 | 25.6 | 26.73 | 29.4 | 29.4 | 29.4 |
| – ($ft^2$) | 540.3 | 356.8 | 434.8 | 438.7 | 462.1 | 246.5 | 193.7 | 286.3 | 288.4 | 288.4 | 288.4 | 288.4 | 275.5 | 287.7 | 316.4 | 316.4 | 316.4 |
| Empty weight – (kg) | 2,970 | – | 4,013 | 4,032 | 4,480 | – | 2,546 | 1,800 | 1,650 | 1,980 | 2,127 | 2,443 | 2,546 | 3,796 | – | 4,258 | 4,560 |
| – (lb) | 6,547 | – | 8,847 | 8,888 | 9,876 | – | 5,612 | 3,968 | 3,637 | 4,365 | 4,689 | 5,385 | 5,612 | 8,368 | – | 9,387 | 10,052 |
| Gross weight – (kg) | 2,960 † | 1,081 | 6,453 | 6,302 | 6,850 | 5,150 | 3,842 | 2,150 ‡ | 2,515 | 2,780 | 2,877 | 3,273 | 3,376 | 5,023 | 5,315 | 5,630 | 6,115 |
| – (lb) | 6,525 † | 2,383 | 14,226 | 13,893 | 15,101 | 11,353 | 8,470 | 4,739 ‡ | 5,544 | 6,128 | 6,342 | 7,215 | 7,442 | 11,073 | 11,717 | 12,411 | 13,481 |
| Speed at sea level – (km/h) | 210.0 | 130.0 | 450.0 | 486.0 | 490.0 | – | – | 198.0 | 350.0 | 322.0 | 341.0 | 374.0 | 356.0 | 455.0 | 449.0 | 410.0 | 458.0 |
| – (mph) | 130.4 | 80.7 | 279.6 | 301.9 | 304.4 | – | – | 123.0 | 217.4 | 200.0 | 211.8 | 232.3 | 221.2 | 282.7 | 279.0 | 254.7 | 284.5 |
| Speed at altitude – (km/h) | 228.0 | – | 530.0 | 513.0 | 520.0 | 570.0 | – | 189.0 | 388.0 | 360.0 | 370.0 | 410.0 | – | 567.0 | 535.0 | 498.0 | 533.0 |
| – (m) | 3,000 | – | 3,000 | 4,500 | 4,500 | 4,600 | – | – | 2,500 | 2,900 | 2,900 | 4,500 | – | 4,900 | 5,000 | 4,800 | 5,050 |
| – (mph) | 141.6 | – | 329.3 | 318.7 | 323.1 | 354.1 | – | – | 241.0 | 223.6 | 229.9 | 254.7 | – | 352.3 | 332.4 | 309.4 | 331.1 |
| – (ft) | 9,800 | – | 9,800 | 14,750 | 14,750 | 15,100 | – | – | 8,200 | 9,500 | 9,500 | 14,750 | – | 16,100 | 16,400 | 15,750 | 16,600 |
| Climb to 5,000m – (min) | 17.0 | – | 8.4 | 6.8 | 7.5 | – | – | – | 12.0 | 15.7 | 14.4 | 16.0 | – | 5.75 | 7.4 | 8.0 | 6.5 |
| – (to 16,400ft – min) | 17.0 | – | 8.4 | 6.8 | 7.5 | – | – | – | 12.0 | 15.7 | 14.4 | 16.0 | – | 5.75 | 7.4 | 8.0 | 6.5 |
| Service ceiling – (m) | 6,400 | 3,120 | 8,000 | 8,200 | 9,000 | – | – | 2,620 | 7,700 | 7,000 | 6,700 | 8,800 | – | 10,800 | 8,900 | 8,700 | 9,700 |
| – (ft) | 20,100 | 10,250 | 26,250 | 26,900 | 29,500 | – | – | 8,600 | 25,250 | 23,000 | 22,000 | 28,900 | – | 35,400 | 29,200 | 28,500 | 32,000 |
| Operational range – (km) | 800 | – | 1,000 | 800 | 2,200 | 700 | – | 400 | 1,050 | – | – | 1,000 | – | 960 | 800 | 900 | 740 |
| – (miles) | 497 | – | 621 | 497 | 1,367 | 434 | – | 248 | 652 | – | – | 621 | – | 596 | 497 | 559 | 459 |
| Take-off run – (m) | 300 | – | 390 | 450 | 500 | 860 | – | – | 250 | – | – | 450 | 350 | 375 | 500 | 390 | 442 |
| – (ft) | 984 | – | 1,279 | 1,476 | 1,640 | 2,821 | – | – | 820 | – | – | 1,476 | 1,148 | 1,230 | 1,640 | 1,279 | 1,450 |
| Landing roll – (m) | 220 | – | 460 | 400 | 450 | – | – | – | 230 | – | – | 280 | 400 | 855 | 500 | 300 | 496 |
| – (ft) | 721 | – | 1,509 | 1,312 | 1,476 | – | – | – | 754 | – | – | 918 | 1,312 | 2,805 | 1,640 | 984 | 1,627 |
| Bomb load – (kg) | 300 | 350 | 600<br>to 1,000 | 600<br>to 1,000 | 800<br>to 1,500 | 400 | 500 | 500 | 200 | 300 | 300 | 400 | 400 | 120 | 400 | 400<br>to 500 | 400<br>to 900 |
| – (lb) | 661 | 771 | 1,322<br>to 2,204 | 1,322<br>to 2,204 | 1,763<br>to 3,306 | 881 | 1,102 | 1,102 | 440 | 661 | 661 | 881 | 881 | 264 | 881 | 881<br>to 1,102 | 881<br>to 1,984 |
| Armament – (mm) | 1 x 7.62 | 1 x 12.7† | 2 x 37<br>1 x 20<br>1 x 7.62 | 2 x 37<br>4 x 20<br>2 x 7.62 | 1 x 12.7<br>2 x 7.62 | 2 x 12.7 | 2 x 12.7<br>2 x 7.62 | 2 x 23<br>1 x 12.7 | 2 x 7.62 | 3 x 7.62 | 3 x 7.62 | 7 x 7.62 | 7 x 7.62 | – | 2 x 7.62 | 2 x 7.62 | 2 x 7.62 |
| Page in main text | 66 | 69 | 67 | 67 | 68 | 42 | 63 | 83 | 64 | 64 | 64 | 64 | 64 | 85 | 85 | 85 | 87 |

* or 9.17m (30ft 0in); † or 3,350kg (7,385lb); ‡ or 2,700kg (5,952lb).

See the Glossary and Notes, pages 14 and 15, for details of measurements units etc.

**Although obsolete, Polikarpov R-5s were used for reconnaissance and light bombing duties during the early stages of the war.**

**Joseph Neman KhAI-51 attack aircraft prototype.**

Table E  **Petlyakov and Myasishchev Dive Bombers**

| | PB-100 | Pe-2 | Pe-2 No.10/35 | Pe-2 No.15/95 | Pe-2 No.4/175 | Pe-2 No.12/307 | Pe-2 No.1/232 | Pe-2B | Pe2I | Pe-2I | Pe-2M | Pe-2K | Pe-2RD | Pe-2M-1 |
|---|---|---|---|---|---|---|---|---|---|---|---|---|---|---|
| Year of Production | 1940 | 1940 | 1941 | 1942 | 1943 | 1944 | 1944 | 1943 | 1944 | 1945 | 1945 | 1945 | 1943 | 1944 |
| Crew | 3 | 3 | 3 | 3 | 3 | 3 | 3 | 3 | 2 | 3 | 3 | 3 | 3 | 2 |
| Powerplant | 2 x M-105 | 2 x M-105 | 2 x M-105RA | 2 x M-105RA | 2 x M-105PF | 2 x M-105PF | 2 x ASh-82 | 2 x M-105PF | 2 x VK-107A | 2 x VK-107A | 2 x VK-107A | 2 x VK-105PF | 2 x VK-105RA | 2 x M-1 |
| Power at altitude – (hp) | 1,050 | 1,050 | 1,050 | 1,050 | 1,180 | 1,180 | 1,380 | 1,180 | 1,450 | 1,450 | 1,450 | 1,180 | 1,050 | 1,300 |
| – (kW) | 783 | 783 | 783 | 783 | 880 | 880 | 1,029 | 880 | 1,081 | 1,081 | 1,081 | 880 | 783 | 969 |
| Length – (m) | – | 12.78 | 12.78 | 12.78 | 12.78 | 12.78 | 12.78 | 12.241 | 13.471 | 13.471 | 13.471 | 13.241 | 12.55 | – |
| – (ft-in) | – | 41-10 | 41-10 | 41-10 | 41-10 | 41-10 | 41-10 | 40-1¾ | 44-2¼ | 44-2¼ | 44-2¼ | 43-5¼ | 41-2 | – |
| Wingspan – (m) | 17.15 | 17.15 | 17.15 | 17.15 | 17.15 | 17.15 | 17.15 | 17.15 | 17.8 | 17.8 | 17.99 | 17.8 | 17.15 | – |
| – (ft-in) | 56-3 | 56-3 | 56-3 | 56-3 | 56-3 | 56-3 | 56-3 | 56-3 | 58-4½ | 58-4½ | 59-0 | 58-4½ | 56-3 | – |
| Wing area – (m²) | 40.5 | 40.5 | 40.5 | 40.5 | 40.5 | 40.5 | 40.5 | 40.5 | 42.5 | 42.5 | 43.5 | 42.5 | 40.5 | – |
| – (ft²) | 435.9 | 435.9 | 435.9 | 435.9 | 435.9 | 435.9 | 435.9 | 435.9 | 457.4 | 457.4 | 468.2 | 457.4 | 435.9 | – |
| Empty weight – (kg) | – | 5,363 | 5,630 | 5,540 | 5,620 | 6,120 | 6,482 | 6,210 | 7,014 | 6,970 | 7,045 | 6,344 | 6,044 | – |
| – (lb) | – | 11,823 | 12,411 | 12,213 | 12,389 | 13,492 | 14,290 | 13,690 | 15,462 | 15,365 | 15,531 | 13,985 | 13,324 | – |
| Gross weight – (kg) | 7,200 | 7,500 | 7,718 | 7,614 | 7,770 | 8,300 | 8,930 | 8,580 | 8,983 | 9,700 | 9,850 | 8,405 | 8,200 | 8,460 |
| – (lb) | 15,873 | 16,534 | 17,014 | 16,785 | 17,129 | 18,298 | 19,686 | 18,915 | 19,803 | 21,384 | 21,715 | 18,529 | 18,077 | 18,650 |
| Speed at sea level – (km/h) | 455.0 | 452.0 | 445.0 | 408.0 | 460.0 | 465.0 | 470.0 | 472.0 | 556.0 | 520.0 | 545.0 | 468.0 | 475.0 | 474.0 |
| – (mph) | 282.7 | 280.8 | 276.5 | 253.5 | 285.8 | 288.9 | 292.0 | 293.2 | 345.4 | 323.1 | 338.6 | 290.8 | 295.1 | 294.5 |
| Speed at altitude – (km/h) | 535.0 | 540.0 | 530.0 | 488.0 | 506.0 | 524.0 | 526.0 | 534.0 | 656.0 | 631.0 | 630.0 | 570.0 | 520.0 | 562.0 |
| – (m) | 6,000 | 5,000 | – | – | – | – | 3,000 | 3,900 | 5,650 | 5,700 | 5,600 | 4,000 | 5,060 | 6,000 |
| – (mph) | 332.4 | 335.5 | 329.3 | 303.2 | 314.4 | 325.6 | 326.8 | 331.8 | 407.6 | 392.0 | 391.4 | 354.1 | 323.1 | 349.2 |
| – (ft) | 19,700 | 16,400 | – | – | – | – | 9,900 | 12,800 | 18,500 | 18,700 | 18,400 | 13,100 | 16,600 | 19,700 |
| Climb to 5,000m – (min) | 6.8 | 9.3 | – | – | – | – | – | 10.5 | 7.0 | 8.4 | 8.8 | 7.8 | 7.05 | 7.2 |
| – (to 16,400ft – min) | 6.8 | 9.3 | – | – | – | – | – | 10.5 | 7.0 | 8.4 | 8.8 | 7.8 | 7.05 | 7.2 |
| Service ceiling – (m) | 12,000 | 8,850 | 8,800 | 8,900 | 8,000 | 7,750 | 7,600 | – | 9,350 | 9,000 | 8,500 | 8,200 | – | – |
| – (ft) | 39,400 | 29,000 | 28,900 | 29,200 | 26,250 | 25,500 | 24,900 | – | 30,700 | 29,500 | 27,900 | 26,900 | – | – |
| Operational range – (km) | – | 1,315 | 1,410 | 1,240 | 1,250 | 1,280 | – | 1,190 | 2,275 | 1,850 | 2,050 | 1,200 | 776 | – |
| – (miles) | – | 817 | 876 | 770 | 776 | 795 | – | 739 | 1,413 | 1,149 | 1,273 | 745 | 482 | – |
| Take-off run – (m) | – | 362 | 412 | 490 | 450 | 500 | 500 | 510 | 650 | 530 | 585 | 525 | 446 | – |
| – (ft) | – | 1,187 | 1,351 | 1,607 | 1,476 | 1,640 | 1,640 | 1,673 | 2,132 | 1,738 | 1,919 | 1,722 | 1,463 | – |
| Landing roll – (m) | – | – | – | – | – | – | – | – | 790 | 485 | 550 | – | 430 | – |
| – (ft) | – | – | – | – | – | – | – | – | 2,591 | 1,591 | 1,804 | – | 1,410 | – |
| Bomb load, normal – (kg) | 600 | 600 | 600 | 600 | 600 | 600 | 600 | 600 | 500 | 1,000 | 1,000 | 600 | 600 | 600 |
| – (lb) | 1,322 | 1,322 | 1,322 | 1,322 | 1,322 | 1,322 | 1,322 | 1,322 | 1,102 | 2,204 | 2,204 | 1,322 | 1,322 | 1,322 |
| Bomb load, max – (kg) | 1,000 | 1,000 | 1,000 | 1,000 | 1,000 | 1,000 | 1,000 | 1,000 | 1,500 | 3,000 | 3,000 | 1,000 | 1,000 | 1,000 |
| – (lb) | 2,204 | 2,204 | 2,204 | 2,204 | 2,204 | 2,204 | 2,204 | 2,204 | 3,306 | 6,613 | 6,613 | 2,204 | 2,204 | 2,204 |
| Armament – (mm) | 4 x 7.62 * | 4 x 7.62 | 2 x 12.7<br>2 x 7.62 | 3 x 12.7<br>2 x 7.62 | 3 x 12.7<br>2 x 7.62 | 3 x 12.7<br>2 x 7.62 | 3 x 12.7 | 3 x 12.7<br>1 x 7.62 | 2 x 12.7 | 3 x 20 | 3 x 20 | 3 x 12.7 | 2 x 12.7<br>1 x 7.62 | 3 x 12.7 |
| Page in main text | 115 | 116 | 120 | – | 123 | – | – | 127 | 128 | 128 | 128 | 128 | 127 | 128 |

\* or 2 x 7.62 and 2 x 20  See the Glossary and Notes, pages 14 and 15, for details of measurement units etc.

Pe-2 bomber in its log-lined dispersal. Note the entry hatch.

More than 10,500 Pe-2s were delivered to the VVS – an extraordinary number for an attack bomber.

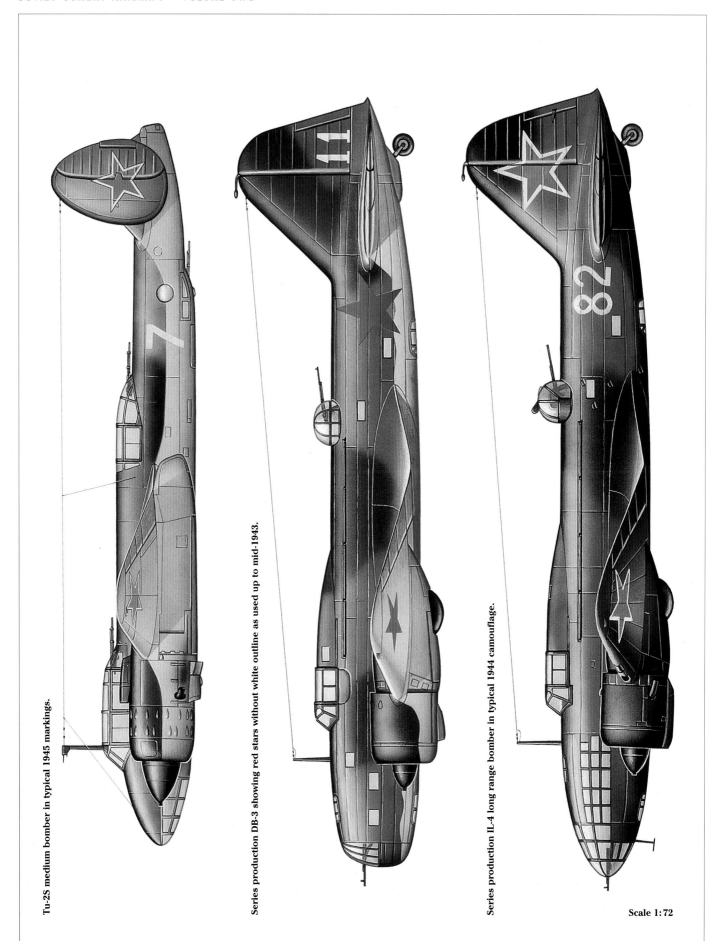

Tu-2S medium bomber in typical 1945 markings.

Series production DB-3 showing red stars without white outline as used up to mid-1943.

Series production IL-4 long range bomber in typical 1944 camouflage.

**Scale 1:72**

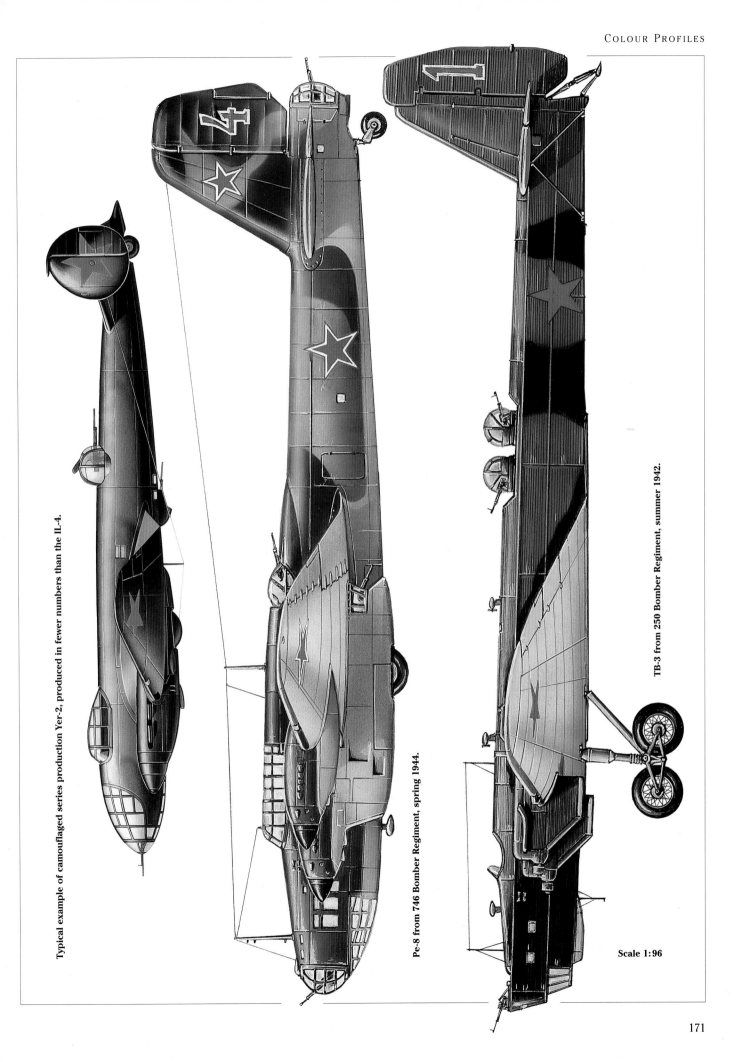

Typical example of camouflaged series production Yer-2, produced in fewer numbers than the IL-4.

Pe-8 from 746 Bomber Regiment, spring 1944.

TB-3 from 250 Bomber Regiment, summer 1942.

Scale 1:96

Table F

## Soviet Long Range Bombers

| | TB-3 production | TB-3 production | ANT-42 prototype | TB-7 (Pe-8) | TB-7 (Pe-8) | Pe-8 | DB-240 | Yer-2 production | Yer-2 production | Yer-2 production | DB-LK | NB(T) | DVB-102 | DVB-102 | DB-2VK108 (VM-16) | VB-2VK-109 | DB-3 | DB-3T | DB-3TP | DB-3 | DB-3F |
|---|---|---|---|---|---|---|---|---|---|---|---|---|---|---|---|---|---|---|---|---|---|
| Year of Production | 1933 | 1936 | 1938 | 1941 | 1941 | 1942 | 1939 | 1941 | 1942 | 1943 | 1940 | 1943 | 1942 | 1943 | 1944 | 1945 | 1936 | 1937 | 1938 | 1939 | 1939 |
| Crew | 6 | 6 | 9 | 10 | 10 | 11 | 4 | 4 | 4 | 4 | 4 | 5 | 4 | 4 | 2 | 2 | 3 | 3 | 3 | 3 | 3 |
| Powerplant | M-17F | M-34FRN | M-34FRNB | AM-35A | M-40 | M-82 | M-105 | M-105 | AM-37 | ACh-30B | M-87B | ASh-82FN | M-120TK | M-71-2TK3 | VK-108 | VK-109 | M-85 | M-85 | M-86 | M-87A | M-87B |
| | 4 x | 4 x | 4 x | 4 x | 4 x | 4 x | 2 x | 2 x | 2 x | 2 x | 2 x | 2 x | 2 x | 2 x | 2 x | 2 x | 2 x | 2 x | 2 x | 2 x | 2 x |
| Take-off power – (hp) | 715 | 830 | 1,200 | 1,340 | 1,500 | 1,400 | 1,050 | 1,050 | 1,400 | 1,500 | 950 | 1,850 | 1,800 | 1,910 | 1,800 | 2,075 | 760 | 760 | 950 | 950 | 950 |
| – (kW) | 533 | 619 | 895 | 999 | 1,119 | 1,044 | 783 | 783 | 1,044 | 1,119 | 708 | 1,380 | 1,342 | 1,424 | 1,342 | 1,547 | 566 | 566 | 708 | 708 | 708 |
| Length – (m) | 24.4 | 25.1 | 22.78 | 23.2 | 23.2 | 23.2 | 16.3 | 16.4 | 16.3 | 16.4 | 9.78 | 15.3 | 18.9 | 18.9 | 13.47 | 14.16 | 14.223 | 14.223 | 15.1 | 14.223 | 14.788 |
| – (ft-in) | 80-0 | 82-4 | 74-9 | 76-1¼ | 76-1¼ | 76-1¼ | 53-6 | 53-9½ | 53-6 | 53-9½ | 32-0 | 50-2¼ | 62-0 | 62-0 | 44-2 | 46-6 | 46-8 | 46-8 | 49-6¾ | 46-8 | 48-6 |
| Wingspan – (m) | 39.5 | 41.8 | 39.0 | 39.13 | 39.13 | 39.13 | 23.0 | 23.0 | 21.7 | 23.0 | 21.6 | 21.5 | 25.17 | 25.17 | 17.8 | 17.8 | 21.4 | 21.4 | 21.4 | 21.4 | 21.44 |
| – (ft-in) | 129-6 | 137-2 | 127-10 | 128-4 | 128-4 | 128-4 | 75-6 | 75-6 | 71-2½ | 75-6 | 70-10 | 70-6 | 82-6 | 82-6 | 58-4½ | 58-4½ | 70-2½ | 70-2½ | 70-2½ | 70-2½ | 70-4 |
| Wing area – (m²) | 230.0 | 234.5 | 188.4 | 188.66 | 188.66 | 188.66 | 72.0 | 72.0 | – | 73.1 | 56.87 | 58.1 | 78.3 | 78.3 | 43.0 | 43.5 | 65.6 | 65.6 | 65.6 | 65.6 | 66.7 |
| – (ft²) | 2,475.7 | 2,524.2 | 2,027.9 | 2,030.7 | 2,030.7 | 2,030.7 | 775.0 | 775.0 | – | 786.8 | 612.1 | 625.4 | 842.8 | 842.8 | 462.8 | 468.2 | 706.1 | 706.1 | 706.1 | 706.1 | 717.9 |
| Empty weight – (kg) | 10,967 | – | 18,000 | 18,571 | 19,710 | 18,790 | 7,070 | – | 8,872 | 10,340 | 6,004 | 8,843 | 10,966 | 12,173 | 6,922 | 7,508 | 4,778 | 4,298 | 5,630 | 5,030 | 5,373 |
| – (lb) | 24,177 | – | 39,682 | 40,941 | 43,452 | 41,424 | 15,586 | – | 19,559 | 22,795 | 13,236 | 19,495 | 24,175 | 26,836 | 15,260 | 16,552 | 10,533 | 9,475 | 12,411 | 11,089 | 11,845 |
| Gross weight – (kg) | 17,200 | – | 28,000 | 33,500 | 33,500 | 36,000 | 11,330 | 11,300 | 13,000 | 14,250 | 10,672 | 13,800 | 14,906 | 16,038 | 9,400 | 9,900 | 8,600 | – | 8,600 | 9,450 | 9,778 |
| – (lb) | 37,918 | – | 61,728 | 73,853 | 73,853 | 79,365 | 24,977 | 24,911 | 28,659 | 31,415 | 23,527 | 30,423 | 32,861 | 35,357 | 20,723 | 21,825 | 19,841 | – | 18,959 | 20,833 | 21,556 |
| Speed at sea level – (km/h) | 197.0 | – | 315.0 | 347.0 | 345.0 | 362.0 | 380.0 | – | 407.0 | 370.0 | 395.0 | 445.0 | 443.0 | 430.0 | 575.0 | 595.0 | 327.0 | 320.0 | 292.0 | 345.0 | 354.0 |
| – (mph) | 122.4 | – | 195.7 | 215.6 | 214.3 | 224.9 | 236.1 | – | 252.9 | 229.9 | 245.4 | 276.5 | 275.2 | 267.1 | 357.2 | 369.7 | 203.1 | 198.8 | 181.4 | 214.3 | 219.9 |
| Speed at altitude – (km/h) | 177.0 | 300.0 | 430.0 | 443.0 | 393.0 | 420.0 | 445.0 | 437.0 | 507.0 | 420.0 | 488.0 | 510.0 | 540.0 | 534.0 | 700.0 | 720.0 | 400.0 | 395.0 | 343.0 | 439.0 | 445.0 |
| – (mph) | 109.9 | 186.4 | 267.1 | 275.2 | 244.2 | 260.9 | 276.5 | 271.5 | 315.0 | 260.9 | 303.2 | 316.9 | 335.5 | 331.8 | 434.9 | 447.3 | 248.5 | 245.4 | 213.1 | 272.7 | 276.5 |
| Climb to 5,000m – (min) | – | – | 16.3 | – | – | – | – | – | – | – | 13.6 | 12.0 | 13.5 | 12.0 | – | 6.0 | 15.1 | 13.0 | 18.2 | 12.1 | 13.6 |
| – (to 16,400ft – min) | – | – | 16.3 | – | – | – | – | – | – | – | 13.6 | 12.0 | 13.5 | 12.0 | – | 6.0 | 15.1 | 13.0 | 18.2 | 12.1 | 13.6 |
| Service ceiling – (m) | 3,800 | ~8,000 | 11,250 | 9,300 | 9,200 | 8,000 | 7,700 | 7,700 | 9,500 | 7,200 | 8,500 | 6,150 | 8,300 | 10,500 | 11,000 | 12,250 | 8,400 | 7,800 | 7,570 | 9,600 | 9,000 |
| – (ft) | 12,500 | ~26,250 | 36,900 | 30,500 | 30,200 | 26,250 | 25,250 | 25,250 | 31,200 | 23,600 | 28,000 | 20,200 | 27,250 | 34,500 | 36,100 | 40,200 | 27,600 | 25,600 | 24,800 | 31,500 | 29,500 |
| Operational range – (km) | 1,350 | – | 3,500 | 3,700 | 6,100 | 4,200 | 4,100 | 4,000 | 2,500 | 5,500 | 2,900 | 3,030 | 3,340 | 3,600 | 2,250 | 2,200 | 4,000 | 1,800 | 1,400 | 3,800 | 3,500 |
| – (miles) | 838 | – | 2,174 | 2,299 | 3,790 | 2,609 | 2,547 | 2,485 | 1,553 | 3,417 | 1,802 | 1,882 | 2,075 | 2,236 | 1,398 | 1,367 | 2,485 | 1,118 | 869 | 2,361 | 2,174 |
| Take-off run – (m) | – | – | – | 470 | 337 | 750 | 580 | – | 760 | 635 | 600 | 660 | 640 | 670 | 500 | 520 | 190 | 190 | 600 | 345 | 390 |
| – (ft) | – | – | – | 1,541 | 1,105 | 2,460 | 1,902 | – | 9,055 | 2,083 | 1,968 | 2,165 | 2,099 | 2,198 | 1,640 | 1,706 | 623 | 623 | 1,968 | 1,131 | 1,279 |
| Landing roll – (m) | – | – | – | – | – | – | – | – | – | – | 550 | 570 | 340 | – | 560 | 460 | 300 | 300 | 600 | 450 | 450 |
| – (ft) | – | – | – | – | – | – | – | – | – | – | 1,804 | 1,870 | 1,115 | – | 1,837 | 1,509 | 984 | 984 | 1,968 | 1,476 | 1,476 |
| Bomb load – (kg) | 2,000 | 2,000 | 4,000 | 4,000 | 4,000 | 6,000 | 4,000 | 4,000 | 4,000 | 5,000 | 2,000 | 4,000 | 3,000 | 3,000 | 3,000 | 3,000 | 2,500 | – | – | 2,500 | 2,500 |
| – (lb) | 4,409 | 4,409 | 8,818 | 8,818 | 8,818 | 13,227 | 8,818 | 8,818 | 8,818 | 11,022 | 4,409 | 8,818 | 6,613 | 6,613 | 6,613 | 6,613 | 5,511 | – | – | 5,511 | 5,511 |
| Armament – (mm) | 4 x 7.62 | 6 x 7.62 | 6 x 20<br>1 x 7.62 | 1 x 20<br>6 x 7.62 | 1 x 20<br>6 x 7.62 | 2 x 20<br>3 x 12.7 | 3 x 7.62 | 1 x 12.7<br>2 x 7.62 | 3 x 12.7 | 1 x 20<br>2 x 12.7 | 6 x 7.62 | 3 x 12.7 | 1 x 20<br>2 x 12.7<br>1 x 7.62 | 1 x 20<br>2 x 12.7<br>1 x 7.62 | 2 x 20 | 2 x 20 | 3 x 7.62 | 3 x 7.62 | 3 x 7.62 | 3 x 7.62 | 2 x 7.62 |
| Page in main text | 140 | 140 | 132 | 132 | 132 | 134 | 90 | 92 | 92 | 92 | 96 | 139 | 111 | 111 | 113 | 114 | 98 | 100 | 100 | 100 | 101 |

See the Glossary and Notes, pages 14 and 15, for details of measurement units etc.

Table F – continued

| | DB-3F | DB-3F | IL-4 | DB-4 | IL-6 | IL-6 |
|---|---|---|---|---|---|---|
| Year of Production | 1940 | 1941 | 1942 | 1940 | 1943 | 1944 |
| Crew | 3 | 4 | 4 | 4 | 5 | 6 |
| Powerplant | M-88 | M-88B | M-88B | AM-37 | ACh-30B | ACh-30BF |
| | 2 x | 2 x | 2 x | 2 x | 2 x | 2 x |
| Take-off power – (hp) | 1,100 | 1,100 | 1,100 | 1,400 | 1,500 | 1,900 |
| – (kW) | 820 | 820 | 820 | 1,044 | 1,119 | 1,417 |
| Length – (m) | 14.788 | 14.788 | 14.788 | 17.85 | 17.378 | 17.378 |
| – (ft-in) | 48-6 | 48-6 | 48-6 | 58-6½ | 57-0 | 57-0 |
| Wingspan – (m) | 21.44 | 21.44 | 21.44 | 25.00 | 26.07 | 26.07 |
| – (ft-in) | 70-4 | 70-4 | 70-4 | 82-0 | 85-6 | 85-6 |
| Wing area – (m²) | 66.7 | 66.7 | 67.0 | 83.0 | 84.8 | 84.8 |
| – (ft²) | 717.9 | 717.9 | 721.2 | 893.4 | 912.8 | 912.8 |
| Empty weight – (kg) | 5,641 | 7,230 | 6,421 | 7,561 | 11,690 | 11,930 |
| – (lb) | 12,436 | 15,939 | 14,155 | 16,668 | 25,771 | 26,300 |
| Gross weight – (kg) | 10,153 | 11,570 | 12,120 | 13,006 | 18,650 | 19,600 |
| – (lb) | 22,383 | 25,507 | 26,719 | 28,672 | 41,115 | 43,209 |
| Speed at sea level – (km/h) | 350.0 | 345.0 | 332.0 | 415.0 | 382.0 | 400.0 |
| – (mph) | 217.4 | 214.3 | 206.3 | 257.8 | 237.3 | 248.5 |
| Speed at altitude – (km/h) | 435.0 | 422.0 | 398.0 | 500.0 | 445.0 | 464.0 |
| – (mph) | 270.3 | 262.2 | 247.3 | 310.6 | 276.5 | 288.3 |
| Climb to 5,000m – (min) | 10.5 | 14.6 | 19.0 | – | 15.7 | 28.7 |
| – (to 16,400ft – min) | 10.5 | 14.6 | 19.0 | – | 15.7 | 28.7 |
| Service ceiling – (m) | 10,000 | 8,900 | 8,300 | 10,000 | 8,000 | 7,000 |
| – (ft) | 32,800 | 29,200 | 27,250 | 32,800 | 26,250 | 23,000 |
| Operational range – (km) | 3,300 | 3,800 | 3,585 | 4,000 | 5,450 | 5,450 |
| – (miles) | 2,050 | 2,361 | 2,227 | 2,485 | 3,386 | 3,386 |
| Take-off run – (m) | 400 | 480 | 530 | – | 600 | 730 |
| – (ft) | 1,312 | 1,574 | 1,738 | – | 1,968 | 2,395 |
| Landing roll – (m) | 500 | 500 | 575 | – | 600 | 650 |
| – (ft) | 1,640 | 1,640 | 1,886 | – | 1,968 | 2,132 |
| Bomb load – (kg) | 2,500 | 2,500 | 2,500 | 3,000 | 4,500 | 4,500 |
| – (lb) | 5,511 | 5,511 | 5,511 | 6,613 | 9,920 | 9,920 |
| Armament – (mm) | 3 x 7.62 | 3 x 7.62 | 1 x 12.7<br>2 x 7.62 | 4 x 7.62 | 3 x 20 | 5 x 20 |
| Page in main text | 101 | 101 | 103 | – | 111 | 111 |

See the Glossary and Notes, pages 14 and 15.

*Top:* **Production DB-3 bomber while at the State Trials at NII VVS.**

*Above:* **The DB-3F bomber had significantly increased take-off weight, nevertheless, owing to the split flaps of increased area and propellers of increased diameter it was capable of take-off from the same airfields as the earlier versions.**

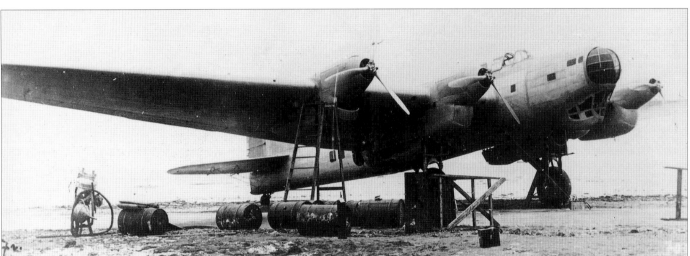

*Top:* **Production DB-3s participating in exercises just prior to the outbreak of the Second World War.**

*Centre:* **Tupolev/Petlyakov ANT-42 prototype prior to manufacturer's tests, fitted with four M-34FRN engines.**

*Bottom:* **Yer-2 powered by ACh-30B diesels which successfully passed its state trials in December 1943.**

Table G

## Tupolev and Arkhangelsky Tactical Bombers

| | ANT-40 | SB-2M100 | SB-2 -M100A | SB-*bis*-2M103 | SB-2M103 No.1/83 | SB-2M103 No.13/221 | MMN-2M105 | AR-2 (SB-RK) | SBB-1 | '103' (58) |
|---|---|---|---|---|---|---|---|---|---|---|
| Year of Production | 1934 | 1936 | 1937 | 1937 | 1938 | 1939 | 1939 | 1939 | 1940 | 1940 |
| Crew | 3 | 3 | 3 | 3 | 3 | 3 | 3 | 3 | 3 | 3 |
| Powerplant | Cyclone | M-100 | M-100A | M-103 | M-103 | M-103 | M-105 | M-105R | M-105R | AM-37 |
| Take-off power x 2 – (hp) | 730 | 750 | 860 | 960 | 960 | 960 | 1,050 | 1,100 | 1,100 | 1,400 |
| – (kW) | 544 | 559 | 641 | 716 | 716 | 716 | 783 | 820 | 820 | 1,044 |
| Length – (m) | 12.3 | 12.273 | 12.27 | 12.27 | 12.27 | 12.27 | 12.78 | 12.5 | 12.27 | 13.2 |
| – (ft-in) | 40-4 | 40-4 | 40-4 | 40-4 | 40-4 | 40-4 | 41-11 | 41-0 | 40-4 | 43-4 |
| Wingspan – (m) | 19.0 | 20.3 | 20.33 | 20.33 | 20.33 | 20.33 | 18.0 | 18.5 | 16.0 | 18.7 |
| – (ft in) | 62-4 | 66-7 | 66-8¼ | 66-8¼ | 66-8¼ | 66-8¼ | 59-0 | 60-8¼ | 52-5¾ | 61-4 |
| Wing area – ($m^2$) | 46.3 | 56.7 | 56.7 | 56.7 | 56.7 | 56.7 | 48.2 | 48.7 | 40.0 | 48.52 |
| – ($ft^2$) | 498 | 610 | 610 | 610 | 610 | 610 | 518 | 524 | 430 | 522 |
| Empty weight – (kg) | 3,132 | 4,060 | – | – | – | 4,768 | 4,820 | 4,430 | 4,415 | 7,726 |
| – (lb) | 6,904 | 8,950 | – | – | – | 10,511 | 10,626 | 9,766 | 9,733 | 17,032 |
| Gross weight – (kg) | 4,717 | 5,628 | 5,732 | 5,905 | 6,175 | 6,380 | 6,500 | 6,650 | 5,961 | 9,950 |
| – (lb) | 10,399 | 12,407 | 12,636 | 13,018 | 13,613 | 14,065 | 14,329 | 14,660 | 13,141 | 21,935 |
| Speed at sea level – (km/h) | – | 326.0 | 371.0 | 357.0 | 358.0 | 375.0 | 405.0 | 410.0 | 455.0 | 482.0 |
| – (mph) | – | 202.5 | 230.5 | 221.8 | 222.4 | 233.0 | 251.6 | 254.7 | 282.7 | 299.5 |
| Speed at altitude – (km/h) | 325.0 | 393.0 | 423.0 | 428.0 | 419.0 | 450.0 | 458.0 | 480.0 | 560.0 | 635.0 |
| – (m) | – | 5,200 | 4,000 | 4,000 | 4,000 | 4,100 | 4,200 | 4,700 | 5,000 | 8,000 |
| – (mph) | 201.9 | 244.2 | 262.8 | 265.9 | 260.3 | 279.6 | 284.5 | 298.2 | 347.9 | 394.5 |
| – (ft) | – | 17,050 | 13,100 | 13,100 | 13,100 | 13,450 | 13,800 | 15,400 | 16,400 | 26,250 |
| Climb to 5,000m – (min) | – | 11.7 | 8.6 | – | 8.6 | 9.5 | 9.3 | – | 5.5 | 8.6 |
| – to 16,400ft – (min)) | – | 11.7 | 8.6 | – | 8.6 | 9.5 | 9.3 | – | 5.5 | 8.6 |
| Service ceiling – (m) | 6,800 | 9,000 | 9,560 | – | 9,600 | 9,300 | 9,000 | 10,100 | 14,100 | 10,600 |
| – (ft) | 22,300 | 29,500 | 31,400 | – | 31,500 | 30,500 | 29,500 | 33,100 | 46,250 | 34,750 |
| Operational range – (km) | – | 2,187 | – | 2,170 | – | 1,900 | 1,000 | 1,500 | 880 | 2,500 |
| – (miles) | – | 1,358 | – | 1,348 | – | 1,180 | 621 | 932 | 546 | 1,553 |
| Take-off run – (m) | – | 350 | – | 270 | 310 | 370 | 360 | – | 400 | 440 |
| – (ft) | – | 1,148 | – | 885 | 1,017 | 1,213 | 1,181 | – | 1,312 | 1,443 |
| Landing roll – (m) | – | 350 | – | – | 400 | 397 | 400 | – | 350 | 730 |
| – (ft) | – | 1,148 | – | – | 1,312 | 1,302 | 1,312 | – | 1,148 | 2,395 |
| Bomb load – kg | 500 | 500 | 500 | 500 | 1,500 | 1,500 | 1,500 | 1,500 | – | 3,000 |
| – (lb) | 1,102 | 1,102 | 1,102 | 1,102 | 3,306 | 3,306 | 3,306 | 3,306 | – | 6,613 |
| Armament – (mm) | 4 x 7.62 | 4 x 7.62 | 4 x 7.62 | 4 x 7.62 | 4 x 7.62 | 4 x 7.62 | 3 x 7.62 | 4 x 7.62 | – | 2 x 20 |
| | | | | | | | | | | 4 x 7.62 |
| Page in main text | 145 | 146 | 146 | 146 | 147 | 147 | 147 | 151 | 152 | 152 |

| | '103U' (59) | '103V' (60) | Tu-2 No.100716 | Tu-2 | SDB (63) No.1 | SDB (63) No.2 | Tu-2D (62) | Tu-2R (Tu-6) | Tu-10 (68) | Tu-2 Standard * |
|---|---|---|---|---|---|---|---|---|---|---|
| Year of Production | 1941 | 1941 | 1943 | 1943 | 1944 | 1944 | 1944 | 1946 | 1945 | 1945 |
| Crew | 4 | 4 | 4 | 4 | 2 | 3 | 5 | 4 | 4 | 4 |
| Powerplant | AM-37 | M-82 | ASh-82FN | ASh-83 | AM-39 | AM-39F | ASh-82FN | ASh-82FN | AM-39FN2 | ASh-82FN |
| Take-off power x 2 – (hp) | 1,400 | 1,700 | 1,850 | 1,900 | 1,870 | 1,870 | 1,850 | 1,850 | 1,850 | 1,850 |
| – (kW) | 1,044 | 1,268 | 1,380 | 1,417 | 1,395 | 1,395 | 1,380 | 1,380 | 1,380 | 1,380 |
| Length – (m) | 13.8 | 13.71 | 13.8 | 13.8 | 13.2 | 13.6 | 14.42 | 13.8 | 13.8 | 13.8 |
| – (ft-in) | 45-4 | 45-4 | 45-4 | 45-4 | 43-4 | 44-7⅓ | 47-4 | 45-4 | 45-4 | 45-4 |
| Wingspan – (m) | 18.8 | 18.8 | 18.86 | 18.86 | 18.86 | 18.86 | 22.06 | 22.06 | 18.86 | 18.86 |
| – (ft in) | 61-8 | 61-8 | 61-10 | 61-10 | 61-10 | 61-10 | 72-4½ | 72-4½ | 61-10 | 61-10 |
| Wing area – ($m^2$) | 48.52 | 48.52 | 48.8 | 48.8 | 48.52 | 48.8 | 59.05 | 59.05 | 48.8 | 48.8 |
| – ($ft^2$) | 522 | 522 | 525 | 525 | 522 | 525 | 635 | 635 | 525 | 525 |
| Empty weight – (kg) | 7,823 | 7,335 | 7,474 | – | – | 8,280 | 8,316 | 8,205 | 8,870 | – |
| – (lb) | 17,246 | 16,170 | 16,477 | – | – | 18,253 | 18,333 | 18,088 | 19,554 | – |
| Gross weight – (kg) | 10,435 | 10,343 | 10,360 | 10,585 | 10,100 | 10,925 | 12,290 | 10,585 | 11,650 | 10,900 |
| – (lb) | 23,004 | 22,802 | 22,839 | 23,335 | 22,266 | 24,085 | 27,094 | 23,335 | 25,683 | 24,029 |
| Speed at sea level – (km/h) | 409.0 | 460.0 | 482.0 | – | – | 547.0 | 465.0 | 509.0 | 520.0 | – |
| – (mph) | 254.1 | 285.8 | 299.5 | – | – | 339.8 | 288.9 | 316.2 | 323.1 | – |
| Speed at altitude – (km/h) | 610.0 | 528.0 | 547.0 | 605.0 | 645.0 | 640.0 | 531.0 | 545.0 | 641.0 | 550.0 |
| – (m) | 7,800 | 3,800 | 5,400 | 8,800 | 6,600 | 6,800 | 5,600 | 5,500 | 8,600 | 5,400 |
| – (mph) | 379.0 | 328.0 | 339.8 | 375.9 | 400.7 | 397.6 | 329.9 | 338.6 | 398.3 | 341.7 |
| – (ft) | 25,600 | 12,450 | 17,700 | 28,850 | 21,650 | 22,300 | 18,350 | 18,050 | 28,200 | 17,700 |
| Climb to 5,000m – (min) | 9.5 | 10.0 | 9.5 | 8.5 | 7.45 | 8.7 | 11.8 | 10.3 | 10.0 | 10.3 |
| – to 16,400ft – (min)) | 9.5 | 10.0 | 9.5 | 8.5 | 7.45 | 8.7 | 11.8 | 10.3 | 10.0 | 10.3 |
| Service ceiling – (m) | 10,500 | 9,000 | 9,500 | 10,400 | 10,100 | 10,100 | 9,900 | 9,050 | 10,450 | 9,350 |
| – (ft) | 34,450 | 29,500 | 31,200 | 34,100 | 33,100 | 33,100 | 32,500 | 29,700 | 34,300 | 30,700 |
| Operational range – (km) | 1,900 | 2,000 | 2,100 | 1,950 | 1,830 | 1,530 | 2,790 | 2,780 | 1,740 | 2,250 |
| – (miles) | 1,180 | 1,242 | 1,304 | 1,211 | 1,137 | 950 | 1,733 | 1,727 | 1,081 | 1,398 |
| Take-off run – (m) | 435 | 516 | 485 | 480 | 470 | 535 | 480 | – | 525 | 475 |
| – (ft) | 1,427 | 1,692 | 1,591 | 1,574 | 1,541 | 1,755 | 1,574 | – | 1,722 | 1,558 |
| Landing roll – (m) | 765 | 640 | 675 | – | – | – | 610 | – | – | 875 |
| – (ft) | 2,509 | 2,099 | 2,214 | – | – | – | 2,001 | – | – | 2,870 |
| Bomb load – kg | 3,000 | 3,000 | 3,000 | 3,000 | 4,000 | 4,000 | 4,000 | – | 4,000 | 3,000 |
| – (lb) | 6,613 | 6,613 | 6,613 | 6,613 | 8,818 | 8,818 | – | – | 8,818 | 6,613 |
| Armament – (mm) | 2 x 20 | 2 x 20 | 2 x 20 | 2 x 20 | 2 x 20 | 2 x 20 | 2 x 20 | 2 x 20 | 2 x 20 | 2 x 20 |
| | 5 x 7.62 | 5 x 7.62 | | 3 x 12.7 | | 2 x 12.7 | 3 x 12.7 | 3 x 12.7 | 3 x 12.7 | 3 x 12.7 |
| Page in main text | 152 | 154 | 155 | 156 | 158 | 158 | 156 | 156 | 158 | 155 |

* Standard for 1946-1947

See the Glossary and Notes, pages 14 and 15, for details of measurement units etc.

Table F -- continued

| | Tu-2T | '62T' | Tu-2DB (65) | Tu-2 (67) | Tu-8 (69) | Tu-2Sh |
|---|---|---|---|---|---|---|
| Year of Production | 1945 | 1946 | 1946 | 1946 | 1946 | 1946 |
| Crew | 3 | 3 | 5 | 5 | 5 | 2 |
| Powerplant | ASh-82FN | ASh-82FN | AM-44TK | ACh-39BF | ASh-82FN | ASh-82FN |
| Take-off power x 2 – (hp) | 1,850 | 1,850 | 2,200 | 1,900 | 1,850 | 1,850 |
| – (kW) | 1,380 | 1,380 | 1,641 | 1,417 | 1,380 | 1,380 |
| Length – (m) | 14.42 | 14.42 | 14.42 | 14.42 | 14.61 | 13.8 |
| – (ft-in) | 47-4 | 47-4 | 47-4 | 47-4 | 47-11 | 45-3¼ |
| Wingspan – (m) | 18.86 | 22.06 | 22.06 | 22.06 | 22.06 | 18.86 |
| – (ft in) | 61-10 | 72-4½ | 72-4½ | 72-4½ | 72-4½ | 61-10 |
| Wing area – ($m^2$) | 48.8 | 59.05 | 59.12 | 59.12 | 61.26 | 48.8 |
| – ($ft^2$) | 525 | 635 | 636 | 636 | 659 | 525 |
| Empty weight – (kg) | – | – | – | – | – | – |
| – (lb) | – | – | – | – | – | – |
| Gross weight – (kg) | 11,423 | 13,500 | 13,450 | 13,626 | 14,250 | – |
| – (lb) | 25,182 | 29,761 | 29,651 | 30,039 | 31,415 | – |
| Speed at sea level – (km/h) | – | – | – | – | – | – |
| – (mph) | – | – | – | – | – | – |
| Speed at altitude – (km/h) | 505.0 | 501.0 | 578.0 | 509.0 | 515.0 | 575.0 |
| – (m) | – | – | – | 6,200 | 5,700 | 5,800 |
| – (mph) | – | – | – | 316.2 | 320.0 | 357.2 |
| – (ft) | – | – | – | 20,400 | 18,700 | 19,000 |
| Climb to 5,000m – (min) | – | – | – | 13.0 | 17.0 | 9.0 |
| – (to 16,400ft – min) | – | – | – | 13.0 | 17.0 | 9.0 |
| Service ceiling – (m) | 7,750 | 7,700 | 11,000 | 8,850 | 7,650 | 10,065 |
| – (ft) | 25,400 | 25,250 | 36,100 | 29,000 | 25,100 | 33,000 |
| Operational range – (km) | 2,075 | 3,800 | 2,570 | – | 3,645 | 2,500 |
| – (miles) | 1,289 | 2,361 | 1,596 | – | 2,264 | 1,553 |
| Take-off run – (m) | | 580 | – | – | 530 | – |
| – (ft) | 1,902 | – | – | 1,738 | – | – |
| Landing roll – (m) | 480 | – | – | 700 | – | – |
| – (ft) | 1,574 | – | – | 2,296 | – | – |
| Bomb load – kg | 3,000 | 3,000 | 4,000 | 4,000 | 4,500 | – |
| – (lb) | 6,613 | 6,613 | 8,818 | 8,818 | 9,920 | – |
| Armament – (mm) | 2 x 20 | 2 x 20 | 2 x 20 | 2 x 20 | 2 x 23 | 2 x 45 |
| | 3 x 12.7 | 3 x 12.7 | 3 x 12.7 | 3 x 12.7 | 2 x 20 | 2 x 37 |
| | | | | | 1 x 12.7 | 2 x 20 † |
| Page in main text | 156 | 158 | 160 | 160 | 160 | 156 |

† Also 1 x 12.

*Above:* **The '103U' prototype.**

*Below:* **Tu-2 prototype with a 57mm RShR anti-tank cannon in the nose.**

# Index

In order to make the index as easy to use as possible, references to oft-quoted subjects, such as the various aircraft types, the designers, test pilots and their OKBs and the factories that built them, test elements of the air force and navy and operational pilots etc have all been omitted as they are readily accessible within each OKB section. Soviet fighter types mentioned 'outside' of their relevant section *are* included in this index.

**The Tu-8 appeared just after the war and was not put into series production.**

Tealing in Scotland was once again the venue for the TB-7 bomber's second visit to the UK. Arriving on 20th May 1942, it brought the Soviet Commissar for Foreign Affairs, Vyacheslav Mikhailovich Molotov for a six-day visit that included being received by the King and concluded with the signing of a Treaty of Alliance and Mutual Assistance between Britain and the Soviet Union. The Soviet delegation left for Washington aboard the TB-7 on 26th May. Note the 'FE' and 'HO'-coded Hawker Hurricanes (most probably of the RAF's No. 56 Operational Training Unit) in the background.
*Philip Jarrett collection*